MO TZU'S RELIGIOUS BLUEPRINT FOR A CHINESE UTOPIA

The Will and the Way

Scott Lowe

The Edwin Mellen Press
Lewiston/Queenston/Lampeter

Library of Congress Cataloging-in-Publication Data

Lowe, Scott, 1950-
    Mo Tzu's religious blueprint for a Chinese utopia : the will and the way /
Scott Lowe.
      p. cm.
    Includes bibliographical references and index.
    ISBN 0-7734-9490-1
    1. Mo, Ti, fl. 400 B.C. Mo-tzu. 2. China--Religion. 3. Utopias.
I. Title.
B128M8.L64   1992
181'.115--dc20   92-4366
                                                    CIP

A CIP catalog record for this book is available
from The British Library.

The Edwin Mellen Press   The Edwin Mellen Press
P.O. Box 450   Box 67
Lewiston, NY 14092   Queenston, Ontario
USA   CANADA L0S 1L0

The Edwin Mellen Press, Ltd.
Lampeter, Dyfed, Wales
UNITED KINGDOM SA48 7DY

Printed in the United States of America

To my parents,
Donald S. and Emily Boyd Lowe

TABLE OF CONTENTS

NOTES ON ROMANIZATION AND CHINESE CHARACTERS

The romanization used in this text is based on the Wade-Giles system with the following modifications:

1. "I" will be written as "yi."

2. Diacritics will only be used in spellings where their absence might cause confusion, e.g. yü, chü, chün, etc., but not che, chen, etc., where their customary use serves no clear purpose for English language readers.

3. Hyphens will not be used in names. Disyllabic names are indicated by the use of the lower case for the initial letter of the second syllable, e.g. Chang Ch'un yi and Ssu ma Ch'ien, where Ch'un yi and Ssu ma are disyllabic personal and family names respectively.

Chinese characters will not be provided for the text of quotations taken from the *Mo tzu* or from modern Chinese sources. The Chinese text for passages quoted from early Chinese books will be given in the body of the monograph. Chinese characters for important terms and concepts will also be given in the main body of the text, where appropriate. An alphabetical list of names and book titles with their Chinese originals will be presented in the appendix.

CHAPTER I

INTRODUCTION

Purpose of the Study

The purpose of this study is to provide new insight into the concerns of the *Mo tzu* 墨子, a Chinese composition of the Warring States period (ca. 475-221 B.C.E.), by analyzing the text from a specifically religious perspective. This will entail an examination of all the significant concepts presented in the oldest textual layers of the *Mo tzu* (henceforth, MT) and an evaluation of the many didactic stories and anecdotes recounted in the MT, in order to determine the hierarchy of concerns expressed in the text. The goal of this analysis is to clarify the ultimate, or religious, concern of the text, as well as detail the means by which this ultimate goal is to be realized. Although this might seem an obvious thing to do, it has never before been attempted.

Mo tzu, or Mo Ti, was a Chinese teacher and social critic who flourished in the latter half of the fifth century B.C.E. and posed the first credible opposition to the teachings and practices of the followers of Confucius. His early disciples were noted for their powerfully expressed teachings of universal love for all humans, regardless of their place of origin or ethnic identifications, and opposition to all offensive war. In the MT, an authentically ancient text that purports to record the words, theories, and deeds of Mo tzu, we can observe the first systematic Chinese attempt to express a vision of an ideal world and detail the methods by which this world can be brought into being.

Like virtually all pre-Han Chinese texts, the MT is not the work of one hand but is a compilation assembled in the centuries following the death of the philosopher named in its title, claiming to present a record of his teachings and actions. As a compilation, the MT contains sections of varying "legitimacy" and interest. For the purposes of this study, it will be most useful to concentrate on those sections of the text thought to be of earliest provenance, and hence arguably closest to the original teachings of Mo Ti.[1] These earliest sections are also the parts of the text most susceptible to religious analysis; the later sections, which will figure far less prominently in this study, are mostly concerned with principles of logic, argumentation, physics, and military defense. Due to the technical nature of these chapters and the neglect that they have received through the centuries, many passages are either unintelligible or subject to an unacceptably wide range of interpretation. But for now, further discussion of the text must be postponed. It will be taken up in the third chapter of this study, where it will be dealt with at great length.

In the rest of this introductory chapter we will first consider the method to be used in this analysis, then we will look briefly at past studies of the MT and introduce the theses to be demonstrated in this study. As this is done, the points of contention between this investigation of the MT and past works will be made clear.

Method

This study approaches the MT from a perspective that we call the "religious" point of view. There are other equally valid ways of approaching the text (and indeed other ways of getting at the "religious" import of the MT). It is hoped that what distinguishes this approach is the definitional clarity with which it begins and the historically accurate analysis that it produces.

Religion is a lexically ambiguous term--it has a large number of special and particular nuances for different scholars, but, unfortunately, it is rarely defined. The manifest reluctance of scholars to define the term with which they are working may be due more to uncertainty about the functions of definitions than it is to confusion over the nature of religion. There are several different intellectual processes subsumed under the name "definition,"[2] but we will concern ourselves here with only one kind, the stipulative definition. In a stipulative definition, one assigns a particular meaning to a word, without making any claims for the absolute truth or lexical accuracy of the meaning now given to the word. This is very useful in that it removes all ambiguity from subsequent use of the term in the work for which it has been defined. It cannot be overemphasized that stipulative definitions do not make statements about ultimate reality--a stipulative definition of religion does not claim to delimit what religion actually is and what it has meant to all people in all times--rather they undertake the relatively modest task of clarifying an individual author's use of a term. It seems probable that many scholars have been unwilling to define religion in their works because they fear that they will inadvertently exclude some aspect of normative or lexical usage, thus laying themselves open to the charge of reductionism. This fear arises perhaps from lack of familiarity with the definitional options open to academic writers. Once it is made clear that a "real" definition is not being attempted, one is free to stipulate whatever meaning one wishes to assign a term, bound, and then quite loosely, only by the dictates of reason and common usage.[3]

For this study, religion is defined as "ultimate concern."[4] Ultimate concern has no arcane or technical nuances here; it simply means that which the text, person, or group in question feels is of ultimate importance and worthy of ultimate allegiance. As such, it need not always be a concern that falls within every scholar's understanding of religion. For the scholar who takes religion to mean that which deals with the supernatural, the mundane ultimate concerns of millions of persons and groups are naturally seen as non-religious. As stipulated here, *all* ultimate concerns are fair game for religious analysis. However, rest assured, we do not plan to present a religious analysis of ultimacy in the life of a rabid Chicago Cubs fan; in this monograph we will confine our attention to an examination of ultimate concern in the text of a school that A. C. Graham has called "the most religious ... of the ancient thinkers."[5]

How can ultimate concern be determined?[6] When studying a living religious thinker or group the task is reasonably straightforward: one asks questions and observes behavior. Unfortunately, since we are dealing with the literary remains of a long dead group, we are unable to look for answers outside the texts that have come down to us from the early centuries B.C.E. We will thus address our questions to the text of the MT itself in the hope that enough answers can be found there to make our study worthwhile. Given the strongly didactic and expository nature of the text, this is not as risky as it might sound. Essential to this approach is our assumption that texts do indeed have meaning independent of their readers' interpretations and projections. While we may never be able to share fully in the worldview and consciousness of the writers of the MT, we can certainly make a serious attempt to understand what they wished to convey through their writing. (The text's authors clearly thought that their message could be understood by any sincere reader, and we may as well share their assumption, since if they are wrong all academic study is ultimately meaningless.)

With many ancient Chinese texts finding the answer to the religious question of ultimate concern requires a great deal of insight, inference, and subjective judgement; although objective data are not lacking, their interpretation is by no means certain and evidence can be marshalled to support several different conclusions. Fortunately the MT is an unusually forthright and homogeneous text; its authors spare no pains to ensure that their message is presented clearly and forcefully. While it is true that some passages are couched in terms whose meaning is now unclear and that parts of the text appear to have been mutilated or miscopied, the text as a whole, and the Essay section in particular, is written in plain unadorned prose. The authors of the text sought above all to communicate their ideas; whatever literary and artistic pretensions they may have had appear to have been thoroughly repressed to serve the greater good of clarity. Therefore it is not necessary to crawl out on an interpretive limb to discover the significant concerns of the MT; the text's concerns are articulated at every opportunity. Rather the task before us is to make sense of an overabundance of concerns, concerns which, each in turn, are presented as being of primary significance.

The guiding assumption in this labor is that the authors (and editors?) of the text are fully rational thinkers whose world views may differ greatly from ours, but whose abilities to think and reason are in no way inferior to our own, though, of course, their styles of proof and argumentation diverge significantly from what we now find compelling. It is therefore unacceptable to treat the text with condescension. In many instances, arguments presented in the text will be clarified and expanded; inferences will be drawn out, but it seems grossly improper to argue along the line of "what the text says is X, but what it really means is Y," where X and Y are not closely related concepts. Respect for the text dictates our assumption that if the authors of the text wished to say Y, then that is what they would have said. Earlier students of the MT have not always been sufficiently sensitive to the actual contents of the text.

The *modus operandi* of this analysis is to allow the text to speak for itself. This may at times seem tedious, but it is the best defense against the oversimplification and reductionism that have plagued previous treatments of the

MT. Therefore in the analysis of the Essay chapters we will examine the text sequentially, point by point. As main ideas become clearly established, less time will subsequently be spent examining the minutia of the text, and it will no longer be necessary to go over the chapters in such fine detail; rather than belabor the obvious, summaries will suffice. In addition to determining the religious, or ultimate, concern presented in the text, it will also be revealing to examine the methods put forward by the text's authors for the realization of this ultimate concern and to document the justifications proffered by Mo tzu for the positions that he takes. This includes considering the types of evidence and styles of reasoning that were thought to be effective in the fourth century B.C.E.

Past Scholarship

It is neither possible nor desirable to provide a complete overview of all previous scholarship on the MT. Although the MT was rediscovered by Chinese intellectuals only in the Ch'ing dynasty, an incredible mass of writings on the text has accumulated since that time. In addition to Chinese treatments of the MT, a great deal has also been written in European languages and Japanese. (The Japanese texts will not be considered at all in this review.)

The vast majority of the discussions of the MT are found as chapters in books on ancient Chinese philosophy; even slighter coverage is given in texts where the MT is presented as part of a sampling of the "one hundred schools" of philosophy that flourished in Warring States China. It would be both exhausting and redundant to deal with all of the broadly similar discussions individually. The numerous book-length studies of the MT written by Chinese scholars in the past century tend to be more concerned with illuminating the meaning of obscure passages and resolving historical questions than with coming to a comprehensive understanding of the system of early Mohist thought, though some authors have certainly attempted that as well. Writers of books in Western languages tend to be more interested than Chinese scholars in the doctrines of Mo tzu and his followers, but they often project their own ideological biases on the text that they are ostensibly interpreting. Few writers in any language have dealt with the MT as a *religious* document; most have simply commented on the "religious" ideas scattered throughout the text and have treated these "religious" ideas as existing on a par with the "political," "economic," "military," "governmental," etc., ideas also expressed by Mo tzu.[7] In any case, since no previous author has attempted a descriptive religious analysis of the MT, it is not necessary to critique the entire literature on the MT to demonstrate the distinctiveness of this study; method alone sets it apart. However, for the sake of contrast and to clarify the advantages offered by the method being used, it will be revealing to consider a few rather questionable inter-pretations of the MT that have been advanced in recent decades. By selecting representative examples from several different approaches to early Mohist thought, both Eastern and Western, a reasonably clear picture of the general tendencies of past scholarship on the MT should emerge. It should be understood that the purpose of this study is not to revolutionize the study of the MT by overturning the findings of previous generations of scholars. The MT is far too straightforward a text to yield wildly varying interpretations--at least to responsible scholars.[8] However, by beginning this study with a clearly stipulated definition of religion, much of the confusion of past studies can be avoided and the fundamental religious unity of the text can be revealed.

The older Western studies of the MT tend to carry a heavy load of intellectual baggage. Judeo-Christian presuppositions and plain ethnocentrism mar otherwise perceptive essays. James Legge's discussion of the MT in *The Chinese Classics* is a representative example of the better sort of this kind of work.[9] Legge was a bright and earnest scholar, but his Victorian upbringing impelled him, and presumably most if not all of his contemporaries, to make what now seem to be excessively normative judgements.[10] Of course, pioneering work like Legge's naturally should be spared the exacting scrutiny given more modern studies. What is surprising is the occurrence of similarly normative attitudes in relatively recent works.

Writing in 1945, Augustinus A. Tseu, a Chinese Roman Catholic, compares Mo tzu's "moral philosophy" with the "natural theology" found in Plato and Aristotle. In addition to his comparative efforts, Tseu seeks to demonstrate that the thought of the MT is in essential conformity with the strictures of Chiang Kai chek's "New Life Movement": "The practical influence of Mo-tze's teachings on the philosophy of life in our modern China is to be seen in the similarity of the principles of the "New Life Movement" with the philosophy of Mo-tze."[11] To Tseu's credit, his purposes in writing *The Moral Philosophy of Mo-Tze* are clearly articulated from the start; although the book is actually rather interesting, it does not do much to advance our understanding of the MT and, in fact, tends to obscure the ideas of Mo tzu by confounding them with the terminology and intellectual constructs of scholasticism.

The writings of scholars from the P.R.C. also tend to serve non-academic agendas, and as a result they often tell us more about the current Chinese ideological line than about the thought of the MT. This is especially regrettable given the outstanding philological skills and unparalleled knowledge of the Chinese classics that some of these scholars possess.[12]

As a rule, scholars from the Chinese mainland do not explicitly define religion but seem to assume that religion embraces anything that is otherworldly, mystical, superstitious, or irrational. This perspective leads to imprecise statements like the following: "Mo Ti's 'religious view' cannot be equated with 'religion' because the content of the will of Heaven (*t'ien chih* 天 治) and the decree of Heaven (*t'ien yi* 天 意) about which Mo Ti talks is in both cases secular."[13] Having implicitly defined religion as something bad, the authors then take those aspects of Mo tzu's thought that they consider "progressive" and label them "secular." This may be a good way to rehabilitate those fragments of traditional Chinese thought judged worth saving by the ideologues of the "New China," but it grossly distorts the systematic unity of Mo tzu's worldview.

Related problems with P.R.C. writings include the tendency to perceive all world views as the inevitable and unvarying product of the class consciousness of their holders and the willingness to interpret all intellectual developments as part of a linear evolution that is determined by the material conditions of the surrounding society. Thus an otherwise outstanding philosopher like Feng Yu lan can say, "Mo tzu and the early Mohist school reflected the demands and aspirations of that era's small private producers, and especially the artisans."[14] Confucius, on the other hand, was a spokesman for the landlord class that had recently evolved from the "slave state nobility." There are instances where this sort of analysis may provide stimulating insights into the social basis of religious thought,[15] but when applied with dogmatic inflexibility and without even acknowledging the existence of other, possibly more significant, causative factors, the results are not very informative.

The "materialist" viewpoint adopted by P.R.C. scholars often leads them to underestimate the influence of non-physical factors in the thinking of others. For instance, Chou Chi chih claims that *li* 利 "benefit" provides the basis for the Mohist reevaluation of traditional concepts of religion, morality, philosophy, and government. There is, as we shall see, some truth in this assertion, but Chou fails to mention that for Mo tzu the reason that *li* is so important is that it is sanctioned by Heaven.[16] By itself *li* is of penultimate concern to Mo tzu; what Mo tzu values more is following the will of Heaven, and since Heaven has decreed that *li* is what it wants for its people, *li* is therefore what the Mohists try to produce through their religious means. Chou's approach to the will of Heaven illustrates the distortions of understanding that issue from imposing one's own biases on the thought of another.[17]

An entirely different set of problems is posed by those writers who are not consciously "normative," that is to say who have no special ideological agenda to pursue, but who are simply too idiosyncratic in their interpretation of the data. If they were obviously biased, then there would be no difficulty in dismissing their work, but these authors are often the most respected scholars in the field of Sinology. As such, their unsupported opinion is often accorded unwarranted credibility.

Henri Maspero, a great pioneer in the study of the Taoist church and a brilliant student of Chinese religion, in his discussion of Mo tzu claims that "his religion was a completely personal religion that consisted first of all in conforming to the will of Heaven, and which by its individualism was opposed to the totally social religion of ancient China."[18] The claim that conformity to the will of Heaven is fundamental to the Mohist faith is beyond reproach, but one can hardly imagine how Maspero decided that organized Mohism was distinguished by its "individualism." Mohism was a "personal" creed in that its adherents made a conscious decision to follow Mo tzu's *tao* 道 , but in its practice Mohism was based upon total obedience to the recognized leader of the Mohist community. (This will be discussed further in the following chapter.) The disciples of Mo tzu may have left the community into which they were born in order to follow Mo tzu, but if they did it meant exchanging one set of duties and obligations for an even more stringent set of demands. Statements of the sort just quoted sound perfectly reasonable, especially when delivered by respected authorities, but when tested against the text of the MT they are often found lacking.[19]

The late A. C. Graham, like Maspero an eminent Sinologist, makes several questionable statements about the Mohists that illustrate both the problem of unsubstantiated opinion and the previously mentioned tendency of scholars, Eastern and Western, to overlook the unity of the MT by classifying the ideas in the text into reified modern categories that certainly did not exist when the text was composed:

> To a modern reader the titles of the 10 triads of chapters seem to cover a curiously heterogeneous variety of subjects, religion ('The will of Heaven', 'Elucidating the spirits'), philosophy ('Rejecting destiny', 'Universal love'), politics ('Elevating worth', 'Conformity with superiors', 'Rejecting aggression'), and miscellaneous questions of morals ('Economy in funerals', 'Economy in expenditure', 'Rejecting music').[20]

In this passage religion seems to be implicitly defined as that which deals with the supernatural; later on the same page, Graham contrasts religious belief and logical thought: "The Mohists, who puzzle us by being at once the most religious and the most logical of the ancient thinkers, also contrive to be both the most pacifistic and the most martial."[21] What exactly is the definition of religion that Graham is assuming we all share? (That which deals with the supernatural and is illogical?) Why is "Universal Love" philosophical and not religious? (Presumably because it is not "supernaturally" based, but in the MT one justification for universal love is that it is what Heaven desires.) The fragmentation of the Mohist ideology created by this type of classification seems unhelpful and unnecessary. Though it is tactless to cavil, one must also point out that the Mohists were neither as pacifistic as the authors of the *Lao tzu* and the *Chuang tzu*, nor were they as "martial" as the "Legalists" (*fa chia* 法家).[22]

The next scholar we will consider in this section is Robin R. E. Yates, whose article "The Mohists on Warfare: Technology, Technique, and Justification" is included in a recently published "thematic issue" of the *JAAR*.[23] Yates's main concern is with the later followers of Mo tzu, a group only considered in passing in this study, but there are several points made by Yates that are germane to the early Mohists and that cannot go unchallenged.[24]

Speaking of the Mohists in general, Yates states that they "were interested in the preservation of boundaries at all costs and therefore they insisted on the preservation of their own groups at all costs."[25] Like the other points soon to be discussed, there is no supporting evidence marshalled to substantiate this assertion. Taken at face value this is a very misleading and historically inaccurate statement. In the following chapter we will examine several accounts from the *Lü shih ch'un ch'iu*, a late Chou dynasty "encyclopedia," that appear to suggest the opposite conclusion: the Mohists valued honor far more than the survival of either the individual or the group.

Another particularly misleading claim is that the Mohists "saw the world as threatening.... Both Heaven and the spirits and ghosts were unpredictable and capricious and hence men had to behave with scrupulous care and attempt to placate and control them."[26] As we shall see in our analysis of the Essay chapters, Mo tzu saw the spirits as fair, impartial, and, above all, morally astute arbiters of human's deeds. There appear to be no indications in the entire MT that Heaven and the spirits are ever unpredictable and capricious; on the contrary, Mo tzu believes that Heaven and the spirits are the guarantors of moral order in the universe. Mo tzu values reverencing Heaven and the spirits and believes that humans should perform sacrifices with regularity and solemn respect, but only the evildoer has any need to fear these "spiritual policemen."

The final claim made by Yates to be considered here is one that runs counter to a major thesis of this study. In a section entitled "Some Reasons Why Mohism Failed," Yates states that,

> Since the Mohists were interested in maintaining the *status quo*, ... they failed to conceive of a total ideal state as did the Confucians (*Hsün-tzu*, *Mencius*, *Chou Li*) and the Legalists, ... They acted always to prevent action, never to create a program for future action [that] would have enabled their idea of universal love to function in the world.[27]

It is possible that the later Mohists, the main subjects of Yates's paper, were more reactive than creative, but it is false to maintain that the Mohists had no vision of an ideal state and no program to bring it into being. This point will be treated at length in the main body of this study, where it will be demonstrated that Mo tzu had a comprehensive vision of the world that he wished to create and an integrated system of means for its realization. Further, I would like to suggest that Mo tzu might best be regarded as China's first fully conscious utopian thinker, and that his formulation of a coherent package of vision and methods is what separates him most clearly from his predecessors and contemporaries.

In the last few years two new studies of the MT have been published. Both take the form of chapters in books discussing the broad field of ancient Chinese thought, and both display impressive scholarship. In *The World of Thought in Ancient China*, Benjamin I. Schwartz gives an excellent summary of the doctrines of the early Mohists. Since he is writing as a political scientist and historian, Schwartz is looking for different things in the text than this study will, but his analysis is both insightful and text-based. Had it been published before this study had begun, this project might well have been abandoned as superfluous; nonetheless, we will find that a religious analysis of the MT produces different insights than that of an historian. When Schwartz attempts to describe the religious outlook of Mo tzu, he confines his remarks to Mo tzu's attitude towards Heaven and the spirits, leading one to suspect that Schwartz views religion as that which deals with the supernatural.[28] Like most other interpreters of the text, Schwartz is inclined to analyze the MT in terms of the standard undefined categories of religion, politics, economics, etc., but this is not the entire story. Schwartz also concurs with a major finding of this study that the MT is a relatively seamless whole that presents a coherent, systematic path to an "utopian" future. In Schwartz's terms, the MT envisions the path to the goal as "a total sociopolitical enterprise."[29] Substitute the word religion for sociopolitical and we must agree wholeheartedly.

Much more difficult to discuss is A. C. Graham's *Disputers of the Tao: Philosophical Argument in Ancient China* and the preceding, and supporting, technical monograph *Divisions in Early Mohism Reflected in the Core Chapters of Mo-tzu*.[30] In recent years, Graham, apparently influenced by biblical scholarship, has undertaken the daunting task of unraveling the tangled webs of authorship in first the *Chuang tzu* [31] and now the MT. In most regards-- philologically, historically, grammatically, philosophically--Graham's work is remarkable; unfortunately, in the case of the MT, one suspects he may have pushed his conclusions further than his facts allow. We will examine his textual arguments in detail in a later chapter; for now a summary of his conclusions will be helpful.

Graham concludes that the Essay chapters of the MT are, in fact, the work of three different, rival schools of early Mohists. By judiciously, and fairly plausibly, rearranging key passages and chapter orders, he manages to come up with a new tripartite division of the Essays, each section of which now shows a reasonable degree of grammatical and philosophical consistency. He names these three textual traditions the "Purist (or Y)," "Compromising (or H)," and "Reactionary (or J)" sects. Leaving aside for the moment the somewhat arguable bases for Graham's shuffling of the text, we should ask what in fact distinguishes these three, presumably hostile, sects. Graham's answer is that the Purist (Y) texts are addressed to "fellow thinkers," come from the North of China, preach a "pure meritocracy," and in their conclusions appeal solely to the "officer gentlemen" (*shih chün tzu* 士君子). The Compromising (H) chapters also come from the North but are less radical in their thrust, appealing to princes and the whole range of nobility in addition to the "officer gentlemen" and reveal a willingness to sacrifice principles in exchange for potential access to political power. The Reactionary (J) chapters are provisionally identified as coming from the Southern Mohists; they seem eager to accommodate to the political realities of the age and are addressed to both the hereditary aristocracy and the "officer gentlemen." Presumably employing modern lexical definition of his terms, Graham declares that the three traditions embrace positions ranging from radical to reactionary, with the Purist chapters being most radical and the Compromising and Reactionary chapters living up to their labels. Graham further asserts that the Purists are closest to the original teachings of Mo tzu, with the Compromising and Reactionary chapters progressively deviating from the Master's positions.[32]

A number of arguments can be arrayed against Graham's analysis, though it would be inappropriate to attempt a full scale refutation here. Without presently contesting Graham's emendation of the text, a few simple objections may suffice to demonstrate why we are not following Graham's new text divisions. First of all, taking the text at face value, it shows a remarkable consistency of concerns. Even if Graham is shown to be correct in his emendations, as modern students of the text, we have no way of knowing which, if any, of the three textual traditions actually represents the thought of Mo tzu. The characteristics that Graham attributes to the three antagonistic schools are all found in abundance in Mo tzu himself, at least as he is presented in the Dialogue chapters, where Mo tzu shows himself to be "Purist," "Compromising," and "Reactionary" by turns. Putting modern labels on what we imagine to be differing strands of Mohist thought is not in the final analysis very helpful in getting at the concerns of the text and certainly cannot tell us what Mo tzu himself believed. Finally, having declared that our purpose is to present the religion of the earliest layers of the MT, it makes more sense to accept the text as it has traditionally been presented. If there are different angles to the MT's message, they should be revealed in a study that treats the text as an organic whole just as much as they should appear in an analysis that dissects and reassembles the text on the basis of hypothesis. However, it is undeniable that early Chinese authors agree in reporting that the followers of Mo tzu divided into three competing, if not warring, sects. This being so, it would be unlikely that their beliefs would remain identical over the years. As one reads further, Graham's hypothesis should be kept in the back of the mind as a possible explanation for the apparent inconsistencies and discrepancies seen in the different Essay chapters.

In this brief survey we have skimmed the surface of the vast body of writings on the MT. Lest it be thought that only the weakest and most vulnerable studies have been singled out for attack, it should be made clear that the works we have considered are among the best to be found. All of them are interesting and significant, providing new insights and suggesting areas open for further research. In the field of religion at least, "perfect" studies are unknown; it is unfair to hold others up to standards that we ourselves fail to meet. However, the position taken in this study is that the more one relies on the text being examined, the better the chances that the resulting conclusions will be accurate, that is to say likely to be recognized as true by the persons being studied. (Assuming, of course, that they could be resurrected for the task.) Therefore in this examination of the MT, the text's concerns will be recorded and examined at face value, not according to some Western theoretical construct.[33] As much as possible, the classifying of Mo tzu's doctrines into convenient categories will be avoided; the price paid for easy understanding is often partial comprehension. By asking what is most important to the authors of the MT, a new perspective on the text will be gained, a perspective that is based on the voiced concerns of the text's authors and that should approximate their worldview.

1 4

Theses

The primary goal of this study is to analyze the religion, or ultimate concern, of the MT. Therefore we have not set out to prove the truth of predetermined hypotheses. Having just said that a major flaw in many previous studies of the text is the tendency of scholars to find in the MT the confirmation of their own theories, it would be especially ironic for us to do the exact same thing in this analysis. However, in the course of researching this study a number of observations began to present themselves, largely as a result of the method being employed, that allow the MT to be viewed in ways that differ subtly, but significantly, from past understandings. These observations will be outlined here in a relatively cursory manner; they shall be developed fully in the following chapters. As one might expect, the theses to be presented vary both in significance and originality; many represent only minor modifications of the scholarly consensus, while others have broader implications. We will start this review with the most basic observations and move to progressively less fundamental points.

One great advantage to be derived from our method is that it enables us to view the *entire* text of the MT as a religious document, though the different sections of the text vary in their religious interest. It is always appropriate to ask the question of religious ultimacy of any part of the text; this enables us to avoid the unnatural division of the MT into restrictive categories that deny the religious significance of ideas labeled "political" or "economic." When viewed from this religious perspective, the text of the MT is found to be remarkably unified and consistent in ideology and intent.

Perhaps the most important insight produced by this method of analysis is the realization that the Mohist religious means: the exaltation of the virtuous, the identification with the superior, universal love, etc., are consciously designed to function in coordination and together form an integrated, systematic method by which the Mohists' ideal world can be produced. The complementary, even synergistic, functioning of the Mohist means, which can individually only be fully implemented when the other means are also instituted, and their vital significance in the Mohists' plans for the transformation of the world has not been fully appreciated in other studies of the MT.[34]

When one asks the religious question of ultimate concern of the MT, it quickly becomes apparent that there is one overriding concern expressed throughout the oldest layers of the text:[35] to bring the greatest possible benefit to the world while excluding all harm from it. In its different wordings, this concern is explicitly stated throughout the Essay and Dialogue sections of the text; where it is not expressly mentioned, it is tacitly implied and forms a part of the underlying assumptions shared by the authors and their readers.

Complementing this somewhat vague ultimate concern are several clear and explicit goals: increasing the population, securing good government and political order, bringing about a state of fellowship among humanity, etc., that can be viewed as the concrete components or manifestations of the Mohists' ultimate concern. Since Mo tzu is not satisfied with the achievement of any one or two of these goals but requires the realization of them all, it is safe to deny them any independent existence as separate desiderata of the Mohist movement distinct from the ultimate concern. This will, of course, be discussed in greater detail later in the study.

The justification for the Mohist ultimate concern is found only penultimately in the benefits to be brought to suffering humanity by its achievement. The ultimate justification for promoting the benefit of the world and alleviating its hardships is to be found in the will of Heaven. Mo tzu claims to be leading the world to follow the will of Heaven, and the Mohist program is, he asserts, based entirely on the commandments that Heaven has provided for the guidance of humanity.[36]

In the remainder of this chapter we will review observations that are less expressly tied up with the methodology of this study; they are more the by-products than the direct results of our method. When looking for the concerns expressed in each chapter of the text, we began to examine the MT in great detail; during this process, other questions were asked that provided new insights into the view of the world held by Mo tzu and the early Mohists. Some of the questions that were asked include: What is the vision of the ideal world being offered? What is the view of human nature expressed in the text? How are Heaven and the spirits perceived and what is their relationship with humans? In addition, the popular image of Mo tzu as an "egalitarian" and anti-traditionalist pacifist came under scrutiny. A synopsis of the conclusions reached in the paper will be presented here. All of these points will be taken up in greater detail when they naturally arise in the course of our analysis.

Mo tzu is a strong advocate of the strict "reward and punishment" methods of social control that have since become identified with the "Legalists."[37] It seems likely that the inflexibly hierarchical and highly regimented internal organization of the Mohists served as a blueprint for the society that they were striving to create.[38] In the Mohist ideal world, the necessities of life: adequate food, clothing, and shelter, are provided for all, but no luxury items of any sort are to be produced. Paradoxically in a world where all goods are drably functional, the rulers and ministers of the state are to have great power, wealth, and prestige. (What they can do with their wealth is an unanswered, and unasked, question.) Mo tzu is unequivocal on this issue; his ideal world is marked by great and well-demarcated distinctions of rank and power, at least within the upper reaches of society. The possible variations in status and wealth among the masses are not mentioned. If the masses are to fulfil a role parallel to that of the rank and file within the Mohist organization, then it may be assumed that the masses will live in a state of social, ideological, and fiscal uniformity. Only in the condition of the ruled is anything resembling egalitarianism to be found.

The ideal man who inhabits the Mohist ideal world is an incorruptible workaholic. Diligent, trustworthy, and competent, he is to be employed only where he can excel. A completely "this-worldly" and non-mystical sage, he is the supreme bureaucrat. Mo tzu assumes the existence of a universal human moral sense and appeals directly to it in many of his arguments. In fact, these arguments simply do not function if all humans do not share a universal sense of right and wrong. According to Mo tzu, humanity shares far more than a common knowledge of right and wrong; the unity of humankind is an essential religious insight of the MT. The Mohist religious means of "exaltation of the virtuous," "identification with the superior," and "mutual love" are all predicated upon a realization of the solidarity of the human race and the development of an increasingly universalized sense of loyalty. (To a lesser extent, nearly all of the Mohist means are dependent for their full realization upon this universalization of the loyalties of humankind.) Mo tzu also gives great credit to the power of the human will; he seems to believe that humans have complete, conscious control over how they act and what they value. Once the readers of the MT see what is right, they are immediately expected to do what is right, with no regard for profit and loss or possible negative consequences. Yet in several places within the MT, Mo tzu does concede that the environment can, at times, mold the masses for the ill, but in most of the text this possibility is ignored. The dominant thrust of the text is to see humans as almost infinitely malleable in the direction of the good and moral; a major goal of the Mohists is to see that the masses are directed towards the actualization of their innate moral capacities.

One of the main reasons that Mo tzu is considered by several of the writers reviewed in the preceding section, and many others besides, to be unusually religious is the attention paid in the MT to Heaven, ghosts, and spirits. As understood by Mo tzu, Heaven and spiritual beings are characterized by their universal moral outlook; they are scrupulously fair and predictable in their dealings with humans. There is a large measure of reciprocity in the dealings of men and spirits--a sort of supernatural *quid pro quo,* but even here the role of the spirits as moral "enforcers" is pronounced; the spirits cannot be casually bribed by the unpenitent guilty.

Mo tzu is not, as some would make him, a rebel but a realist; his system of religious means is designed to transform society from within. Although he is not often supportive of the leaders of the Chinese states of his time--his religious means entitled "exaltation of the virtuous" is designed to produce a new meritocracy with which to replace the hereditary rulers of the day--he has no plans for fundamentally altering the existing political system. However, it is important to realize that Mo tzu's apparent endorsement of the status quo often embraces a hidden agenda and is always true to his religious goal. That Mo tzu is more a "traditionalist" than an iconoclast is shown by his extensive reliance on the written works of the Chinese literary mainstream--books later assumed to be the property of the "Confucian school"--and his strong advocacy of what scholars assume to be the traditional values of Chou China (family relationships, filial devotion, worship of Heaven and spiritual beings, etc.).

Like the theoreticians of all the other early Chinese schools, excepting the "Legalists," Mo tzu looks back on an ideal past from the vantage of a corrupt present. In the past, name and form corresponded; now there are high titles with no accompanying power, great status with no wealth. The task of the Mohists is to recreate the ideal world of the past in this degenerate time. Just as the Confucians found their ideal model in the founding years of the Chou dynasty, and the authors of the *Chuang tzu* found their golden age in the time before the advent of the sage kings, so Mo tzu looked back to the Hsia dynasty of an already legendary antiquity for his inspiration.[39]

The last point to be considered here is the nature of Mo tzu's widely mentioned "pacifism." Like many other multivocal words, pacifism often means different things to the persons using the term. If pacifism is taken to mean the opposition (nonviolent, of course) to all forms of war or violence, then Mo tzu and his followers were emphatically not pacifists. The Mohists reluctantly, but effectively, assisted in the defense of besieged states once all other alternatives for forestalling conflict had been exhausted. However, if taken in a broader sense to mean espousing a policy for ensuring a state of universal peace and non-aggression among the nations, then the Mohists could be considered exemplary pacifists, pacifists who believed so strongly in their mission that they were willing to die for the cause of world peace.[40]

We will now turn to a discussion of the era in which Mo tzu lived and consider what is known of the details of his life and those of his followers.

Notes

[1] Closeness to the thought of Mo Ti cannot, of course, be determined solely by the date of composition of a passage; however, it is probable that the analysis of the earliest sections of the text will give the clearest picture available of the goals and means of Mo tzu and his early followers. Even so, it is quite likely that it will never be possible to demonstrate that any particular concept in the text originated with Mo tzu or even that it played a significant role in his thought. This, fortunately, is beside the point of this paper. The MT will be treated as a *reasonably* coherent and consistent expression of the thought and beliefs of a school of like-minded individuals; whether any one individual ever espoused all the ideas in the text is immaterial.

[2] For a fuller exploration of this concept see Richard Robinson, *Definition* (Oxford: Oxford University Press, 1950).

[3] If one wished, it could be stipulated that in one's writing "religion" denotes a unit of mass equal to four kilograms. While this is permissible under the rules governing stipulative definitions, it is hard to imagine what productive purpose could be served by such an assignment of meaning. We shall steer clear of such egregious extremes.

[4] This particular approach was first suggested by Robert Baird, who took the term "ultimate concern," though not its interpretation, from Paul Tillich. See Robert D. Baird, *Category Formation and the History of Religions* (The Hague: Mouton and Co., 1971), p. 18.

[5] A. C. Graham, *Later Mohist Logic, Ethics, and Science* (Hong Kong: The Chinese University Press, 1978), p. 4. While it is unclear by what criteria Graham has made this determination, his words suggest that the heady freedom of stipulation has not led us too far from scholarly consensus in selecting a text for analysis.

[6] Since this is a religious study, it will not be proper to appropriate the method of one of the many schools of psychology or psychoanalysis in making our inquiries. We are thus somewhat hampered in our ability to probe beneath the surface of the beliefs and doctrines espoused by the writers of the MT. While it is reasonable for a religious analysis to pursue the implications of stated doctrines and positions and to infer the nature of ideas, beliefs, and goals not directly expounded in the text, it is, it seems to us, unacceptable to project upon the text a framework of psychological constructs that would almost certainly be rejected by the text's authors.

[7] For a striking example of a modern scholar regarding the MT as a chaotic melange of unrelated doctrines from different fields of study, of which "religion" forms one component, see A. C. Graham, *Logic*, pp. 3-6. In treating the "religious" thought of the MT in this manner, Graham is simply continuing the approach to the text followed by almost all modern writers on the MT. For another substantial English language example see Y. P. Mei, *Motse: the Neglected Rival of Confucius* (London: Arthur Probsthain, 1934).

[8] Chin Tsu t'ung and several later Chinese writers have argued that since Mo tzu's doctrines clearly are not "Chinese" and yet are neither "Buddhist" nor "Brahmanical," Mo tzu must be an Arab teaching the doctrines of Islam (*hui chiao*

回教). Chin gets around the obvious problems of chronology by claiming that Mo tzu is teaching the doctrines of *hui chiao* (ordinarily translated by "Islam") as they were understood *before* the time of the Prophet. The particulars of Chin's and several others' theories are given in Fang Shou ch'u, *Mo hsüeh yüan liu* (Taipei: Chung hua shu chu, 1957), pt. 2, pp. 87-100. While the claim that Mo tzu was a follower of Islam is perhaps the most unorthodox explanation for Mo's philosophical antecedents, Fang also refutes other theories that put Mo tzu's place of birth in the West. It is most revealing that these scholars should have felt the need to go so far afield to explain the origin of Mo tzu's thought, since to most non-Chinese the teachings of the MT apparently harmonize well with the other Chou dynasty traditions. Evidently, the intellectual strangle-hold assumed by "Confucian" orthodoxy made the rival philosophical systems of the Chou dynasty seem impossibly "foreign" to scholars steeped in the later literary tradition. See Fang, *Mo hsüeh yüan liu*, pt. 2, pp. 17-85.

[9] James Legge, *The Chinese Classics*, 5 vols. (Oxford: Clarendon Press, 1895), 2:100-122.

[10] However, given that scholarly styles come in and out of fashion with some regularity, who can say that normative pronouncements might not in the future become the hallmark of committed scholarship?

[11] See Augustinus A. Tseu, *The Moral Philosophy of Mo-Tze*, (Taipei: China Printing, Ltd., 1965), pp. 13-14. Note that Tseu sees a causal link between Mo tzu's thought and the principles of Chiang's movement.

[12] The least useful of this "scholarship" is that which is unabashedly produced for the purpose of ideological indoctrination. Rather than calling it "scholarship," it might more accurately be termed "didactic historical revisionism." Though by no means the worst of the lot, Jen Chi yü's *Mo tzu* (Shanghai: Jen min ch'u pan she, 1961) gives a good feel for the genre.

[13] Hsin Kuan chieh, Meng Teng chin, and Ting Chien sheng, eds. *Chung kuo ku tai chu ming che hsüeh chia p'ing chuan*, 3 vols. (n.p.: Ch'i lu shu she, 1980), 1:148. Evidently any concern with "this worldly" matters is automatically defined as secular and therefore outside the purview of religion. On p. 145 of the same volume the authors assert that Mo tzu is simply cloaking his own ideas with the authority of Heaven in order to facilitate their acceptance. While this is of course possible, it is hardly something that can be stated as a fact.

[14] Feng Yu lan, *Chung kuo che hsüeh shih hsin pien* (Peking: Jen min ch'u pan she, 1964), p. 142.

[15] I certainly do not want to assert that religious values are never influenced by social conditions--it is obvious that they often are--but it is equally obvious that one's social station is not the sole determining factor shaping the development of one's religious thought.

[16] See Hsin Kuan chieh, ed. *Chung kuo ku tai chu ming che hsüeh chia p'ing chuan*, 1:126.

[17] Perhaps what is most important here is the unwillingness of P.R.C. scholars to take ancient philosophers at face value. As they see it, if Mo tzu expresses reverence for the "will of Heaven," this does not mean that he truly wishes to do Heaven's bidding but only that he is appropriating the name of Heaven to give his

own ideas more clout. If Confucius reveres the courtly rituals of the Chou dynasty, this is only because he is an apologist for the landlord class who wishes to befuddle the masses and distract them from the real causes of their misery. At odds with the naivete found in doctrinaire mainland Chinese writings is their profound underlying cynicism, though most of the oddities in P.R.C. scholarship can perhaps be explained by the ideological constraints under which these scholars are forced to write and publish.

[18] Henri Maspero, *La Chine antique, Annales du Musée Guimet*, no. 71 (Paris: Presses Universitaires de France, 1965), p. 389.

[19] Maspero is such a fine scholar that one feels rather petty pointing out minor flaws selected from the vast body of his work; however, this is precisely the point being made: reputable scholars make eminently reasonable pronouncements that on closer inspection turn out to be unsubstantiated.

[20] Graham, *Logic*, pp. 3-4.

[21] Graham, *Logic*, p. 4.

[22] Here it must be admitted that a great deal depends on one's definitions of "pacifistic" and "martial." If by pacifistic one means the complete opposition to all violence, then the authors of the *Chuang tzu* have it all over the Mohists. If by martial one means warlike, then the defensive stance of the Mohists is not "martial" at all and has to bow down before the warmongering militarism of Shang Yang.

[23] Robin R. E. Yates, "The Mohists on Warfare: Technology, Technique, and Justification," *JAAR*, vol. 47, no. 3S, thematic issue, *Studies in Classical Chinese Thought* (September 1979).

[24] Unlike the objections raised earlier in this section, the ones to be presented now are more of substance than of method; however, Yates clearly must have an interpretive framework that is dictating some of the wholly undocumented conclusions that are drawn, even though he never tells his readers what it is. For example, consider the claim that,

> because the group was considered as a whole, they were not interested in the elaboration of status differentiation between age groups and social groups as were the Confucians. It was for this reason that they objected to elaborate funeral rituals which were the expressions of such differentiation and the process by which new status relationships were created. (Ibid., p. 561)

Since Mo tzu is painfully explicit that his objection to extravagant funerals is founded on the waste that they entail, Yates had to go outside the MT to reach the conclusion quoted above. Reading further one finds that Yates's labored and superfluous explanation is based on "anthropological analysis of other traditional societies." From this analysis Yates infers that "Mo tzu himself understood the social and religious nature of such expenditure."(Ibid.) To argue in this manner without providing solid textual support for one's assertions seems grossly unfair to Mo tzu.

[25] Ibid.

[26] Ibid., p. 562.

[27] Ibid., pp. 563-564.

[28] Benjamin I. Schwartz, *The World of Thought in Ancient China* (Cambridge, MA: Harvard University Press, 1985), p. 170.

[29] Ibid., p. 138.

[30] A. C. Graham, *Disputers of the Tao: Philosophical Argument in Ancient China* (La Salle, IL: Open Court, 1989) and A. C. Graham, *Divisions in Early Mohism Reflected in the Core Chapters of Mo-tzu* (Singapore: National University of Singapore, Institute of East Asian Philosophies, 1985).

[31] A. C. Graham, "How Much of *Chuang tzu* Did Chuang tzu Write?" *JAAR*, vol. 47, no. 3S, thematic issue, *Studies in Classical Chinese Thought* (September 1979).

[32] Graham, *Disputers*, pp. 35-36 and 51-53, and Graham, *Divisions*, pp. 20-28.

[33] This may seem naive and superficial to some readers. It is important to realize that the distortions and misrepresentations that have been produced in past studies are due to lack of sensitivity to what the text actually says. The simplicity of the method being advocated in this monograph is more apparent than actual; to interpret a text with the minimum of distortion is a daunting task, and one that is rarely achieved to full satisfaction. Even the concept of "ultimate concern" can be disparaged as an alien imposition; Mo tzu never explicitly details his hierarchy of concerns, so our interpretation requires a measure of inference. Whenever one infers, one runs the risk of error. However, as will be discussed later, the MT repeatedly states that one should talk about that which is most important; on this basis, it is reasonable to suppose that the authors of the MT will focus unremittingly on their deepest concerns.

[34] As mentioned in the preceding section of this chapter, Yates seems particularly insensible to this crucial insight. It shall be demonstrated in the fourth, fifth, and sixth chapters of this study that the Mohist means constitute a system for world transformation that is far more comprehensive than anything attributable to Mencius, to take only one example.

[35] This study will primarily be focussed on the "Essay" and "Dialogue" sections of the text for reasons that are discussed in Chapter III. For more information on the divisions of the MT the reader is referred to that chapter.

[36] Though the cynical may object, we will take Mo tzu at his word on this and other points. It has long been observed by Western writers that Chinese philosophers almost invariably attribute their own ideas to Heaven and in this way give further weight to their opinions. In the case of certain later and more sophistic philosophers, one might suspect that this attribution is not entirely sincere; however, with Mo tzu we have someone who appears to be one of the most earnest men to have ever lived, a man who insists upon the complete identity of word and deed. In the MT, Mo tzu gives every evidence of actually believing his claim to be modeling himself on Heaven; it seems only right to accept his claim at face value. For an early example of a Western writer observing that the Chinese regularly claim that their personal beliefs are directly inspired by Heaven see Alexandra David-Neel, *Socialisme chinois: le philosophe Meh-ti et l'idée de solidarité* (London: Luzac and Co., 1907), p. ix.

[37] By "Legalist" we mean the philosophies of social control expounded by Shang Yang, Han Fei tzu, etc. Though as a technical term "Legalist" is imprecise

and even slightly misleading--"Authoritarian" or "Totalitarian" might better fit the facts--it is a term widely used and commonly understood.

[38] This is especially probable since Mo tzu and his immediate followers seem to have been extremely strict in insisting on the absolute correspondence of means and ends. It is hardly conceivable that Mo tzu would have planned to structure his organized followers one way and society another.

[39] The Hsia dynasty is traditionally dated to ca. 2205-1766 B.C.E. Even, or perhaps especially, in the time of Mo tzu very little factual information about the Hsia was in circulation.

[40] One frustrating aspect of many discussions of Mo tzu is the tendency for authors to use terms like "pacifism," and of course "religion," without making the slightest effort to define or descriptively qualify what is meant by the words.

CHAPTER II

THE LIFE AND TIMES OF MO TZU

The Milieu

At this point it will be useful briefly to consider the social and political circumstances in which Mo tzu and his followers lived, though we will not attempt to provide an exhaustive social history of China in the fifth century B.C.E.

Mo tzu lived during the last years of the "Spring and Autumn" period (722-481 B.C.E.) and the early decades of the period of the "Warring States" (ca. 475-221 B.C.E.). This was a time of great technological innovation and social change, during which the old feudal order continued its disintegration and a new period of social mobility began. By considering a few of the most important developments of the time, an adequate, though not exhaustive, understanding of the background of Mo tzu's teaching can be achieved. The issues covered will necessarily seem spotty, but their significance should become apparent as the following chapters are read. Once this has been done, we will then examine the teachings and actions of Mo tzu and his early followers.

Late in the Spring and Autumn period an inventor, or inventors, unknown to us, designed the first Chinese ox-drawn, iron-tipped plow. This seemingly minor innovation proved to have wide ranging and profound consequences. The new plow allowed farmers to expand greatly the land area under cultivation: individual farmers could handle larger plots, and areas previously deemed marginal for cultivation could now be productively utilized. This resulted in a dramatic increase in the total area of land under cultivation and certainly facilitated, if it did not directly produce, the rapid population growth and economic expansion that began soon thereafter.[1] The increase in agricultural productivity and ensuing surpluses of grain provided for the first time the wherewithal for the emergence of powerful merchants, a large artisan class, and, ultimately, a class of non-laboring yet non-aristocratic intellectuals and philosophers.

According to scholars from the People's Republic of China, another result of the increase in agricultural efficiency was that the "basic social unit of production changed from the patriarchal clan to the family."[2] If true, this suggests that individuals would be a bit less firmly locked into their inherited social position and that individual initiative might more easily find its rewards. Hsü Cho yün believes that the entire social system of Spring and Autumn China was overturned by the end of the Warring States period,[3] which certainly suggests that the period in question was one of unusual turmoil and social change. As families broke free from the feudal and clan systems, they were able to leave their ancestral homes to seek virgin land to cultivate. These areas newly brought under cultivation, having never before been settled, were naturally devoid of any previously existing system of social hierarchy. The independent homesteading families that settled these areas clearly experienced a degree of social mobility unimaginable in previous centuries.[4] Unfortunately, a great deal of the mobility experienced in the next several centuries was downward. Peasants who owned land could also lose it--a fate unknown to the earlier generations who were tied to the land on feudal manors. Roving bands of landless peasants were to become an important factor in the general lawlessness of the Warring States period.[5]

Hsü Cho yün enumerates four causes underlying the dramatic rise of a wealthy, and therefore powerful, merchant class in the late Spring and Autumn and early Warring States periods: (1) The consolidation of states provided ever larger areas under the control of individual governments. This greatly enlarged the areas in which merchants could safely operate. (2) Transportation routes improved significantly. (3) States became increasingly interdependent due to localized specialization of production, both agricultural and industrial. (4) The widespread use of money facilitated the spread of commerce.[6]

The development of efficient commercial networks further stimulated the trend towards occupational specialization and the large scale manufacture of iron, bronze, and ceramic goods.[7] As more consumer goods became available, the merchants responsible for their distribution became wealthier and more influential. Over time, these merchants became great landlords at the expense of the peasantry, while many peasants, it seems, voluntarily left the land to seek their fortunes in manufacturing and commerce.[8] As a result, there was a noticeable shift in the population away from the countryside and towards the developing urban areas.

At the beginning of the Spring and Autumn period, China was organized into many separate states led by hereditary feudal lords who owed at least nominal allegiance to the Chou emperor.[9] However, the bonds linking the Chou emperor with his vassal lords had been growing progressively weaker through the centuries that had elapsed since the original investitures. Throughout the Spring and Autumn period, feudal lords, disregarding the strictures of the Chou court, engaged in increasingly ruthless wars of acquisition and conquest. By the dawn of the Warring States period, the hundreds of small fiefdoms established by the Chou had been consolidated into roughly twenty independent and contesting states, of which six were especially large and bellicose. Yet despite the violent turmoil of the time, China was culturally unified and the vying states were well-linked through mutually profitable trade, a shared system of writing, and the active exchange of political, philosophical, and religious ideas.[10]

As the growing population of literate city dwellers observed the chaos surrounding them and contemplated the apparently random twists of fate that led some to riches and others to ruin, religious skepticism became increasingly common, and the acceptance of traditional piety became harder and harder to maintain. It seemed that Heaven did not punish lawbreakers, at least not if they were politically well-connected, and good deeds only rarely brought the rewards that were once thought to be automatically bestowed. New schools of thought began to appear that offered novel solutions to the increasingly complex problems confronting the rulers and administrators of the surviving states.[11]

One of the areas that received a great deal of attention during the late Spring and Autumn period was the "art of war," and as a result the goals and methods of warfare were completely rethought. Military campaigns in the early Spring and Autumn period were slapdash affairs. Armies were most often "small, inefficiently organized, usually ineptly led, poorly equipped, badly trained, and haphazardly supplied."[12] Samuel Griffith reports that "many campaigns ended in disaster simply because the troops could find nothing to eat."[13] Although this early warfare was amateurish, there was nothing comical about it. Inept or not, the armies of the Spring and Autumn period still took a dreadful toll on the civilian population, but their damage can hardly be compared with what was to come.

In the Spring and Autumn period, military commanders were usually aristocrats who received their commission by virtue of their birth. Warfare was conducted according to an elaborate and archaic code, which moderated the death toll. Battle skills such as archery and charioteering took years to master and were therefore the exclusive province of those with the leisure to learn them. Peasants more commonly fueled the war machines with their grain and labor than with their skill in arms. All this was to change as the Spring and Autumn period drew to a bloody close.

The most common military engagement of the Warring States period was the infantry attack, in which thousands or tens of thousands of peasant footsoldiers armed with lances and swords met in personal combat. Armies were huge, well-disciplined, and commanded by professional generals chosen for their skill and competence.[14] The introduction of the crossbow, generally dated to ca. 400 B.C.E., further transformed the way the Chinese waged war, since a formidable offensive weapon could now readily be mastered in a matter of weeks instead of the years normally required to learn archery.[15] Conscription, while not unknown in the Spring and Autumn period, became universal by the time of the early Warring States; the new battle techniques and accompanying innovations in strategy made huge peasant armies both effective and necessary, while the deadly earnestness with which campaigns of conquest were pursued ensured that every ruler who desired to survive secured the largest and most efficient army possible. It seems probable that the most talented peasant draftees were able to make a career of military service and rise to the rank of professional officers. This in itself provided a great deal of social mobility in the Warring States period.[16]

While military service provided an avenue of upward mobility for a few, the devastation of war inflicted downward mobility on far more individuals. The entire population of many contested areas was forced to flee before the contending armies as their fields and homes became battlegrounds; those captured were either enslaved or killed.[17] For those of humble origins, opportunities for personal advancement had never been greater, yet at the same time the peril and uncertainty of the age left many longing for peace.

It seems probable that literacy was also coming within the reach of the most talented commoners. The sons of merchants, industrialists, and the growing class of landlords had the time and money needed for education. At the same time, the polygamous hereditary nobles were producing far more children than they could ever hope to support. The succeeding generations descending from the nobility often had little more than their education to separate them from the masses. Fortunately, in the right person this education proved to be a useful commodity, as the idea of private academies began to gain acceptance. The literate descendants of the aristocracy and their relatively wealthy commoner pupils soon came to be known under the collective designation of *shih* 士 "knights," a title once reserved for aristocratic warriors.[18]

It is widely believed that, starting with Confucius, the *shih* began founding academies to train aspiring administrators and military tacticians for service in the courts of the remaining rulers. While some of the teachers certainly desired to transmit the culture and morality exemplified by the political paragons of the past-- keeping body and soul together at the same time--it is likely that the majority of their students were motivated primarily by desires for personal advancement, as were their employers, who desperately sought stratagems and formulae that would give them a "winning edge" in the fierce struggle for survival and dominance.[19] The founders of these schools constructed a great variety of philosophical and political theories that were predictably united, despite their different approaches, by their concern with questions of statecraft. The questions that these teachers attempted to answer include the following: What is the ideal state? What brings the greatest security and prosperity to the state? How can lasting order be secured? What is the role of the sage ruler? How should his ministers behave?, etc. So far as we know, all these early schools promoted their version of the ideal man and attempted to define his behavior. (Though I favor the use of inclusive language wherever appropriate, here it probably is not; the early Chinese philosophers were primarily trying to define the roles proper to males, and only rarely were women even mentioned, though it must be conceded that the character *jen* 人 "man" that the philosophers use may often refer to human beings in a generic sense.)

The earliest private teacher of whom we have any certain knowledge is Confucius. Several of Confucius's immediate disciples did very well for themselves, rising to chief executive positions in feudal states; this undoubtedly did a great deal to enhance the prestige of private education in the eyes of talented commoners. Other disciples went on to become teachers themselves, founding their own schools in the tradition of Confucius and further propagating literacy and education among the masses.

Mo tzu is the first teacher known to history who founded a school distinct from the Confucian tradition. For several decades after Mo tzu's death, the Mohists and Confucians seem to have dominated the intellectual landscape of China, but in the following century a great efflorescence of philosophies and schools spread across the warring states--so many in fact that later generations of Chinese speak of the "one hundred schools" of the late Warring States era.

The followers of Confucius and Mo tzu, known as *ju* 儒 and *mo che* 墨者 respectively, continued to flourish throughout the period of the Warring States despite the competition posed by the proliferating schools and their distinctive teachings on the true Way (*tao* 道). The significance of these two pioneering schools can hardly be overstated, for not only did they take the opening positions in the great war of ideas that was to shape the entire future course of Chinese civilization, but to a great extent they, along with the "Taoists," played a seminal role in defining the terms and conditions under which the debate was conducted.

The Life and Social Background of Mo tzu

When one considers how great Mo tzu's impact on Chinese intellectual history has been, it is rather astonishing that more biographical details of his life have not survived. Even the name by which our philosopher has been known is now under scrutiny. Writing in 1917, Chiang Ch'üan stated that

> With the exception of the Mohists, all the "nine schools," like the *Ju* (Confucians), *Tao* (Taoists), *Ming* (School of Names), *F a* (Legalists), *Yin Yang* (School of *Yin* and *Yang*), *Tsung Heng* (School of Diplomats), *Tsa* (Miscellaneous), and *Nung* (School of Agriculturalists), take their school's name from the purpose of their learning. When you hear their name, then you know what branch of learning they pursue.[20]

Reasoning by analogy, Chiang concluded that *Mo* "dark" must refer to the exposure-blackened faces of the followers of Mo Ti (the *Mo* named Ti).[21] If this theory is correct then Mo tzu means something like "the philosopher of the *Mo*," where *Mo* is the descriptive name of the school and not the founder's surname. Ch'ien Mu developed a similar theory based on another early meaning of the word *mo*: the branding by which minor felons were punished in Chou China. According to Ch'ien the Mohists were men who worked as hard as convicts, and presumably looked as careworn as them too.[22] These speculations are mentioned not because they need to be resolved here but only to indicate how little certain knowledge we have of the founder of the Mohist school.[23]

Mo tzu's dates are also uncertain, but through the analysis of evidence provided by several early Chinese texts, and that contained internally in the MT, scholars have arrived at a general consensus. The first mention of Mo tzu in a dynastic history occurs in the *Shih chi* of Ssu ma Ch'ien (154-86 B.C.E.): 蓋 墨翟宋之大夫，善守禦為節用。或曰並孔子時，或曰在其後。 "Generally Mo Ti, a great official of Sung, was good at military defense and at making frugal expenditures. Some say he was contemporaneous with Confucius; others say he came later."[24] What is most notable about this passage is its inaccuracy and uncertainty: modern scholars generally reject all claims that Mo tzu held high office, and even in this early source Mo Ti's dates are in question.

A century later, Pan Ku (32-92 C.E.) gave a definite opinion in his *Han shu*: 在孔子之後 "(Mo tzu) came after Confucius."[25] We have no way of knowing what evidence Pan Ku used in making his determination, but perhaps he simply observed what for most scholars is the "bottom line" in the debate: the MT contains a great number of criticisms, both explicit and implied, of the followers of Confucius. Therefore Mo tzu must have lived at a time when Confucians were widely known throughout China. This suggests that Mo tzu's teaching career commenced well after the death of Confucius (ca. 479 B.C.E). Pan Ku sets no time for Mo tzu's death, but since Mo tzu and his followers were roundly condemned by Mencius (372-289 B.C.E.), who complained that "the words of Yang Chu and Mo Ti fill the empire,"[26] all modern scholars with whom I am familiar assume that Mo tzu's followers must have been flourishing when the *Mencius* was composed, and therefore Mo tzu probably died well before the *Mencius* was written. Naturally, when dealing with ancient history, affairs are never this simple; a great number of complicated schemes for determining Mo Ti's dates have been promoted by scholars, some plausible, others not.[27] After all is said and done, the discrepancies in the best scholars' suggested dates are not great: Hu Shih settles on 500-490 B.C.E. to 425-416 B.C.E.[28] Feng Yu lan suggests ca. 475 to ca. 390 B.C.E.[29] Fang Shou ch'u favors 490 B.C.E. to 403

B.C.E.[30] We will not be far afield if we situate Mo tzu firmly in the fifth century B.C.E.

Mo tzu's place of origin has also been a subject of debate for several thousand years. During most of that time the two leading contenders have been the ancient Chinese states of Lu and Sung. In the *Shih chi* passage already quoted, it was claimed that Mo tzu was a "great official" in Sung. Further evidence that he was a man of Sung is adduced from the famous story in which Mo tzu prevented an attack on Sung that was being planned by Ch'u.[31] Of course, Mo tzu is famous for rushing to defend unjustly attacked states; there is no reason to assume that his defense of Sung came from any personal involvement with the state. Further evidence of a secondary sort has been added by scholars through the centuries, but, on the whole, the claim that Mo tzu came from Sung is not impressively documented.

Much more plausible are the authors who assert that Mo tzu came from Lu, the home state of Confucius. A great quantity of internal evidence from the MT points to Lu as Mo tzu's base of operations, if not his ancestral home. A number of passages describe Mo tzu as going out from Lu towards some other state or returning to Lu after traveling elsewhere. According to Chang Ch'un yi, by using the directions to other states that are given in the text, viz. "traveling south to Ch'u" or "northward going to Ch'i," etc., one can by a process of triangulation determine that Lu is the state from which the writer is viewing the world.[32] As weak as these proofs seem, when taken as a whole they form a far stronger case for Lu than the Sung partisans have been able to muster for their choice.[33] If the evidence for Lu is rejected, then it seems clear that Mo's origins must be considered unknown and unknowable, pending discovery of new information.

The social class and family background of Mo tzu are known only indirectly by piecing together hints scattered through the MT and other pre-Han Chinese texts. Though the evidence scholars have assembled is necessarily circumstantial, Mo tzu's lower class origins can now be considered reasonably well-established. In his *Mo hsüeh yüan liu*, Fang Shou ch'u has collected some of the reliable pre-Han evidence for Mo tzu's roots in the artisan class. While some of Fang's assertions are too speculative to be accepted, the general thrust of his presentation is reasonable and worth recapitulating. (In the following summary, supplementary material from the MT has been added to flesh out the outline of ideas.) In the

Dialogue chapter "Esteem for Righteousness" there is a story recounting Mo tzu's attempt to meet with King Hui of Ch'u. Mo tzu gave the king some books (presumably from his own hand) which the king read and liked. Yet the king did not use the books and, pleading old age, sent a retainer, Mu Ho, to see Mo tzu off:

> When Mu Ho received Master Mo tzu in audience, Mo tzu gave a speech of persuasion to Mu Ho. Mu Ho was greatly pleased by it and addressed Master Mo tzu saying, "I'll grant that your ideas are really good, but my king is one of the world's great kings. Won't he then say, "These are the works of a commoner" and not use them?[34]

Fang goes on to demonstrate that the term *chien jen* 賤人, translated above as "commoner," was more descriptive than pejorative in the time of Mo tzu; all members of society below the level of *shih* 土, or "knights," were called *chien jen*. (Confucius, Fang notes, was also referred to as a *chien jen*, though he certainly seems to be of higher status than Mo tzu.)

Reasoning further, Fang quotes a passage from the Dialogues where Mo tzu claims that he neither serves a lord nor engages in agriculture. This, coupled with a MT passage where Mo tzu claims that a single, functional linchpin that he has made is far more valuable than a fancy mechanical bird fashioned by Kung shu P'an, a famed artificer and mechanic, leads Fang to assert that Mo tzu was a carpenter and chariotmaker. In other classical works, Mo tzu joins Kung shu P'an as a master of technical innovation, but even in these tales Mo tzu always emphasizes the superiority of honest craftsmanship over clever, but useless, invention. From the evidence presented by the chapters on military defense found in the final section of the MT, Fang concludes that Mo tzu's skills reached beyond mere carpentry to embrace a comprehensive knowledge of military technology. Fang is careful to note that Mo tzu's lowly birth and blue-collar occupation were not incompatible with a high level of education and goes on to list several possible groups with whom Mo tzu may have studied as a youth.[35] We will return to this after considering other evidence regarding Mo tzu's social station.

In non-Mohist pre-Han sources, Mo tzu's social position is discussed without the circumspection we expect, and see, on the part of his followers. In the *Lü shih ch'un ch'iu* version of the story where Mo tzu defends Sung from the unprovoked attack of Ch'u, Mo introduces himself by saying 臣北方之鄙人, "I, your subject, am a lowly man of the North."[36] The author of the *Hsün tzu* attacks the idea that rulers should do actual work, saying that 為 之 者，役 夫 之 道 也，墨 子 之 説 也 "doing it oneself is the way of a serf. [This is] Mo tzu's theory."[37] While it is quite possible that these passages reflect the polemical intent of their authors and as such cannot be taken as unbiased witnesses to Mo tzu's social station, the fact remains that _all_ known mentions of Mo tzu's social station place him in the lower classes. If a single reference to Mo tzu as an aristocrat survived, we might have to reconsider the accuracy of these ancient sources, but as it now stands we have no choice but to assume that Mo Ti was a man of very humble origins.

Despite his low social station, it is clear that Mo tzu was well educated by the standards of his time. In the "Esteem for Righteousness" chapter of the MT we read,

> When Mo tzu traveled south to serve Wei [an ancient Chinese state], a very large number of books were piled up on the crossbar [of his chariot]. Hsien T'ang tzu saw it and considering it strange said, "My dear Sir, you have taught Kung Shang Kuo saying, 'Simply consider the crooked and the straight [wrong and right] and that is all.' Now why is it that you are carrying so many books?" Master Mo tzu replied, "Formerly Duke Tan of the Chou dynasty read one hundred articles each morning and saw seventy gentlemen in audience every night. Therefore Duke Tan assisted the emperor and his achievements have reached up till the present ... how dare I discard this [example, or perhaps "these books"]?"[38]

In a story quoted above we read that Mo tzu presented books to King Hui of Ch'u. It is strongly implied in that passage that Mo tzu wrote the books himself, which is another indication that Mo tzu was exceptionally literate for a commoner.[39] The many MT citations of ancient texts tend to lend further credence to the claim that Mo tzu was an accomplished scholar, though it must be acknowledged that since the MT was composed after the death of Mo tzu, those passages that purport to present Mo's actual speech could well have been doctored by the addition of literary allusions in order to make Mo tzu appear better educated than he actually was. However, there is no reason to assume that a determined, bright, and ambitious commoner would have had no access to education fifth century B.C.E. A number of writers have observed that, beginning in the time of Confucius, a new social and intellectual milieu began to emerge in the Middle Kingdom. One aspect of this changing environment was the development of private "schools" where noted thinkers engaged a small group of students in dialogue and, perhaps, more formal instruction. Very little evidence for the existence of these schools in the fifth century B.C.E. has survived to modern times, but several early Chinese texts record traditions that, if correct, would indicate that Mo tzu studied in at least one of these early "academies." In the "Tang jan" 當染 chapter of the *Lü shih ch'un ch'iu* we find the following:

魯惠公使宰讓請郊廟之禮於天子, 朿亘王使史角往。惠公止之, 其後在於魯。墨子學焉。

> Duke Hui of Lu sent Tsai Jang to request the rites of the "suburban temple" [where annual sacrifices to Heaven were held] from the emperor. Emperor Huan ordered Shih Chiao to go [to Lu]. Duke Hui detained him, and his descendants remained in Lu. Mo tzu studied with them.[40]

What Mo tzu might have studied with these descendants of Shih Chiao is anyone's guess, for we see no evidence in the MT that Mo tzu was well versed in the rituals of Imperial sacrifices. However, Shih Chiao's progeny, living far from the emperor's court, may well have branched out into other areas of learning, areas of wider appeal that could provide them with remunerative local employment. It is certainly possible that they may have taught basic literacy and etiquette to talented and ambitious local youths.

The *Huai nan tzu* reports that Mo tzu studied with followers of Confucius (presumably when Mo was still young); although seemingly quite different from the claim made in the *Lü shih ch'un ch'iu*, it is possible that the two stories have a single origin:

墨子學儒者之業, 受孔子之術, 以為其禮煩擾而不說。厚葬靡財而貧民, 服傷生而害事。姑背周道而用夏政。

> Mo tzu studied the Confucian calling and received Confucius' arts, yet he considered their rituals bothersome and was not pleased [with them]. Rich burials squander wealth and therefore impoverish the people. Mourning injures life and thereby harms affairs. Therefore he turned his back on the way of the Chou and used the governmental [methods] of the Hsia.[41]

If the descendants of Shih Chiao had become early teachers of the "Confucian" way during their long sojourn in Lu, then these two accounts can be read as supplementing and supporting each other. It would not be terribly surprising to find that literate specialists in Imperial ritual, when exiled far from the emperor's court, would ally themselves with the early followers of Confucius. However, all speculation aside, these two independent accounts strongly suggest that at some time in his early life Mo tzu became acquainted with the ritual practices of the upper classes and grew to dislike them. Mo tzu was clearly familiar with the literary texts that have come to be associated with the Confucian tradition and is shown quoting extensively from them in the MT;[42] we can say with confidence that he received some kind of education in his early years. To the best of our knowledge, a "Confucian" education seems to have been the only kind available outside of the private tutoring given to the sons of nobles, so it is likely, though by no means certain, that the accounts in the *Lü shih ch'un ch'iu* and the *Huai nan tzu* are based on fact.

The Teachings and Actions of Mo tzu and His School

As previously indicated, we have only sparse information about the actions and events marking Mo tzu's adult career, and what little is known cannot fully be relied upon. Early students of the MT generally believed that Mo tzu served Sung in some official capacity, either as the "great official" (*tai fu*) mentioned in the *Shih chi* and *Han shu* [43] or as an envoy from Sung to the state of Wei.[44] Modern scholars have often questioned the veracity of these reports of Mo tzu's lofty position in Sung, especially since the internal evidence in the MT strongly suggests that Mo tzu was a person of low social standing throughout his life.[45]

What can be known for certain is that Mo tzu traveled a great deal to propagate his ideas and that he was the founder of his own school. In a number of places the MT tells of students seeking out Mo tzu in order to become his pupils; the text even shows Mo tzu somewhat deceitfully luring promising students to his school, by holding out promises of future wealth and position.[46] From all indications it seems probable that Mo tzu was quite successful as a teacher. In the famous passage in the "Kung shu" chapter of the MT where Mo tzu dissuades Kung shu P'an and the King of Ch'u from attacking Sung, Mo tzu's clinching argument is that no matter what happens to him personally, his second in command, Ch'in Ku li, is waiting on the walls of the Sung capital with three hundred of Mo tzu's trained and devoted disciples, all of whom are willing to die in the defense of Sung.[47] Any teacher who can command such loyalty from three hundred followers must certainly be regarded as successful!

The *Huai nan tzu*, an early Han dynasty text, confirms this picture of Mo tzu as the leader of a fanatically devoted band of disciples, although Mo tzu is credited with somewhat fewer followers in this non-Mohist text:

墨子服役百八十人。皆可使赴火蹈刃，死不還踵，化之所致也。

Mo tzu's disciples numbered one hundred and eighty. All could be commanded to rush into fire or tread on the edge of swords, and [when faced with] death they would not turn on their heels. This is the extreme of [personal] transformation.[48]

Although Mo tzu's disciples apparently displayed remarkable obedience to his command and formed highly disciplined, though voluntary, troops, the main goal of many of his followers seems to have been securing well-paid positions of power in the upper levels of the governments of feudal states. In the MT we find many indications that Mo tzu was quite successful in placing his "graduates" in good positions. One example will illustrate the sort of evidence the text provides: "Master Mo tzu sent Kuan Ch'in ao to recommend[49] Kao Shih tzu in Wei. The lord of Wei gave him [Kao] great emoluments and established him among the ministers."[50]

Who were these disciples who followed Mo tzu so fervently while apparently also seeking to better their position in society? The general trend in modern MT scholarship is to view Mo tzu's followers by and large as educated men of relatively low social status. A. C. Graham calls the Mohist movement "a confluence of merchants, craftsmen, and déclassé nobles, briefly emerging as a power in the cities as the feudal order disintegrates."[51] The early Mohists are clearly not self-conscious proponents of class struggle; they do not appear to view themselves as opponents of the established, though crumbling, order. Like the Confucians, they seek to influence society through appointment to office and through the propagation of their ideology. Whatever their class background, they believe that the creation of the ideal world will come through the restoration of the enlightened rule practiced by the sage kings of Chinese antiquity, not from the overthrow of the feudal system. However, the early Mohists are not "yes men" or apologists for the status quo. As we shall see, the teachings of the MT are in many ways unique in Chinese intellectual history; the distinctive point of view presented in the MT may well reflect the thinking of many members of that large segment of Chinese society, the merchants and craftsmen, that elsewhere finds no expression in the entire body of classical Chinese literature.[52]

The organization of the Mohist movement is far more restrictive than that of the other Warring States schools for which we have information. In fact had the modern press been in existence in the fourth century B.C.E., the early Mohists would probably have been labeled a "cult," and their exploits would have been splashed across the headlines at every supermarket checkout lane. Certainly it is hard to imagine a follower of Mencius or Hsün tzu subjecting himself to the rigors viewed as commonplace by the Mohists: "When Ch'in Ku li had served Master Mo tzu for three years, his hands and feet were thickly calloused, and his facial features were blackened; having placed himself in bondage, he did not dare ask what he wished."[53] After undergoing years of demanding training, those Mohists who were finally placed in powerful and remunerative positions still remained remarkably obedient to their master:

> The Master Mo tzu sent Sheng Ch'o to serve Hsiang Tzu Niu. Hsiang Tzu Niu invaded the territory of Lu three times, and Sheng Ch'o three times followed him. Upon hearing of it, Master Mo tzu sent Kao Sun tzu to bring him [Sheng Ch'o] back saying, "I sent Ch'o in order to stop pride and rectify depravity. Now as for Ch'o, his emoluments are lavish and he deceives his master [by not providing proper moral guidance?]. His master invaded Lu three times, and three times Ch'o followed him.... It is not as if [I] did not cause Ch'o to understand it, it is that emoluments triumphed over righteousness.[54]

What is most striking about this passage is that Mo tzu was evidently successful in his recall attempt. Since Sheng Ch'o had already fallen from Mo tzu's good graces, why did he not stay on with Hsiang Tzu Niu, an action perfectly in accord with the prevailing moral currents, rather than return to the Mohist camp where he was certain to face censure? It is unlikely that Mo tzu had great leverage with Hsiang Tzu Niu, judging from the latter's behavior, so we may assume that Mo tzu would have been unable to engineer his disciple's dismissal. Evidently Mo tzu wielded enormous influence over his followers even after they had completed their period of schooling, and somehow he managed to control aspects of their behavior while they were serving other masters and at odds with his teaching. (The prevention of aggressive war is a pillar of the Mohist program.) Elsewhere in the MT we read of former students who send substantial wealth back to Mo tzu, though this is apparently due more to respect and appreciation than to any direct coercion.[55]

The *Huai nan tzu* passage recently cited also gives a clear indication of the morally disciplined tenor of the Mohist movement and the unswerving, self-abnegating obedience of Mo tzu's disciples. In contrast to the personal relationship of master and disciple that ends with the death of either of the parties, the Mohists successfully institutionalized their bonds of devotion by creating the office of *chü tzu* 鉅子, or "great leader," to whose command all Mohists owed allegiance. The rank and file Mohists owed their loyalty to whomever held the office of *chü tzu*; when the office was passed along, the allegiance of the Mohists followed. After Mo tzu's death, Ch'in Ku li was appointed the first *chü tzu*. (The term does not seem to have been used while Mo tzu was alive.) The title was subsequently passed down through a succession of leaders, presumably until the Mohist organization came to an end at the close of the Warring States period. From stories told in the *Lü shih ch'un ch'iu* about the actions of two of these *chü tzu*, a clear impression of the roles and powers conferred by the title can be formed.[56]

The story that comes first in the chronology of Mo tzu's successors recounts the demise of Meng Sheng, a man thought to be the second *chü tzu* of the Mohists (the successor to Ch'in Ku li). Meng Sheng was the friend and confidant of Yang Ch'eng Chün, the lord of a fortified city in Ch'u. Meng Sheng was placed in charge of Yang Ch'eng Chün's domain and given half of a jade tally as a sign of his authority. While Meng Sheng was in charge of the city, Yang Ch'eng Chün grievously offended the rulers of Ch'u and was forced to flee the state, thereby forfeiting his claim to his territory. When the troops of Ch'u came to take over Yang Ch'eng Chün's domain, Meng Sheng was faced with a dilemma. Reasoning aloud he is credited with saying,

受人之國與之有符。今不見符而力不能禁。不能死不可。

I have received a man's state and share a tally with him. Now I do not see a [matching] tally [presented by the representatives of Ch'u], but my strength is unable to prevent [Ch'u from taking control]. If I cannot die, then that is unacceptable.[57]

One of Meng Sheng's disciples attempts to reason with his master, pointing out that his death will not benefit Yang Ch'eng Chün in any way and, even worse, will cut off the line of succession of the Mohists. Meng Sheng is unconvinced and replies with a moving soliloquy:

吾於陽城君也，非師則友也，非友則臣也。不死
自今以來求嚴師必不於墨者矣，求賢友必不
於墨者矣，求良臣必不於墨者矣。死之所以行
墨者之義而繼其業者也。我將屬鉅子於宋
田襄子。田襄子賢者也。何患墨者之絕世也。

In my relationship with Yang Ch'eng Chün, if I am not a teacher then a friend, or if not a friend then a minister. If I do not die, then from now on [those who] seek a worthy friend certainly will not do so among the Mohists, and [those who] seek a good minister certainly will not do so among the Mohists. It is that whereby my death carries out the righteousness of the Mohists and continues their affairs. I will entrust [the office of] *chü tzu* to T'ien Hsiang tzu of Sung. T'ien Hsiang tzu is worthy. Why grieve that the Mohist line will be cut off?[58]

The story ends with the death of Meng Sheng and one hundred eighty-three of his followers.[59]

The second account of the actions of a Mohist leader recounted in the *Lü shih ch'un ch'iu* concerns a *chü tzu* from the state of Ch'in named Fu Tun. Fu Tun's only son killed a man under circumstances that are not mentioned in the story.[60] King Hui of Ch'in, feeling sorry for the old man who is about to lose his only heir, pardons Fu Tun's son and urges the *chü tzu* to accept this royal dispensation. Fu Tun replies:

墨者之法曰殺人者死，傷人者刑。此所以禁殺
傷人也。夫禁殺傷人者，天下之大義也。王
雖為之賜而令吏弗誅，腹䵍不可不行墨者
之法。

The law of the Mohists says "He who kills a man dies, and he who injures a man is punished. This is that whereby we prevent the killing and harming of others. Now preventing the killing and harming of men is the greatest righteousness in the world. Although you, the king, have bestowed [a pardon] on his behalf and have commanded your officials not to punish him, Fu Tun cannot but carry out the Mohists' law.[61]

True to his word, Fu Tun refused the king's pardon and immediately had his son executed.

From these stories it is quite clear that the *chü tzu* were remarkably rigid in adhering to their Mohist principles, even when by so doing they brought about their own deaths, and those of their children and followers as well. The decision of the *chü tzu* appears to have been final--though at least one *chü tzu* was willing to listen to his disciples' remonstrances--and was followed by the entire Mohist community.[62] Not only did the *chü tzu* hold the power of life and death over their disciples, but they were bound by higher standards than the law of the land. Fu Tun's refusal of the royal pardon for his son shows the extent to which model Mohists could deny self-interest in their strict adherence to Mo tzu's laws.[63] The impression of the Mohists garnered from the MT and the early non-Mohist sources is strikingly consistent. The followers of Mo tzu seem to have inherited their leader's unwavering belief in moral absolutes and to have shared his conviction that righteous behavior is to be found only in the perfect correspondence of ideal and action, word and deed. Absolutely honest and utterly predictable, at least to those conversant with their teachings, the early Mohists were stalwart defenders of the innocent; even their detractors seem to have been impressed by the Mohists' principled asceticism.[64] However, as one might expect, such fanaticism exacts a toll, and as a result the Mohists do not come across as men with well-balanced personalities, at least by modern standards. They seem to have been terribly severe, earnest, and humorless men. From the following assessment of the Mohist *tao* given in the *Chuang tzu* we can sense the tenor of the men who chose to make this *tao* the focus of their lives:

其生也勤其死也薄其道大觳。使人憂使人悲
其行難為也。恐其不可以為聖人之道。反天
下之心，天下不堪。墨子雖獨能任，奈天下
何。離於天下，其去王也遠矣。

Their life toil, their death meagre, their *tao* is very harsh. It makes
people grieve and makes people sad; its actions are hard to do. I
fear it cannot be the *tao* of the sages. It goes counter to the hearts of
the world's [people] and the world cannot endure it. Though Mo
tzu by himself was able to sustain it, what about the world? It is far
from [the people of] the world, and it is far from true kingship.[65]

The *Chuang tzu* has overstated its case: Mo tzu was not the only man able to endure his *tao*. However the *Chuang tzu* is surely right in claiming that the severity of the Mohist path made it unsuitable for the masses.

The doctrines Mo tzu taught can be drawn from the text of the MT itself, and the largest part of this paper will be devoted to that task; however, at this point we should try to determine very generally what the curriculum of Mo tzu's school might have been. Mo tzu's greatest emphasis seems to have been on the intensive study of the religious means preserved for us in the Essay chapters of the MT, with attention directed to both theoretical understanding of the means and consideration of the practical methods for their implementation. It cannot be overemphasized that these means were seen as complementary and as constituting a coherent system of interlocking methods all leading to the same goal. The following speech attributed to Mo tzu makes this point forcefully:

> Master Mo tzu said, "Whenever you enter a state you must select your task and work at it. If the state is disorderly, then talk to them about exaltation of the virtuous and identification with the superior. If the state is poor, then talk to them about economy of expenditures and simplicity in funerals. If the state delights in music and is submerged in wine, then talk to them about the condemnation of music and anti-fatalism. If the state is perverse and without rituals, then talk to them about reverencing Heaven and serving spirits. If the state is engaged in robbing, invading, and oppressing, then talk to them about universal love and the condemnation of offensive war. Therefore I say, 'select your task and work at it.'"[66]

Any one of these means (exaltation of the virtuous, identification with the superior, economy of expenditures, simplicity in funerals, etc.) can serve as a starting point for the rectification of a state's government, and each state is likely to have an area where the need for rectification is most apparent, but none of the warring states was limited to a single set of faults. From a Mohist point of view, all needed to be completely overhauled, and the task facing the Mohist missionary was finding a place to begin; once he started on one of the Mohist means, the others inevitably would be drawn into play, for the full realization of any one of the means necessarily requires the implementation of the others.

To determine the rest of the contents of the Mohist curriculum we will have to be a bit more speculative, but even here we will rely on relatively strong evidence drawn from the MT to reach conclusions with a high probability of truth. The Mohists are perhaps best known to moderns as the men who rushed about ancient

China rescuing innocent states from unwarranted and unprovoked attacks, but the evidence in the MT itself would suggest that this is a very partial and one-sided view of the Mohists, or at least of the earliest followers of Mo tzu. In the MT, Mo tzu and his disciples appear above all to have been scholars and debaters. Their first line of defense was always the persuasive speech; in the entire "Dialogue" section of the text, where the purported words and actions of Mo tzu are recorded in an anecdotal fashion, there is only one mention of a Mohist defense of a city, and that comes after five accounts of non-military intervention.[67] Though the evidence is less complete than we might wish, it seems clear that Mo tzu and his followers sought above all to *persuade* others of the folly of wars of conquest. Only when persuasion failed did the Mohists assist the beleaguered states in their defense, and then it was in the capacity of tacticians and engineers, not footsoldiers. However, on this last point the evidence is equivocal. There is one passage in the MT that mentions the death of a disciple in battle, in a way that makes warfare seem an integral part of the Mohist training:

> There was a man of Lu who entrusted his son to Master Mo tzu for teaching. The son was killed in battle and the father blamed Master Mo tzu. Master Mo tzu replied: "You wanted me to teach your son and now his studies have been fulfilled; he died in battle and you are resentful. This is like wanting to sell [something] and after selling it becoming resentful.[68] Is that not absurd?[69]

Against this one mention of a disciple's violent death can be arrayed numerous statements attributed to Mo tzu that explicitly denigrate training in the martial arts, while praising study and scholarship. Mo tzu did not value study for its own sake; Mohist scholarship was designed to further the goals of the movement and therefore had to be pursued expeditiously, using a minimum of time and resources. As the following quote makes clear, Mo tzu was well-aware of the limited ability of humans to absorb new knowledge and acquire new skills; studying the martial arts simply was not cost efficient for the early Mohists:

> There were several [disciples] who came to Master Mo tzu to learn archery. Master Mo tzu said, "No way! Wise persons must measure what their strength can accomplish and work on that. The "national knights" [a term denoting the most outstanding *shih* in the land] are unable to fight a battle while at the same time assisting others. Now you are not "national knights," so how can you possibly become both scholars and archers?[70]

In an argument with a self-righteous recluse living in the wilds south of Lu, Mo tzu specifically rejects the occupations of farmer and weaver before addressing soldiering in this passage narrated in the third person:

> Ti has certainly thought of putting on armour and carrying a lance in order to rescue the feudal lords from their distress. If successful, then [he would still only] equal one man's military might. Now, that one man's military might cannot resist three armies has long been evident.[71] Ti thinks this cannot compare with propounding the *tao* of the former kings and seeking out their theories, understanding the words of the sages and investigating their speeches, and having done that then first persuading kings, dukes, and great men and next persuading ordinary folk and commoner *shih* [to follow the sage kings' teachings.] If kings, dukes, and great men use my words, the states will definitely be ordered. If ordinary folk and commoner *shih* use my words, then their actions will definitely be good.[72]

It seems safe to say that even though the later followers of Mo tzu became renowned as military strategists and technicians, Mo tzu and his early followers were primarily in the business of argument and persuasion. The development of the Mohists' military role seems to have been gradual and late--the product of necessity rather than choice--though it is not contrary to the ideology expressed in the earliest textual layers of the MT. It seems unlikely that many Mohists were accomplished men-at-arms--their relatively small numbers alone would have prevented them from having a significant impact on battlefields where armies composed of tens of thousands of soldiers were commonplace--rather they used their scholarly skills and knowledge of mechanics to devise the remarkable defensive hardware and strategies described in the last chapters of the MT. How much of this military technology existed in the time of Mo tzu is unknown, but it is not improbable that he personally initiated the study of the methods of defensive warfare that was so characteristic of his later followers.

The demise of the Mohist movement is even less clearly documented than its origins, but it may prove useful to discuss a few of the things that are known, without attempting to consider everything that has been written about this murky period of history. After Mo tzu's death, the Mohist schools continued to thrive for several hundred years. During this time their academic concerns continued to evolve and became increasingly sophisticated. The impetus provided by Mo tzu's early interest in effective persuasion eventually led to the development of a corpus of logical propositions (found in chapters 40-45 of the modern editions of the MT) that are indispensable for understanding the theses of late Warring States sophists like Hui Shih and Kung sun Lung. A. C. Graham suggests that the later Mohists had lots of time for logical and scientific thinking in the third century B.C.E., since their opportunities for playing a significant role on the stage of Chinese politics had effectively ended.[73]

As the chaos of the Warring States period was replaced by a unified empire under first the short-lived Ch'in dynasty (221-207 B.C.E.) and later the long, relatively stable Western Han (206 B.C.E.-25 C.E.), there was little or no room for the presumably lower-class Mohists to exert an influence on governmental affairs. Perhaps even more importantly there was no real *need* for Mohist input. China enjoyed a reasonable degree of internal peace and prosperity under its well-developed bureaucratic government; the skills that the Mohists had so diligently acquired were basically irrelevant to the age. Under these circumstances, the Mohists seem simply to have faded away.[74] Though there is some lukewarm debate over precisely when the Mohists last existed as a movement, the general conclusion is that they died out in the Western Han.[75] In any case, the history of the Mohist movement is of only peripheral interest to this study, of course, and will not be pursued further.

We will next consider what is known of the origins, transmission, and authenticity of the MT.

45

Notes

[1] Joseph Needham, gen. ed., *Science and Civilisation in China*, 7 vols. (Cambridge: Cambridge University Press, 1954 -), vol. 6 pt. 2 (1984): *Agriculture*, by Francesca Bray, p. 168.

[2] Hsin Kuan chieh, Meng Teng ching, and Ting Chien sheng, *Chung kuo ku tai chu ming che hsüeh chia p'ing chuan*, 1:124.

[3] Hsü Cho yün, *Ancient China in Transition* (Stanford: Stanford University Press, 1965), p. 1 and elsewhere.

[4] S.F. Teiser, "Engulfing the Bounds of Order: the Myth of the Great Flood in *Mencius*," *Journal of Chinese Religions*, nos. 13 and 14 (Fall 1985 and 1986), p. 21.

[5] Hsü Cho yün, *Transition*, p. 116.

[6] Ibid.

[7] Ibid., p. 127.

[8] Ibid., pp. 129-130.

[9] The emperors of the Chou dynasty were, in principle if not in fact, the rulers of China from ca. 1122 to 256 B.C.

[10] Cheng Te k'un, *Chou China*, Archaeology in China, vol. 3 (Cambridge: W. Hefler and Sons, 1963), p. 302.

[11] That the individual was still subservient to the community is tellingly revealed by the fact that although the full weight of the problems caused by the breakdown of traditional values was borne by the individual, the solutions proposed, with the exception of the writings of the "Taoists," all deal with the problems on the level of the state.

[12] Samuel B. Griffith, *Sun Tzu: the Art of War* (Oxford: Oxford University Press, 1963), p. 7.

[13] Ibid.

[14] Ibid., p. 9.

[15] Ibid.

[16] Hsü, *Transition*, pp. 69-74. Hsü distinguishes two talents that were especially valued and rewarded: fierceness in battle and skill in strategic planning. Using Han dynasty sources, Hsü plausibly documents his claim that in virtually all of the "warring states" men of humble origins rose to command great armies.

[17] Ibid., p. 68.

[18] Jen Chi yü, *Mo tzu*, p. 17. There is a good deal of inconsistency and imprecision in the use of the term *shih*. Some ancient Chinese authors seem to use it as a class term reserved for those with noble antecedents. Others seem to be more willing to use it for educated non-aristocrats. In the *Shih chi* Confucius refers to himself as a commoner (*chien jen*), which is puzzling unless we understand it as a

polite term of self-deprecation, for Confucius actually came from aristocratic stock. See the *Shih chi* citation in Fang Shou ch'u, *Mo hsüeh yüan liu*, p. 15.

[19] Hsü, *Transition*, pp. 100-104.

[20] Chiang Ch'üan, *Tu tzu chih yen* quoted in Ch'en Yüan te, *Chung kuo ku tai che hsüeh shih* (Taipei: Chung hua shu chu, 1962), pp. 191-192.

[21] Chiang's theory is fleshed out in Graham, *Logic*, p. 6, note 9.

[22] Ch'ien Mu, *Mo tzu* (Shanghai: Commercial Press, 1931), pp. 1-7.

[23] Whether Mo is our philosopher's surname or not makes little difference to this study; furthermore, the various theories offered so far by scholars are nearly equally flawed, so there is little basis for choosing among them. We are not alone in spotting the faulty logic of these attempts to overturn the assumptions of the past two millennia; others appear to take these speculations as a personal affront. In his indignation over the branding theory, the P.R.C. writer Jen Chi yü refers darkly to the ruminations of "imperialist running-dog scholars like Ch'ien Mu." See Jen Chi yü, *Mo tzu*, p. 5.

[24] Ssu ma Ch'ien, *Shih chi* (n.p.: T'ung wen ying tien k'an, 1903), chapt. 74, p. 6.

[25] Pan Ku, *Erh shih wu shih*, vol.1 (Taipei: K'ai ming shu tien; reprint ed., 1969), p. 435.

[26] D.C. Lau, trans., *Mencius* (Middlesex: Penguin Books, 1970), p. 114.

[27] All of the methods for dating Mo tzu are based on the dates, estimated and known from other sources, for events and persons mentioned in the MT. The matter becomes tricky when references to certain events and persons are rejected as interpolations, while others are accepted as part of the original text. Some scholars show little discrimination in their treatment of references to known persons and events in the MT, giving equal weight to those cited rhetorically and those linked directly to the life of Mo tzu. Given that the text is multi-layered and that stories from a later time could have been inserted into the text by editors and copyists seeking to clarify points original to Mo tzu, this approach seems shaky at best. The aforementioned method might serve to determine the date at which a chapter reached its present form, but it is in no way adequate to ascertain the dates of Mo tzu. The most plausible and consistent results are obtained by those scholars who confine their consideration to events and persons linked directly to Mo tzu in the text. These writers are uniform in placing Mo tzu in the fifth century B.C.E.

[28] Hu Shih, *Chung kuo che hsüeh shih ta kang* (Taipei: Commercial Press, reprint ed., 1970), pp. 145-147.

[29] Fung Yu lan, *Chung kuo che hsüeh shih hsin pien* (Peking: Jen min ch'u pan she, 1964), p. 140.

[30] Fang, *Mo hsüeh yüan liu*, pp. 10-14.[31] This story is found in several early Chinese works. The MT version is in the chapter entitled "Kung shu." See MTCC, pp. 615-618.

[32] Ibid., pp. 753-755.

[33] If Lu is, in fact, Mo tzu's ancestral home, this adds a shred more credibility to the tradition, recorded in the *Huai Nan tzu* (ca. 122 B.C.E.), that in his youth Mo

tzu studied with followers of Confucius, since most authorities believe that the Confucian tradition first prospered in Confucius's home state of Lu. The strongest argument against the Lu theory is provided by modern philological studies that indicate that the MT is not written in what Bernhard Karlgren has termed the "Lu dialect." This is not an insurmountable objection however. Others have used this fact as evidence of Mo Ti's lower class origins; by this reasoning, the MT is written in the dialect of artisans and craftsmen. Steven Durrant correctly suggests that if the MT was recorded by the disciples of Mo tzu, then it should be written in *their* dialect and should reflect their origins, not Mo tzu's. See Stephen Durrant, "An Examination of Textual and Grammatical Problems in Mo Tzu" (Ph.D. dissertation, University of Washington, 1975), pp. 10-11.

[34] MTCC, p. 569.

[35] Fang, *Mo hsüeh yüan liu*, pp. 15-17.

[36] *Lü shih ch'un ch'iu*, CTCC, vol. 6, p. 282.

[37] *Hsün tzu hsin chu* (Peking: Chung hua shu chu, 1979), p. 172.

[38] MTCC, p. 574. The passage continues and makes the point that once one has learned enough and thought deeply on the lessons contained in books, it is no longer necessary to read. What is important here for us is the fact that Mo tzu was a voracious reader, something apparently quite unusual for the time.

[39] What these books might have been is unknown. Most scholars now assume that all compositions written by Mo tzu have long been lost, but it is always possible that the MT may incorporate fragments of these original works.

[40] *Lü shih ch'un ch'iu*, CTCC, vol. 6, p. 20.

[41] *Huai nan tzu*, CTCC, vol. 7, p. 375.

[42] Interestingly, the one "Classic" that Mo tzu never quotes is the *Yi ching*.

[43] The *Shih chi* quotation has been given in a preceding section of this chapter; the *Han shu* quote cannot be viewed as an independent source since its information was most likely drawn from the earlier *Shih chi*.

[44] The belief that Mo tzu served as an envoy to Wei is grounded in a contested MT passage that currently reads: 子墨子南遊使衛 "The Master Mo tzu traveled south to serve as an envoy to Wei." Since at least one early MT text lacks the character *shih* 使 "to serve as an envoy," Chang suggests that the corrected text might read: 子墨子南遊於衛 "The Master Mo tzu traveled south to Wei." MTCC, p. 574.

[45] Liang Ch'i ch'ao effectively demolishes the plausibility of all accounts that make Mo tzu an official of Sung by examining the rest of the MT text. He finds that there are simply *no* traces or signs of any sort indicating that Mo tzu ever held a high position in Sung, or anywhere else for that matter. Further, Liang marshals a good deal of evidence for his claim that Mo was not an official of Sung. Logic is on Liang's side, though given the time span separating us from the events in question, nearly anything is possible. See Liang Ch'i ch'ao, *Mo tzu hsüeh an* (n.p., 1921; reprint ed., Taipei: Chung hua shu chu, 1966), p. 3.

[46] In the "Keng Meng" chapter of the MT, Mo tzu tells a desirable recruit that if he studies in Mo tzu's academy, he will become an official. One year later, when the promised position has not materialized, the man confronts Mo tzu only to be told, in effect, that he has been tricked into studying, but that it was for his own good! See MTCC, pp. 590-591. In this tale of "benevolent" deception, one suspects we catch a glimpse into the thinking of a man with a mission who *knows* that he is right.

[47] Ibid., p. 618. A very similar version of this story is told in the *Lü shih ch'un ch'iu*, but no mention of the disciples waiting in Sung is made in this later and somewhat truncated retelling of the tale. See *Lü shih ch'un ch'iu*, CTCC, v. 6, p. 282.

[48] *Huai Nan tzu*, CTCC, v. 7, p. 357.

[49] Following the gloss given by Yeh Yü lin in his *Mo tzu hsin shih* (Tainan: Ta hsia ch'u pan she, 1982), pp. 251-252. Yeh will henceforth be cited as MTHS.

[50] MTCC, p. 561.

[51] Graham, *Logic*, p. 10.

[52] Ibid., p. 6.

[53] MTCC, p. 653. That the demands Mo tzu placed on his disciples were not merely physical is suggested by the following quote: "The Master Mo tzu said, 'My ideas are sufficient for all uses. Discarding my ideas to think on your own is like discarding the harvest to pick up [individual] heads of grain.'" (Ibid., p. 578.)

[54] Ibid., pp. 611-612.

[55] See, for example, the story of Keng Chu tzu. Ibid., pp. 556-557.

[56] We are assuming that the *Lü shih ch'un ch'iu* is a reliable witness to the events it records and that the stories it recounts about the actions of the Mohists are basically accurate.

[57] *Lü shih ch'un ch'iu*, CTCC, vol. 6, p. 243.

[58] Ibid.

[59] This story incidentally provides valuable evidence for the attempts to establish Mo tzu's dates. The Mohist defense of Yang Ch'eng Chün's realm is variously dated to 400 B.C.E. (Jen Chi yü, *Mo tzu*, p. 11.) and 381 B.C.E. (Graham, *Logic*, p. 4.) If, in fact, Meng Sheng is the second *chü tzu* of the Mohists, then Mo tzu must have died at least several decades before the event in question. Further, if taken as factual, this story provides direct counter-evidence to the extraordinary, and unsupported, claim made by Robin R. E. Yates that the Mohists "insisted on the preservation of their own groups at all costs." Since it is very clear from both the MT and non-Mohist contemporary sources that the Mohists were far more concerned with sticking to principle than with survival, it is hard to imagine the basis for Yates's assertion. See Yates, "The Mohists on Warfare: Technology, Technique, and Justification," p. 561.

[60] As it turns out, the Mohist application of punishment appears to be completely inflexible; all circumstances that we might consider mitigating are irrelevant for them and hence do not merit mention.

[61] *Lü shih ch'un ch'iu*, CTCC, vol. 6, pp. 10-11.

[62] This is not to say that individual Mohists did not on occasion break discipline. The two disciples of Meng Sheng who were sent to confer the title of *chü tzu* on T'ien Hsiang tzu provide a good example. When they told T'ien Hsiang tzu that they intended to return to Yang Ch'eng to die with Meng Sheng, T'ien Hsiang tzu pointed out that he was now the new *chü tzu* and forbade them to go. They went anyway. Evidently their martyrdom was more important to them than mere obedience. Ibid., p. 243.

[63] It also suggests that the Mohists, by ignoring the civil laws whenever they were in conflict with Mo tzu's teaching, may have formed a "state within the state"--a potential source of conflict with the governments of the Warring States period, increasingly concerned as they were with all-embracing ideological and political control.

[64] See, for example, the "T'ien Hsia" chapter of the *Chuang tzu*.

[65] Ch'en Ku ying, ed., *Chuang tzu chin chu chin yi* (Taipei: Shang wu yin shu kuan, 1975), p. 941.

[66] MTCC, pp. 607-608.

[67] Ibid., pp. 567-618. The one reference to Mohist military forces occurs on p. 618 at the end of the "Kung shu" chapter.

[68] Following the gloss of Yeh Yü lin given in his MTHS, p. 293.

[69] MTCC, p. 604.

[70] Ibid., p. 593.

[71] The translation of the last two sentences is imprecise but, I hope, essentially correct.

[72] Ibid., p. 605.

[73] Graham, *Logic*, p. 21.

[74] Ibid., pp. 64-65.

[75] See, for example, Lo Ken tze, *Chu tzu k'ao suo* (Peking: Jen min ch'u pan she, 1958), p. 173. Most of the evidence used to date the end of the Mohists as a formal movement is exceedingly weak. The general procedure followed by scholars interested in this question is to comb through Han dynasty literature looking for the last datable references to the Mohists. Durrant has located a relatively obscure mention of the Mohists in the *Yen t'ieh lun* (written in 81 B.C.E.). Unfortunately, the passage in question tells of a gathering of Confucians and Mohists without providing any date for their meeting. All the reader knows is that sometime before 81 B.C.E. persons identified as Mohists were still alive. (I have not been able to date any of the persons named in the passage.) This by itself is not particularly useful information, though it suggests to Durrant that the movement survived into the Han dynasty. See Durrant, "Examination," p. 44.

CHAPTER III

THE *MO TZU*

The History of the Text

Before going on to analyze the religion of the MT, we should consider what is known about the history of the text's transmission from the Warring States period up till the present. After reviewing the text's history we will go on to consider questions of its authenticity, authorship, and time of composition.

As can easily be imagined, the turmoils of the last two thousand years of Chinese civilization have seen to it that virtually no early Chinese texts have survived to modern times completely intact. Those few works that were saved from the infamous book-burning of Ch'in Shih Huang Ti (traditionally dated to 213 B.C.E.) were lost soon afterwards when the Ch'in imperial archives were sacked by the rebel armies that struggled for power upon the death of the first Ch'in emperor.[1] While this was perhaps the most dramatic setback suffered by literature in general, there were untold other incidents leading to the loss, in whole or part, of thousands of other works. Even when no calamity was involved, mere neglect was sufficient to lead to the loss of a text: unless re-copied repeatedly all texts not carved in stone or metal were in danger of perishing. A text that fell out of favor for a few centuries was likely to be lost forever. Many of the books listed in the "Yi wen chih," the earliest Chinese bibliography still extant (found in chapter 30 of the *Ch'ien Han shu*, are known by name alone; for others all we have is a late forgery that appropriates the name of the earlier, lost text.[2] Obviously when dealing with a text believed to be from the Warring States period it is prudent to scrutinize its history carefully. Only then can one know if the text actually originates from the time when it was purported to have been written, if it is most likely an accurate representation of the school whose views it is claimed to represent,[3] and if the text that we currently possess has been abridged, lengthened or otherwise seriously altered through the years.

The literary detective work involved in uncovering the past of an ancient Chinese text is immense and requires the efforts of many scholars over a number of years before the complete picture can be pieced together. We are fortunate that quite a few talented Chinese and Japanese scholars have invested years of their time in researching the MT and even more fortunate that Stephen Durrant has collected, synthesized, and evaluated their efforts. In the following abridged history of the MT, we are heavily indebted to Durrant for his careful analysis of the many Chinese and Japanese sources.[4]

The first mention of the MT in a bibliography occurs in Pan Ku's *Ch'ien Han shu*, "Yi wen chih" (chapter 30): 墨子七十一篇。 "MT, seventy-one chapters."[5] It is significant that this first bibliographic entry on the MT shows a length of seventy-one chapters for the text; our current MT has only fifty-three chapters, though the titles of a further eight chapters have been preserved. If the *Ch'ien Han shu* entry is correct, and it is the consensus of modern authorities that it is, then eighteen chapters of the MT have been lost since the Han. For eight of these chapters the title is known; for the other ten even that has been lost.

The next reference to the MT is in Kao Yu's commentary (written ca. 210 C.E.) to the *Lü shih ch'un ch'iu*: 墨子名翟。魯人，作書七十二篇。 "Mo tzu was named Ti. He was from Lu and wrote a book of seventy-two chapters."[6] As Durrant points out, the simplest explanation for the discrepancy in the lengths of the text seen in the two citations is that Pan Ku saw a MT text without a table of contents, while the text Kao Yu saw was provided with one that he counted as a separate chapter.[7] This theory was earlier advanced by Sun Yi jang.[8]

Unfortunately, many of the later references to the length of the text refer to *chüan* 卷 "volumes" rather than *p'ien* 篇 "chapters." This makes it rather more difficult for us to determine when chapters may have been lost from the text, since individual chapters within a volume can be lost without changing the number of volumes in a text.[9]

Throughout the Sui (581-618 C.E.) and T'ang (618-907 C.E.) dynasties there are repeated references to the MT, and many works from this period quote from the MT text. Since a large number of the quotations are no longer found in the

MT, Durrant assumes that they are taken from the eighteen chapters that have been lost.[10] If this is the case then it is reasonable to infer that at least some of the missing eighteen chapters were extant in the T'ang, though it is possible that the quotations in question were taken from earlier collectanea that preserved bits and pieces of chapters that were lost before the T'ang, rather than taken from the MT itself.[11] The T'ang references to the MT generally cite the number of volumes without mentioning the number of chapters.[12] In the T'ang, fifteen volumes, or sixteen volumes including a one volume table of contents, seems to be the norm for the MT.

Durrant cites six Sung dynasty (960-1279 C.E.) references to the MT. The text described in each instance comprises fifteen volumes. There is also a mention of a three volume abridged text.[13] This abridged text turns up repeatedly in later bibliographies, but its history is tangential at best to our concern here.[14] Two of the six Sung references to the MT additionally specify that the text is divided into sixty-one chapters.[15] This sixty-one chapter version would appear to be intermediate to the Han seventy-one chapter version and the current fifty-three chapter text.[16]

What are we to make of this spotty and uncertain history? We can be fairly certain that at least ten chapters had been lost from the MT by early Sung times. Whether all sixty-one chapters existed in their entirety or were in some cases merely represented by their titles cannot be determined. Since the present MT comprises fifty-three full chapters and eight more chapter titles without accompanying text, it is certainly possible that the Sung texts of the MT were essentially the same as the modern exemplars.[17]

There are four extant MT texts that can be traced back to the Ming dynasty (1368-1644 C.E.).[18] Since our modern texts are based upon these Ming texts, we should briefly consider them at this point.[19]

1. The *Tao Tsang* text (TT). This text is found in the *Cheng t'ung tao tsang*, the Ming dynasty Taoist Patrology completed in 1445.[20] Since this version of the text deletes a Sung dynasty taboo character, it is thought to be a Sung text. The TT version of the MT is considered by some authorities to be relatively uncorrupt and was used by Pi Yüan as the basis for his emended text.[21]

2. The Wu K'uan text (WK). This text was used by Sun Yi jang in his collation of the MT alongside the texts utilized by Pi Yüan. Its name is derived

from the fact that the text Sun acquired was hand copied by the Ming scholar Wu K'uan (1435-1504 C.E.). As Sun notes, "it is missing the first five volumes and it is largely identical to the TT text."[22] The WK text is unavailable, so we must rely on Sun's assessment that it is very similar to the TT text. Durrant suggests that they are either both descendants of a single earlier text or that one has been copied from the other.[23]

3. The Chih Ch'eng text (CC). This rare text was printed in 1552 and named after the city in which it was published. Its importance derives from the fact that Pi Yüan used it in his groundbreaking collation of the MT, and therefore all subsequent editions of the MT have presumably incorporated some of its readings.[24] The CC text is thought to have origins independent of the TT text, so the possibility exists that its antecedents may be older than the TT text.

4. The T'ang Yao ch'en text (TYC). This is the text reprinted in the well-known *Ssu pu ts'ung k'an* series (SPTK).[25] This text, dated 1554, seems to be much more closely related to the TT edition than to the CC text. In one chapter alone, Hu Shih found ten places where the CC text differs from the TT text. In all but one of these instances, the TYC text agrees with the TT text.[26] It seems probable that the TYC text was used as the basis for the Mao K'un text which was once popular in Japan.[27]

These four Ming dynasty texts are the basic source materials from which later, scholarly collations of the MT have been assembled. In addition to these more or less complete MT texts a number of abridged texts have also survived from the Ming. These shorter texts, several of which clearly derive from the previously mentioned Sung dynasty three volume MT, are generally considered to be unreliable and have played only a minor role in the collation of modern editions of the MT.[28]

In the early years following the Manchu conquest of China in 1644, many of China's most talented scholars turned away from government service and found solace in the study of antiquity. An early leader in this new academic trend was Ku Yen wu (1613-1682 C.E.). From his research into the causes underlying the fall of the Ming to the barbarian Ch'ing conquerors, Ku concluded that the intellectual blinders imposed upon the literati by the rote acceptance of Neo-Confucian orthodoxy, which was required for success in the imperial examinations, had so stifled independent thinking and creativity as to make barbarian conquest almost inevitable. To remedy this lamentable state of affairs, Ku advocated re-interpreting the legacy of the Classics by going back to the early commentaries of the Han dynasty. The resulting school of "Empirical Research" developed what Immanuel C.Y. Hsü has termed a "proto-scientific approach" to the study of antiquity.[29] The scholars of this school brought their critical scrutiny to bear on ancient phonetics, philology, etymology, and, most importantly for us, textual criticism. With Neo-Confucian orthodoxy in disrepute, the time was ripe for a reawakening of interest in ancient texts like the MT that stood outside the Confucian mainstream. The MT exercised further fascination by virtue of its obscurity. Since it had attracted very little scholarly attention in the past, relatively few emendations and "corrections" had been made to the text; it therefore preserved many ancient characters and phrases that provided fertile ground for phonetic, philological, and etymological investigation.[30] Not surprisingly numerous well-known Ch'ing dynasty scholars made serious studies of the text. Among their number were Lu Wen ch'ao (1717-1796), Pi Yüan (1730-1797), Wang Nien sun (1744-1832), Wang Yin chih (1766-1834), Yü Yüeh (1821-1907), and Sun Yi jang (1848-1908).[31]

Pi Yüan, with the assistance of Lu Wen ch'ao, produced the first modern collation of the MT. By comparing the available editions of the MT and collecting quotations preserved in other works, Pi established a relatively reliable edition of the text that has served as the foundation for all later textual criticism.[32]

A second landmark in the study of the MT is the text produced by Sun Yi jang, *Mo tzu hsien ku* (MTHK). Sun's MTHK was first published in 1894; an updated and expanded version printed in 1907 is one of the texts relied upon in this study. Both Y. P. Mei and Burton Watson used Sun's MTHK as the basis for their translations of the MT.[33]

The final text that we will consider is Chang Ch'un yi's *Mo tzu chi chieh* (MTCC). Chang's text, first published in 1931, relies largely on Sun's MTHK; its strongest point lies in its collection of commentary from scholars working after Sun Yi jang. Since Chang collects most of the important work of his predecessors without deviating greatly from Sun's excellent text, his MTCC will be the main MT edition referred to in this study.

Text Divisions, Authenticity, Authorship, and Time of Composition

In the preceding outline of the history of the MT text, we have seen that a collection of very similar texts all titled *Mo tzu* has been passed on from the Han dynasty to the present without, so far as we can tell, any break in the continuity of transmission. While it seems likely that chapters have been lost from the text in the course of the last several thousand years, it does not appear probable that significant additions have been made to it.[34] Having sketched the transmission of the text from the Han to the present, we should now tackle the trickier questions of provenance and authorship.

When asking the question of authorship of any pre-Han text we must first consider the nature of early Chinese text compilation. Although pre-Han texts are often named after a particular thinker and may in some cases even contain writings from the hand of their purported author, in most cases what we have are collections of writings from different authors and different times that often, though not always, share some similarity in outlook. Since the intent of these ancient authors appears to have been to represent the teachings of the particular school to which they belonged, the identity of the writer of any specific passage seems to have been a matter of little or no consequence.[35] Therefore, when reading a text from this period we do not necessarily expect the consistency of outlook and doctrinal uniformity that may sometimes be found in the works of a single author. However, it is not unreasonable to assume that these works were placed together by their compilers with intelligence and purpose; when a book purports to present the views of a particular man and his school we should not be surprised to find a related, coherent community of concerns expressed throughout the text.

The Divisions of the Text and Their Authenticity

Students of the MT have long noticed that certain groups of chapters seem to fit together, sharing a unity of style and occasionally of subject matter, and have come up with very similar schemes for grouping the chapters of the text.[36] The five-fold division proposed by Hu Shih is convincing and will prove quite adequate for our purposes. It will be most convenient to discuss the five divisions in the order in which they appear in the text.

1. The first seven chapters of the book form a unit that Durrant has called the "Epitomes."[37] The first three of these chapters are thought to be late additions to the text, in both style and content far removed from the rest of the text.[38] The last four chapters, while also apparently late additions to the text, are much more in keeping with the rest of the MT. Hu Shih has suggested that they are assembled out of leftover pieces culled from the body of the MT by early editors.[39] Y. P. Mei goes further with this line of thinking and suggests that the last four of the Epitomes were written as a sort of appendix to the MT in which some of the main ideas of the text are summarized.[40] The grammatical analysis done by Durrant shows that the Epitomes do not exhibit certain grammatical features found in the following "Essay" section of the text. From this Durrant concludes that the Epitomes must be regarded as "linguistically separate" from the main body of the MT; however, Durrant correctly cautions that just because the Epitomes are grammatically distinct from the Essays we should not therefore treat the Epitomes as a unit and assume that they share a common origin and authorship.[41] For our analysis of the religion of the MT, it is clear that the first three chapters of the Epitomes should be discarded. The last four chapters can conceivably be used should they be needed, but since they present in condensed form ideas more fully developed elsewhere, this should not be necessary.

2. Chapters eight through thirty-nine will be termed the "Essays." These chapters, seven of which have been lost, constitute a series of lectures on eleven different topics.[42] The chapters are organized in groups of three; each member of a triad shares the same chapter name followed by one of three designations: *shang* "upper," *chung* "middle," or *hsia* "lower."[43] (Rather than following the Chinese text literally, it will prove more convenient to substitute the numbers 1, 2, and 3 for the designations "upper," "middle," and "lower." With this system we will refer to Essay chapters as "Universal Love 2," "Will of Heaven 3," etc.) Although seven of the original thirty-two chapters are no longer extant, the losses have been well distributed so that each of the eleven subjects is represented by at least one surviving chapter, and sometimes by two or three. Scholars have long been puzzled by the occurrence of these triads of chapters, each concentrating on one particular topic. Although there are variations among the members of a triad, the differences are slight when compared with the similarities: the basic themes,

organization and even wording are usually similar and sometimes identical within the chapters making up a triad.

Henri Maspero believes that the style of the Essays is that of oration directly transcribed, which explains the many repetitions and uneven tempo of the discourses.[44] If true, this would tend to suggest that the Essays preserve, more or less directly, the words of Mo Ti. This is the impression one actually gets when studying these chapters; it seems almost as if one were reading three separate sets of notes taken at the same lecture. Ch'en Chu has advanced a theory that makes just this point. Ch'en argues that the chapters in the triads are too similar to be the records of different lectures or the accounts of competing sects, but are most probably the collected notes of three of Mo Ti's followers assembled after the master's death into something like our present text.[45] Although this is an argument I find reasonably plausible it is neither the oldest explanation nor the one most widely accepted among Sinologists.

The *Han Fei tzu,* a late Chou dynasty text, speaks of the separation of Mohists into three sects after the death of the master:

自墨子之死也，有相里氏之墨，有相夫氏之墨，
有鄧陵氏之墨。故孔墨之後，儒分為八，墨離
為三。取舍相反不同，而皆自謂真。

> After the death of Mo tzu there were Hsiang Li's Mohists, Hsiang Fu's Mohists, and Teng Ling's Mohists. Therefore, after Confucius and Mo tzu, the Confucians divided into eight [sects] and the Mohists separated into three. In collecting and discarding they are mutually opposed and differ, yet they each call themselves true [Confucians and Mohists].[46]

Yü Yüeh (1821-1906) is the first modern scholar on record to connect this account from the *Han Fei tzu* with the three part division of the Essay discourses:

> Mo tzu died and then the Mohists split into three. There were Hsiang Li's Mohists, Hsiang Fu's Mohists, and Teng Ling's Mohists. Now when we look at "Exaltation of the Virtuous," "Identification with the Superior," "Universal Love," "Condemnation of Offensive War," "Economy of Expenditures," "Simplicity in Funeral," "Will of Heaven," "On Ghosts," "Condemnation of Music," and "Anti-Fatalism" [the Essay chapters], they are all divided into three chapters, an upper, a middle and a lower. The words and sentences are slightly different but the main ideas are identical. I suspect that these are the differences in the versions passed on by the three schools of Hsiang Li, Hsiang

Fu, and Teng Ling. Men of a later time put them together to make a book.[47]

This theory that three chapters of each triad are the texts of the three different Mohist sects has been accepted by A. C. Graham,[48] Liang Ch'i ch'ao,[49] Y. P. Mei,[50] and Henri Maspero[51] among others. These writers further assume that each of the divisions of the text (*shang* "upper," *chung* "middle," and *hsia* "lower," or 1, 2, and 3 in our labeling) are the work of one of the schools. While it is certainly tempting to suppose that the three chapters of each triad are the texts of the three rival Mohist schools, until recently there was little evidence available that supported the theory. Further, several arguments of varying persuasiveness were mounted against it. As already mentioned, Ch'en Chu wondered why the texts of rival schools would show so little difference. Certainly doctrinal disputes are not the only reason for antagonistic sects to arise--struggles for authority, personality clashes and differences in praxis are obvious causes of sectarian proliferation--yet it does seem peculiar, given that the varying sects must have had some grounds for disagreement even if we do not know what they are, that no sign of this difference is detectable in the text. A more substantive argument is furnished by Durrant's grammatical analysis of the chapter triads. Of the Essay chapters as a whole he concludes that the distinctiveness of their language "points to the conclusion that they reflect an attempt to reproduce the systematic teachings of Mo Ti in the language which he spoke."[52] However, that this attempt was not altogether successful is revealed by variations from chapter to chapter within a triad; it appears that some writers were more adept than others in approximating the actual language spoken by Mo Ti.[53] More telling for the point at hand is his discovery that there is no discernable correlation between distinctive grammatical features and the *shang*, *chung*, and *hsia* chapters analyzed as three separate groups.[54] In other words, all the *shang* (or *chung* or *hsia*) chapters taken as a whole do not show greater grammatical uniformity than the *shang*, *chung*, and *hsia* chapters of any individual triad might display. This seems to indicate that, from a grammatical point of view, there are no grounds for assuming common authorship within each of the various strata of the triads.

Unfortunately, affairs are never so neatly wrapped up. As mentioned earlier, A. C. Graham has recently brought his formidable linguistic skills to bear upon the divisions of the MT, with startling conclusions. Graham first observes that Durrant inadvertently erred in his count of the occurrences of the non-final particle *hu* 乎. A correct count would have revealed that the use of non-final *hu*, a distinctive grammatical characteristic, occurs in only one of each of the triad chapters; Graham has labeled these chapters the H series. Graham then goes on to demonstrate that other discrete series of chapters can be identified on the basis of distinctive grammatical features. One series (named Y) is identified by the tendency to use the formula "Master Mo tzu *pronounces* " 子墨子 言 曰 throughout the essay. (Nearly all essays start with this formula but soon drop it in favor of the simpler "Master Mo tzu *says* " 子墨子曰.) The third series (J) is identified by a distinctive quotation formula in which the character *jan* 然 is used after the titles of books being quoted. He concludes that the Essay section of the MT is in fact the work of three different auctorial or editorial traditions, though due to displacements in the ordering of chapters, the three traditions do not correspond exactly to the current organization of chapters into *shang*, *chung*, and *hsia* series.[55]

Graham then moves a few passages, rearranges the text, and presents his new organization of the chapters. In this version of the MT the triads are ordered sequentially Y, H, and J, with the Y chapters always the shortest and the H chapters the longest. Graham speculates that when the Han dynasty editors of the MT compiled the current text, they sorted out the chapters in the order YHJ, but by this time a number of J chapters had already been lost. To fill in the gaps, the editors found "digests," short summaries of Mohist doctrines that were presumably already in circulation, and inserted them in the text so that there could be three versions of each essay. Unfortunately, instead of placing the "digests" where the missing J chapters should have been, the editors inserted them in the Y position, thus pushing the Y chapters into the H position and the H chapters into the J slot, and thereby skewing the sequence out of order and producing our current arrangement. By this reckoning, "Universal Love 1," "Condemnation of Offensive War 1," and "Economy of Expenditures 1" are not proper essays at all but are "digests" placed in the Y position in the YHJ series, and in a roundabout way filling in for the lost J chapters in their triads.

Although Graham's arguments are fascinating and show great ingenuity, they cannot be taken as proven. There are simply too many exceptions to the rules and special allowances made for anomalies for Graham's reconstruction to be accepted without reservations. For example, instances of the phrase "Master Mo tzu pronounces" are found in some of the H chapters as well as in the Y chapters for which this phrase is an identifying characteristic. To explain this apparent irregularity, Graham notes that this wording is only used when the theories of other schools are being refuted. Therefore, the five instances where H chapters use a phrase supposedly diagnostic of Y chapters do not "count."[56] Enough examples of equally tortured reasoning exist to give one the impression that Graham first intuitively grouped his chapters and then searched for the features that proved their kinship.[57] Furthermore, there is no evidence whatsoever for the existence of the "digests" that Graham posits were substituted for missing essays. Graham has repeatedly demonstrated an amazing sensitivity to the nuances of Classical Chinese style and grammar, so we should not by any means write off his assertions; however, at this point it might be more prudent to wait for further evidence before taking them as proven fact.

Of greater concern for this study is Graham's reading of political positions in his newly discovered series of chapters. Are the three versions of any chapter sufficiently different to reflect antagonistic political stances? Well, yes and no. If Graham's reconstruction is correct, then it appears that the Y series is notable for the paucity of its quotations and appeals to the authority of the sage kings. This clearly could be the result of conscious choice and might well reflect this series' editors' aversion to traditional sources of political legitimation; however, this is by no means certain. In a preceding section of this study we have commented on Graham's claim that the Y, H, and J chapters were produced by schools that were Purist, Compromising, and Reactionary respectively. It may be worth repeating that these categories (Purist, etc.) are modern, evaluative, normative projections onto ancient texts. Furthermore, they are evaluations made on the basis of subtle and slight literary evidence. For all we know, it may someday be discovered that, contrary to expectations, the "Compromising" wing of Mohism was the most vigorous of all Mohist factions in the military defense of attacked states; we just do not have the facts. It seems rash to evaluate an activist tradition on the basis of minor variations of emphasis in basically similar texts.

Most importantly, it is impossible to determine where Mo tzu himself stood on this supposed political spectrum. The very terms Graham assigns carry heavy implications; it seems clear that Graham believes that the Purist tradition is closest to the teachings of the master. Why should this necessarily be so? Might not Mo tzu have been a great compromiser--it would certainly fit with his emphasis on the practical--and the "Purist" wing of his followers been a schismatic sect of fanatics? As stated earlier, the Dialogue section of the MT reveals a teacher who can be stern, principled, self-righteous, clever, and conniving by turns. The tendencies Graham sees in the Essay series are all to be found in the master himself. Since our goal is to discover the patterns of ultimate concern in the oldest sections of the MT, it still seems most appropriate to accept the Essay section of the text as a reasonably consistent and unified whole.

At the very least, Graham's recent research clearly undercuts *all* positions in a longstanding debate over the priority of the three text levels. While one suspects that the following positions will have to be reconsidered, or discarded, in the light of Graham's hypotheses, they still merit a brief summary and provide insight into the history of scholarly debate over the Essays.

Alfred Forke argues that the similarities within the chapters of a triad are so great that the chapters could not possibly have been written independently. He believes that the three chapters of each triad are based upon an *ürtext*. Assuming that texts evolve from the simple to the complex, he takes the shortest version of every chapter (often the *shang* "upper" chapter) to be the basis for the other redactions.[58] Though Forke's hypothesis seems unlikely to be true, it could perhaps still be rehabilitated.

Fang Shou ch'u argues against the suitability of Western evolutionary assumptions for the analysis of ancient Chinese texts. He observes that the trend in Mohism is from the verbose and inelegant to the concise and refined;[59] the more precise and shorter chapters should therefore be of later provenance. This leads Fang to the conclusion that the *shang* chapters were written not first but last.[60] This argument is not without merit. As we shall see in our examination of the "Logic" chapters, later Mohist writings are extremely dense and place a great emphasis on the precise use of language. Unfortunately, both Forke and Fang are arguing reasonable positions based upon their individual perceptions of underlying trends, not quantifiable facts. While text redactions may in general *tend* to become more elaborated with the passing of time, we have no certainty that this is the case with the MT. Fang's counter argument might seem more plausible than Forke's in this particular case, but neither theory can be proven or falsified. Graham did not publish anything dealing with the question of priority, and in fact seems to view the

6 2

texts as the simultaneous products of contemporaneous schools, but it is not inconceivable that he may have had opinions on this issue as well. For now, the order in which the chapters were composed appears to be relatively unimportant.

With what then are we left? Although scholars may differ over the circumstances under which the Essays were committed to writing, they are uniform in accepting their basic usefulness for understanding the doctrines of early Mohism. Hu Shih states that although the Essay chapters have suffered from some late interpolations (the "Fei yüeh," "Condemnation of Music," and "Fei ju," "Anti-Confucianism," chapters are especially suspect in his eyes), overall the chapters can be taken as faithfully representing the thoughts, and even the words, of Mo Ti.[61]

The subject matter treated in the Essay chapters dovetails perfectly with the Mohist doctrines mentioned in Chou and Han sources. Kojima Kenkichiro has demonstrated that Chou and Han sources laud or attack Mohism "on virtually every major teaching appearing in the MT text today."[62] Generally speaking, the late Chou texts that mention Mo Ti or later Mohists are not enthusiastic advocates of the Mohist cause nor do they systematically present and critique Mohist doctrines, nonetheless they probably give a fair idea of the popular views of Mohism held by the literati of the Warring States period. The *Chuang tzu, Hsün tzu, Lü shih ch'un ch'iu, Chan kuo ts'e,* and *Mencius* all comment on Mohism in ways that seem very much in keeping with what we can learn from the received text of the MT. The following passage from the *Chuang tzu* is particularly complete in its assessment:

不侈於後世，不靡於萬物，不暉於數度，以繩
墨自矯而備世之急，古之道術有在於是者。墨
子禽滑釐聞其風而說之，為之大過已之大循。
作為非樂，命之曰節用。生不歌，死無服。墨子
汎愛兼利而非鬥，其道不怒。又好學而博不異
不與先王同，毀古之禮樂。

Not setting an extravagant example for later generations, not wasteful with material things, not splendid in ceremonial observances, regulating oneself with carpenter's line and blacking [metaphor for rules and regulations], and in that way relieving the distress of the world, as for the ancients' "arts of the *Tao* " some lay in this. Mo Ti and Ch'in Ku li heard of these practices and delighted in them, but they did them to excess and followed them too literally. He [Mo, or They?] wrote "Condemnation of Music" and exhorted [their followers] to "Economy of Expenditures." In life they did not sing; in death there was no mourning. Mo tzu advocated universal love and mutual benefit and therefore opposed war; his Way was non-violent. He also loved to study and was widely learned, [he sought to appear] not different [from others] but was not the same as the kings of antiquity, and he reviled the music and rites of the past.[63]

As we shall see when we turn to the analysis of the "Essays," the criticisms of the Mohists expressed in this *Chuang tzu* passage are very apropos to the MT text that we currently possess. Although this correspondence of ancient criticism and modern text is very close, it does not of course *prove* that the received MT is the same as the pre-Han text or even that it was produced by the Mohist school, but it is certainly strongly suggestive of that conclusion. In dealing with affairs of such antiquity this may be as close to certainty as we can get.

3. Chapters forty through forty-five will be called the "Logic" chapters for want of a better title. These six chapters are both extremely difficult and extremely corrupt. Further they cover an astonishing range of topics; in a series of short propositions and definitions they touch upon problems of logic, mathematics, mechanics, optics, ethics, psychology, economics, politics, and grammar.[64] Before A. C. Graham's pathfinding study of these chapters, they were, in my opinion anyway, virtually unreadable. The problems with the text led Liang Ch'i ch'ao to say that

> When it comes to the hardest to read and most fascinating of ancient writings, there is nothing to compare with the six MT chapters of "Ching shang," ["Canon 1"]; "Ching hsia," ["Canon 2"]; "Ching shuo shang," ["Exposition of Canon 1"]; "Ching shuo hsia," ["Exposition of Canon 2"]; "Ta ch'u," ["Major Illustrations"]; and "Hsiao ch'u," ["Minor Illustrations."][65]

The authorship of these chapters is usually attributed to "Neo-Mohists," a term coined by Hu Shih to describe these later followers of the Mohist school.[66] The following *Chuang tzu* passage gives us a glimpse of these argumentative Neo-Mohists and their topics of disputation:

相里勤之弟子，五侯之徒，南方之墨者，苦獲，己齒，鄧陵子之屬，俱誦墨經而倍譎不同，相謂別墨，以堅白同異之辯相訾，以觭偶不仵之辭相應。

Hsiang li Ch'in's disciples, the followers of Wu Hou, the Southern
Mohists: K'u Huo, Chi Ch'ih, Teng Ling tzu, and their ilk, all recite
the Mohist canons and opposing and deceiving [each other] over
their differences call each other "heretical Mohists" [Hu's term,
Neo-Mohists, does not fit too well in this context]; with disputations
on "hard and white" and "differences and similarities" they rebuke
each other and answer each other with propositions on the not
matching of "odd and even."[67]

"Hard and white" and "odd and even" were common subjects for the
disputations of the sophists at the end of the fourth century B.C.E. in China. A. C.
Graham suggests that the Neo-Mohists were responsible, in part, for introducing to
China the concern for precision of thought and definition that disputation on these
subjects requires.[68] It is obvious to modern readers of the text that the level of
sophistication displayed in these chapters, and the type of intellectual issues
engaged, belong to a time clearly removed from that of Mo Ti, yet Pi Yüan and
Liang Ch'i ch'ao both believed that the Logic chapters were the work of Mo tzu
himself. Pi based his attribution on the absence in the Logic chapters of the formula
"the Master Mo tzu said" (*tzu Mo tzu yüeh* 子墨子曰). Since Mo tzu's disciples
would certainly take advantage of every opportunity to refer to the master with
reverence, the fact that his name is not once mentioned in the Logic chapters
necessarily implied to Pi that Mo Ti must be their author![69] As we shall see, this
inference is insupportable. Liang Ch'i ch'ao's error is more interesting. Citing the
Chuang tzu passage quoted above, Liang argues that if the contending Mohist
schools "all recited the Mohist canons (*Mo ching* 墨經)," then the canons must
have been written at an early point in the history of the movement. Liang reasons
that the two Logic chapters named "Canon" ("Ching shang," "Canon 1," and
"Ching hsia," "Canon 2") are the work of Mo tzu, though containing later
emendations and interpolations, while the two chapters entitled "Exposition of
Canon 1" and "Exposition of Canon 2" ("Ching shuo shang" and "Ching shuo
hsia") contain some of the original oral explanations given by Mo Ti along with the
formulations of later teachers of the text.[70]

Hu Shih effectively demolishes Liang's argument by demonstrating that the
"Mohist canons" referred to by the *Chuang tzu* are what we have called the Essay
chapters. The Logic chapters that have the word "canon" in their titles are the
product of the Neo-Mohists and are not likely to have been recited as venerated
texts by their own creators. The "canons" referred to in the *Chuang tzu* must have

existed before these "heretical Mohists" arose and began disputing about "hard and white" and "differences and similarities."[71]

Perhaps the most convincing objection that Hu raises to Liang's theory is based on the contrast between the logical method expounded in the Essays and the the precise logical system of the Logic chapters. However noteworthy the early Mohist attempts at developing a method of reasoning may be, they are a far cry from the tightly reasoned propositions of the Logic chapters; it is inconceivable that the two systems, one so rudimentary and the other so sophisticated, could be the product of the same man or time.[72]

That the Logic chapters were composed at a late date is generally accepted by modern Sinologists. A. C. Graham argues that the process of developing the definitions and propositions of the Logic chapters probably began sometime before 300 B.C.E. and continued well into the third century B.C.E.[73] Similarly, Hu Shih suggests the dates of 325-250 B.C.E. for the time period in which Neo-Mohist thought flourished.[74] Both authors agree that the style and content of the Logic chapters mark them as works originating no earlier than the middle of the fourth century B.C.E. Graham examines the rigidly controlled use of language in the chapters and identifies a large number of technical terms used in the works-- further illustrating the distance in time and thought separating the Neo-Mohists from the early followers of Mo Ti.[75]

Given that the Logic chapters must postdate Mo Ti by one hundred years or more, what use can we make of them in this study? It seems clear that we must relegate them to a very minor position. The Logic chapters are fascinating (and mystifying) documents of a late and highly distinctive strand of Mohist thought. As evidence of the evolution of a group's, or part of a group's, thought after the death of its founder they are invaluable, but only where that later thought serves to clarify terms and concepts presented in earlier strata of the MT can it prove useful in our study.

4. The next five chapters, numbered forty-six through fifty, will be referred to as the "Dialogues." Comprising Mo Ti's answers to questions from both opponents and disciples, descriptions of encounters and battles of wits purportedly engaged in during Mo Ti's lifetime, and various anecdotes and aphorisms, the short paragraphs of the Dialogues were clearly compiled with didactic intent. Unlike the ponderous and repetitive Essays, the Dialogues display a leaner style that many

authors compare to that of the Confucian *Analects*. Although this comparison is basically accurate, the Dialogues quite fortunately tend to furnish a bit more context for the Master's sayings than do the *Analects*, which makes their meaning more accessible.

Throughout the Dialogue chapters, Mo Ti is referred to as "Master Mo tzu," leading many scholars to assume that the chapters were compiled by Mo Ti's disciples. Hu Shih suggests that the Dialogues were written by disciples soon after Mo tzu's death and contain firsthand recollections of the Master's words and actions. In his opinion "they contain much material that is far more important than that in the Essays."[76] Henri Maspero states that the first three Dialogue chapters are the preserved fragments of actual conversations with Mo tzu that were collected soon after his death; the last two chapters also preserve remembered accounts of Mo Ti's life and words but were committed to writing at a later date.[77]

In some editions of the MT, the first of the Dialogue chapters, "Keng chu p'ien," contains the words *tzu Ch'in tzu* "the Master Ch'in tzu";[78] from this one mention of Master Ch'in, some scholars have reasoned that the "Keng chu p'ien," or perhaps only a part of the chapter, is the work of the disciples of Mo tzu's disciple Ch'in Ku li.[79] This is certainly a possibility, but it is of course equally possible that while copying the text a disciple of Ch'in Ku li came upon his master's name and quite naturally added the first, honorific *tzu*. In any case, it seems probable that this section of the text dates back to a time when disciples still lived who had memories of Mo Ti's life, acts, and words.

Steven Durrant's grammatical analysis of the Dialogue chapters is inconclusive: he finds that the Dialogues are written in "the eclectic language of the later Chou period."[80] Individual episodes may well have been drawn from "linguistically disparate sources," but there is no compelling evidence to suggest that these chapters are not the work of disciples writing within several generations of Mo tzu's death.[81]

On the basis of the evidence cited above, we will be using the Dialogues as a major source for our inquiry into the religion of the early Mohists. Along with the Essays, these chapters provide us with our most reliable and accessible source materials on Mo Ti and his early followers.

5. The final eleven extant chapters of the MT deal with various strategies for military preparation and defense. This section abounds in technical terms of

uncertain meaning; the text presupposes a familiarity with late Warring States military equipment and procedures that modern scholars have not yet acquired--the lack of which makes the "Defense" chapters arguably the most difficult section of the MT to decipher. Faced with the immense labors necessary to decode these chapters, and the marginal rewards that restoring a work on warfare seems likely to bring to students of philosophy and literature, scholars have historically elected to allow the Defense chapters to continue their slide towards oblivion. Only recently have new studies appeared, particularly Ts'en Chung mien's *Mo tzu ch'eng shou ke p'ien chien chu*, that dispel some of the confusion enveloping these chapters, but much work remains to be done before we can claim fully to understand this section of the MT.[82]

As with the other divisions of the MT, the origins of the Defense chapters are shrouded in mist, but since these chapters have only recently come under scholarly scrutiny there is even less consensus on their provenance than we find for the rest of the text. Hsü Cho yün writes that "the authenticity of this last group [the Defense chapters] was questioned by the Ch'ing scholars, and it has now been fully proven that these chapters were forged by Han tacticians."[83] What is "fully proven" to one scholar is highly suspect to another; Fang Shou ch'u thinks that seven of the eleven chapters are clearly products of the late Chou, while four display *yin-yang* and "five elements" influences that suggest a Han dynasty authorship.[84] Joseph Needham is of the opinion that no one really knows when these chapters were written but thinks "they may well date from between -300 and -250."[85] If Needham is correct, then all the Defense chapters are the product of the late Warring States period.

One thing upon which all scholars seem to agree is that the Defense chapters are a relatively late addition to the text. The repeated appearance in these chapters of Mo Ti's disciple Ch'in Ku li (often with the title "Master Ch'in") tends to support this perception. While it is reasonable to suppose that the Defense chapters were written by followers of Mo Ti and that they display the techniques and reflect the concerns of one aspect of the later Mohist tradition, there is very little of religious interest in these chapters for one studying the early followers of Mo tzu. The significance of the Defense chapters for this analysis may lie less in their content than in the very fact that they were written, for their existence tends to lend support to the early accounts of Mo Ti's life and deeds and drive home just how important defensive military action is in the tradition of the followers of Mo tzu.

In summary, we have concluded that the received MT is most likely a direct descendant of the earliest known exemplars of the text and, insofar as can be determined, is largely or entirely the product of the school, or schools, professing allegiance to Mo Ti. The MT is divided by scholars into five divisions, each with its own distinguishing characteristics, that are of varying usefulness for this study. We will make no use of the Epitomes since the first three chapters are probably spurious and the others only summarize the main points of the Essays. The Essay and Dialogue chapters seem to be the oldest strata of the text and will be taken as our primary sources in the analysis of the teachings of Mo Ti and his early followers. Being the products of a later age, the Logic and Defense chapters can provide only secondary evidence regarding the practices and beliefs of the early school.

We will now turn to the analysis of the Essays.

Notes

[1] It has been pointed out by many authors that the effects of the book burning may not have been as complete as the Ch'in emperor wished. Nonetheless, most of the pre-Ch'in "classics" that still exist are thought to have been reconstructed (from memory, preserved text fragments, etc.) during the Han. See Fung Yu lan, *A History of Chinese Philosophy*, 1:15-16.

[2] Burton Watson, *Early Chinese Literature* (New York: Columbia University Press, 1962), pp. 4-5.

[3] It is commonly believed that nearly all pre-Han texts are not the work of an individual author but the product of a group of disciples or a school of thinkers. The *Hsün tzu* and the *Han Fei tzu* are possible exceptions to this generalization. They were also written at the very end of the period in question.

[4] Stephen Durrant, "Examination."

[5] *Erh shih wu shih*, p. 435.

[6] *Lü shih ch'un ch'iu*, CTCC, vol. 6, p. 18.

[7] Durrant, "Examination," p. 48.

[8] Sun Yi jang, *Chiao pu ting pen Mo tzu hsien ku*, with an Addendum by Li Li (reprint ed., Taiwan: Yi wen yin shu kuan, 1969), p. 1187.

[9] Durrant, "Examination," p. 48.

[10] Ibid., p. 53.

[11] Ibid.

[12] The one T'ang citation of the MT that refers to the number of chapters in the work states: "Mo tzu wrote a book of thirty-five chapters." This is most perplexing since it seems to indicate that a T'ang text of MT existed that was significantly *shorter* than the current text. A number of explanations for this odd circumstance have been proffered, the most plausible of which is that in this text several groups of chapters have been lumped together and each new group counted as one chapter. If all chapters in the "Essay" section of the text dealing with the same subject matter are counted together, we end up with a text of thirty-nine chapters. With several more consolidations, the number thirty-five could be reached. (Ibid., pp. 53-54.)

[13] Ibid., p. 55.

[14] The fifty-three chapter MT text that we will use in this study is believed to be a direct descendant of the seventy-one chapter text cited in the *Ch'ien Han shu*. A. C. Graham argues that the three volume MT was the only version readily available to literate Chinese from the T'ang to the Ch'ing (1644-1911 C.E.). See Graham, *Logic*, p. 68.

[15] Durrant, "Examination," p. 55, quoting the *Chih chai shu mu* of Ch'en Chen sun (1236 C.E.).

[16] As Durrant points out, the current text of MT has sixty-one chapter titles in the table of contents, while the text consists of only fifty-three chapters. It is possible that the Sung bibliographers had a text very similar to the current version and

counted all sixty-one chapter titles in the table of contents as if they were full chapters. A counter argument can be made from evidence drawn from the *T'ai p'ing yü lan* (TPYL), an "encyclopedia" dating from the early years of the Sung (ca. 983 C.E.). Since many of the quotes in the TPYL attributed to the MT are not found in the present text, it can be argued that chapters no longer extant must have circulated in the Sung. Of course, it could also be argued that the TPYL drew its material not from the MT but from pre-Sung literary collections. (Ibid., pp. 56-57.)

[17] Ibid., p. 61. Durrant notes that the practice of counting chapters that exist in title alone was continued by later bibliographers.

[18] Ibid., p. 63.

[19] Unless otherwise noted, all of the following information on the Ming dynasty MT texts is drawn from ibid., pp. 63-68.

[20] Graham, *Logic*, p. 74.

[21] Though since superseded, Pi Yüan's pioneering work on the MT marks the beginning of modern study of the text. His emended text was a great improvement over all preceding MT texts and has itself served as the basis for later, more accurate reconstructions.

[22] Sun, MTHK, p. 11.

[23] Durrant, "Examination," p. 65.

[24] One of the most frustrating aspects of Pi Yüan's MT arises from Pi's failure to cite the sources from which he draws his variant readings. For this reason it is often impossible to determine which text(s) are being followed in any specific passage.

[25] SPTK, vol. 24.

[26] Cited in Durrant, "Examination," p. 87.

[27] Ibid., p. 68.

[28] Ibid., pp. 68-69.

[29] Liang Ch'i ch'ao, *Intellectual Trends in the Ch'ing Period*, trans. Immanuel C. Y. Hsü (Cambridge: Harvard University Press, 1959), p. 129.

[30] Chou Fu mei notes on page one of her *Mo tzu chia chieh tzu chi shih* (Taipei: Taiwan University, 1965) that the MT preserves a large number of ancient words and loan graphs that have long since been edited out of more extensively studied texts.

[31] Durrant, "Examination," p. 70.

[32] Ibid., p. 72.

[33] See Mei, *Rival*, p. 52, and Burton Watson, *Mo Tzu: The Basic Writings* (New York: Columbia University Press, 1963), p. 16.

[34] Durrant, "Examination," p. 314, argues that chapters were lost and not simply consolidated since there are many apparently authentic MT quotations in early Chinese collectanea that are without parallels in our current text. The large number of these quotations would seem to indicate that a significant chunk of the text has

been lost from our current MT. Given the relative obscurity of the MT and the low regard in which its prose was, and is, held by the literati, it seems quite improbable that any self-respecting literary forger would seek to insinuate new material into its text. Further, the various sections of the MT all have their respective, distinctive styles; there is no evidence that any divisions of the text have been seriously tampered with.

[35] See Watson, *Literature*, p. 124, and Fung, *History*, pp. 19-20 for a fuller exposition of these ideas.

[36] Hu Shih divides the text into five distinct sections, while Fung, by collapsing Hu's first two sections together, comes up with only four sections. Both divide the final three sections identically. See Fung, *Chung kuo che hsüeh shih hsin pien*, p. 140, and Hu Shih, *Chung kuo che hsüeh shih ta kang*, pp. 151-152. Mei, *Rival*, pp. 52-57 follows Hu Shih very closely.

[37] Durrant, "Examination," p. 11.

[38] Hu Shih, *Chung kuo che hsüeh shih ta kang*, p. 151. It should be noted that not everyone agrees with this assessment. Pi Yüan argued that the first two epitomes, "Befriending the Learned" and "Self-Cultivation," were from the hand of Mo Ti himself! This would be exciting if true, but unfortunately Pi's argument is exceedingly weak: he believed that since these chapters dispensed with the honorific *tzu Mo tzu* "Master Mo tzu" they must have been written personally by Mo tzu. Using this same reasoning, Pi claimed that the Logic chapters, now universally regarded as a late addition to the text, must also have been written by Mo Ti. See Pi Yüan, *Mo tzu chu* (1783, reprint ed., Taipei: Kuang wen shu chu, 1965), p. 1b.

[39] Hu Shih, *Chung kuo che hsüeh shih ta kang*, p. 151.

[40] Y. P. Mei, *Rival*, p. 53.

[41] Durrant, "Examination," p. 15.

[42] Most scholars mention only ten subject areas, apparently feeling that the "Anti-Confucian" chapters do not form a separate subject area, since attacking another school is not the same as advancing theses of one's own.

[43] The one exception to the three part division is the group of "Anti-Confucian" chapters. As far as it is known, only two of these chapters have ever existed.

[44] Maspero, *La Chine antique*, p. 391.

[45] Fang Shou ch'u, *Mo hsüeh yüan liu*, p. 41

[46] *Han Fei tzu*, CTCC, vol. 5, p. 351.

[47] MTHK, preface by Yü Yüeh, pp. 5-6.

[48] Graham, *Logic*, p. 3.

[49] Liang Ch'i ch'ao, *Mo tzu hsüeh an* (Shanghai: Chung-hua shu chu, 1936), p. 6.

[50] Mei, *Rival*, p. 54.

[51] Maspero, *La Chine antique*, p. 390.

[52] Durrant, "Examination," p. 317. This is similar to the conclusion of Maspero noted above.

[53] Ibid., p. 317.

[54] Ibid., p. 318.

[55] Graham, Divisions, pp. 2-10. Graham's reasoning is far more complex and detailed than this summary indicates. In some ways this complexity is reassuring, though one has to wonder at the elaborate reasoning needed to explain the many discrepancies, anomalies, and irregularities that prevent the data from fitting neatly into the mold.

[56] Ibid., pp. 4-6.

[57] This is not to say that Graham's arguments, taken individually, are implausible. They are not. However, the number of suppositions and emendations one must accept before the data truly fit Graham's reconstruction is too large to inspire confidence in his hypotheses.

[58] Me Ti: des Socialethikers und seiner Schuler philosophische Werke, p. 23, cited by Durrant, "Examination," pp. 19-20. Forke is correct in noticing that the lengths of the chapters within the triads tend to increase from shang to chung to hsia. Lo Ken tse gives the number of characters in each chapter of the Essays in Chu tzu kao so (Peking: Jen min ch'u pan she, 1958), p. 179. Using his count, the mean number of characters in each extant chapter of the three text strata can be computed as follows: shang, 947; chung, 1596; hsia, 2105.

[59] A. C. Graham has also remarked upon this tendency in Mohist writings. Graham, Logic, pp. 7-8.

[60] Fang Shou ch'u, Mo hsüeh yüan liu, pp. 41-58.

[61] Hu Shih, Chung kuo che hsüeh shih ta kang, p. 151.

[62] Kojima Kenkichiro, Chu tzu pai chia k'ao, pp. 186-187, quoted in Durrant, "Examination," p. 45.

[63] Ch'en Ku ying, ed., Chuang tzu chin chu chin yi, pp. 940-941.

[64] At least Graham claims to find all these topics in this section of the MT. Graham, Logic, pp. 25-54. Graham has done an extraordinary job of deciphering the technical vocabulary and sorting out the displaced passages of this section of the MT. It is fairly easy to look at his translation of the Logic chapters and agree with his interpretation; it would be infinitely harder to do the translation oneself!

[65] Liang Ch'i ch'ao, Mo tzu hsüeh an, p. 35.

[66] Hu Shih, The Development of the Logical Method in Ancient China, 2nd ed. (Shanghai, 1922; reprint ed., New York: Paragon Book Reprint Co., 1963), p. 59.

[67] Ch'en Ku ying, Chuang tzu, p. 941.

[68] Graham, Logic, p. 19.

[69] Pi Yüan, Mo tzu chu, p. 1b.

[70] Liang Ch'i ch'ao, Mo tzu hsüeh an, p. 35.

[71] Hu Shih, Chung kuo che hsüeh shih ta kang, p. 185.

[72] Hu Shih, Development, p. 83.

[73] Graham, Logic, p. 53.

[74] Hu Shih, *Development*, p. 61.

[75] Graham, *Logic*, pp. 167-227.

[76] Hu Shih, *Chung kuo che hsüeh shih ta kang*, p. 152.

[77] Maspero, *La Chine antique*, p. 391. Unfortunately Maspero does not support his assertions with evidence, though he almost certainly had some.

[78] MTCC, p. 562. Chang notes that two other modern texts drop the first *tzu*, which yields the ordinary name Ch'in tzu.

[79] One instance of this can be seen in Pi Yüan, *Mo tzu chu*, p. 3.

[80] Durrant, "Examination," p. 317.

[81] Ibid., pp. 316-317.

[82] See Ts'en Chung mien, *Mo tzu ch'eng shou ke p'ien chien chu* (Peking: Ku chi ch'u pan she, 1958).

[83] Hsü Cho yün, *Transition*, p. 187.

[84] Fang Shou ch'u, *Mo hsüeh yüan liu*, p. 54.

[85] Joseph Needham, *Science and Civilisation in China*, vol. 2: *History of Scientific Thought* (Cambridge: Cambridge University Press, 1956), p. 166.

CHAPTER IV

ANALYSIS OF THE ESSAYS 1

Introduction

In our analysis of the religion of the MT we will use, as already mentioned, the criterion of ultimate concern to identify what is specifically *religious*, as opposed to philosophical or supernatural, in the text. However, this alone does not really get at the heart of Mo tzu's teaching[1]; if we desire to do so we must also consider other related and significant matters. This chapter and the following two will be devoted to the religious analysis of the Essay chapters; in addition to a consideration of the ultimate concern of the Essays as a whole, we will also examine the religious means presented in each triad of Essay chapters, and consider how the Mohist system was designed to recreate the ideal world of the sage kings of antiquity. Once we have discussed goals and means we will examine the arguments presented in the text in support of the Mohist agenda in order to understand better the full import of Mo tzu's positions and to see more clearly the extent to which the Mohist tradition is an outgrowth of the mainstream literary culture of Warring States China.

Unlike many writers of Chinese philosophical and religious texts, Mo tzu was not interested in mystifying his message or cloaking his ideas in vague, if evocative, language;[2] the ultimate concern of the MT is stated clearly and unambiguously in many places throughout the text, though the wording often varies. One of the most general statements of ultimate concern is found in "Universal Love 2" where it is presented in the guise of a description of the actions of a benevolent man, or sage:[3] "The master Mo tzu said: 'The reason that the benevolent man acts must be to promote the good of the world and to exclude harm from it.'"[4] Throughout the MT we find this concern for the welfare of the world expressed in a variety of ways and approached from a number of different angles.

The expressed components of the commonweal vary from description to description, but the consistent thrust of the text is unmistakable. The ultimate concern of the early Mohists is then to promote all actions and policies perceived to bring true benefit to the people of the world while at the same time making coordinated efforts to escape from, or eliminate, all courses of action that harm the general good. As we move from this most general statement of early Mohist ultimacy to the actual means designed to realize Mo tzu's religious goal, the formulations in the text become increasingly pragmatic and specific.

At first remove from the Mohist ultimate concern, or perhaps a subset of it, are the broad concrete goals that, if realized, would produce the benefit to society at large that Mo tzu desires. These goals, to bring about good government, to increase the population, to achieve a state of brotherhood among men, etc., can reasonably be viewed both as ends in themselves and as means to the highest goal--societal well-being. For the purpose of our analysis we could reasonably view these Mohist desiderata as either the concrete components of the Mohist ultimate concern or as the highest level means for achieving that ultimate concern. For example, when viewed from the vantage point of ultimate concern, the Mohist concept of good government is clearly a means for producing an ideal society. However, this concept can equally well be regarded as a goal of the Mohist program, since good government is one of the essential qualities of a state where the Mohist ideals have been realized. To avoid unnecessary confusion and to ensure a measure of consistency, we will henceforth refer to these broad goals not as means but as the concrete, specific components of the Mohist ultimate concern, or alternately as a subset of the ultimate concern. By so doing we are not in any way attempting to obscure the interdependent nature of the Mohist means and goals.

What we will term the "primary means" are the ten major topics of the Essay chapters (exaltation of the virtuous, identification with the superior, universal love, etc.). By making each of these means the topic of three essays,[5] the early Mohists left a clear indication of the importance that these means held in their program of social transformation.[6] These primary means are themselves often the goals of what we shall term the "secondary means." We may again look at one of the early Essay chapters for an illustration. The exaltation of the virtuous is certainly one means for securing an ideal society, but its implementation presents several difficulties that must themselves be resolved through subsidiary means. It is all very well to talk of employing and promoting the virtuous, but whence are the necessary numbers of skilled, honest, and capable men to come? Mo tzu suggests several ways to increase the number of worthies in the state; his methods for doing this are examples of secondary means. Generally speaking, the secondary means are intended to be directly implemented by the rulers of states; although for over two millennia critics have attacked them as thoroughly unrealistic, it is likely that Mo tzu offered them in all sincerity as practical stratagems for implementing his primary means.

In the remainder of this section of the study we shall consider each of the triads of Essay chapters, taking them in the order in which they appear in the current text. As previously indicated, the triads will be first described and analyzed according to our scheme of goals, primary means and secondary means. Methods of argument and the types of proof used in the chapters will be examined for the light they shed on the preconceptions, assumptions, and values of the early Mohists. Claims made by earlier students of the text that in the light of this study appear to be untenable will be dealt with as appropriate. After all of the triads of Essay chapters have been analyzed in this and the following two chapters, a concluding section will summarize the findings scattered through the three chapters to draw a relatively comprehensive picture of the religion of the Essays.

Exaltation of the Virtuous[7]

As we proceed through the Essays a repeated pattern, or structural formula, will emerge in almost every chapter: the chapter begins either with a statement of a desired goal or a description of a situation harmful to the common good. This opening is then followed by a Mohist prescription for achieving the desirable goal or alleviating the harmful condition, as the case may be. Since all the original chapters entitled "Exaltation of the Virtuous" are still in existence, we have three separate essays on this topic to compare.

Chapters 1 and 3 have very similar openings; though worded differently, one paraphrase will serve to convey the gist of both of them: The master Mo tzu said: "Nowadays all the world's rulers want their states to be wealthy, their people numerous, and their laws enforced in an orderly manner, yet what they obtain is, in fact, the opposite of what they desire. Why is this? It is that they do not have the exaltation of the virtuous as the basis of their government."[8]

The beginning of "Exaltation of the Virtuous 2" nicely complements the concerns expressed in "Exaltation of the Virtuous 1" and "Exaltation of the Virtuous 3":

> The Master Mo tzu said: "Now when emperors, dukes and high officials rule the people, manage the altars of earth and grain, and regulate their states, they desire to administer and stabilize and in that way not lose them. Why do they not see that the exaltation of the virtuous is the root of government?"[9]

The claim advanced in these opening lines is that the exaltation of the virtuous is "the root [or basis] of government." Good government, we remember, is one of the specific components of the Mohist ultimate concern and as such shares in the qualities of both the Mohist ultimate concern and the highest category of means for attaining that concern. While we have chosen to refer to good government and the other related goals as subsets of the Mohist ultimate concern, or religious goal, it may prove helpful to keep the instrumental nature of these goals in mind. If one desires good government, then, the text claims, one must understand that the employment and promotion of the virtuous is the way to realize it. The exaltation of the virtuous is therefore a primary means for the realization of the Mohist ultimate concern.

The wealthy states, flourishing populations, and orderly jurisdictions named in these sentences as the things desired by the world's rulers form a subset of the Mohist religious goal, or ultimate concern. Here, as elsewhere in the text, the authors of the MT skillfully present their religious desiderata *not* as the particular and idiosyncratic goals of their own organization but as the natural, shared aims of all civilized leaders. In so presenting their religious goals the Mohists are not necessarily completely disingenuous; the Mohist ultimate concern does, in fact, have wide appeal and is sufficiently practical and mundane to interest the most "secular" of rulers. However, enlisting the readers' sympathy for the Mohist vision of the ideal world is not the major task of the MT; the variations on the Mohist goal are listed almost without comment in many sections of the MT, for it is understood by the early Mohists that their goals are shared, at least in part, by nearly all readers of the text and therefore do not require proof. Rare is the ruler who does not at least claim to desire greater prosperity and security for his people. Where the

Mohists encounter the greatest difficulty is in selling their religious *means* to a skeptical, cynical world.

The greater part of the three chapters on the "Exaltation of the Virtuous" is spent demonstrating that the employment of the virtuous will, in fact, result in superior, orderly government, that the virtuous in every state can and should be increased, and that the exaltation of the virtuous was one of the *modi operandi* of the sages of antiquity. Demonstrating that the employment of the virtuous leads to ideal government is, of course, proof of the efficacy of the primary means presented in the chapter. Showing how and why the virtuous in every state can and should be increased is the presentation and justification of a secondary means. The claim that the exaltation of the virtuous was one of the methods of the sages is another attempt to buttress the primary means--it also reveals a great deal about the thinking of the early Mohists.

Before going on to discuss the content of the chapter it will be worthwhile to consider what Mo tzu meant by his use of the term *hsien* 賢 which is consistently translated here as "the virtuous." Bernhard Karlgren, the outstanding Swedish Sinologist, gives "wise," "worthy," and "superior" as Chou dynasty meanings for the word.[10] The dictionary *Tz'u Hai* gives the following early meanings: "talented," "hardworking," and "the best of a particular thing."[11] Of course, dictionary entries can only point us in the general direction of the MT's probable meaning for the term; for a fuller understanding of what "the virtuous" really means we must look at the text. As a work of the early centuries B.C.E., the Essay section of the MT naturally does not define its terms in a modern academic manner,[12] but in this case it does give a description of how the virtuous *behave* when given positions of authority:

> When the virtuous rules a state he goes to court as soon as it is light and returns home when it is late, all the while listening to lawsuits and managing the government. This is why the state is well-governed and the penal codes are just. When the virtuous serves as an official he goes to bed late and rises early, collecting taxes from the passes, markets, mountains, forests, and weirs in order to fill the governmental storehouses. For this reason the storehouses are filled and goods are not dispersed. When the virtuous governs a district he goes out early and returns late, plowing the fields, planting and gathering in the beans and grains.[13] This is why the beans and grains are plentiful and the people have enough to eat. Therefore when the state is well-governed, the penal code is just;

when the governmental storehouses are full, the masses are prosperous.[14]

Based on this passage, it seems that the distinguishing characteristic of "the virtuous" is his diligence and capacity for work. Competence and honesty are perhaps implied qualities of this ideal official, but great spiritual insight and superhuman moral rectitude do not seem to be required. The Mohist ideal of human behavior, at least as it is presented in this description, is notable mostly for its attainability. Unlike the "cloud riding immortals" of later Taoist literature who "ascend to Heaven in broad daylight," the ideal person of the MT, the *hsien*, differs from the common run of humanity only in degree, not in kind. Given sufficient determination and a willingness to sublimate individual benefit to the well-being of society, anyone with above average managerial ability should be able to become one of "the virtuous." One must bear in mind the rather mundane nature of this ideal person and not be misled by the English language implications of the word "virtuous."

The three chapters on exalting the virtuous offer two forms of proof for the efficacy of this primary religious means: assertions based on common sense and observation, and the precedent of practices attributed to the sage kings of antiquity.[15]

In the first category we find the following persuasion:

How do we know that the exaltation of the virtuous constitutes the basis of government? I say that when the noble and wise rule the stupid and base, then there is order. When the stupid and base rule the noble and wise, then there is disorder. This is how we know that the exaltation of the virtuous is the basis of government.[16]

This observation is presented as self-evident; the reader is expected to accept it at face value, for no further evidence, either logical or historical, is provided to back it up. The second example in this category illustrates a genre much used in the MT: the argument from analogy. Mo tzu constantly complains that the rulers of his time understand small matters but are ignorant of important affairs. His reasoning runs as follows: when rulers want a coat made they know they cannot do it themselves, and so they hire a competent tailor. When they have a cow or sheep to be slaughtered they cannot kill it themselves, so they hire a good butcher. In these two instances they know to exalt the worthy and employ the capable. Only when it comes to rectifying disorder in the state do they fail to know to employ the virtuous.[17] The style of reasoning from analogy used in this passage must have been viewed as effective by Mo tzu, for we find it repeated throughout the Essay and Dialogue chapters.

With these two examples we exhaust the logical arguments presented in the text for the usefulness of exalting the virtuous. A large percentage of the rest of the chapters is devoted to illustrations of the practice during the reigns of the sage kings.[18] Along the way the reader is shown how a "secondary means," the nurturing and increase of the ranks of the virtuous, was prosecuted in high antiquity. We are told that:

> Therefore, anciently the sage kings deeply revered the exaltation of the virtuous and the employment of the capable. They did not collude with their male relatives; they were not partial to the wealthy and noble, nor did they dote on the good looking. As for the virtuous, they raised and exalted them, enriched and ennobled them, and made them officials. The unworthy they suppressed and cast aside; they impoverished them, made them commoners, and used them as laborers. Thereupon the people were all encouraged by their [the sage kings'] rewards and feared their punishments and led each other in becoming virtuous. That is why the virtuous were numerous and the unworthy few. This is what is meant by the exaltation[19] of the virtuous.[20]

A surprisingly large number of points are made in this passage; although they are fleshed out more fully elsewhere in the chapters, we can clearly see them here. First we are told that the exaltation of the virtuous was honored and actually practiced by the sage kings. As practiced by the sage kings, the exaltation of the virtuous was an effective means for social transformation; the number of good persons increased while that of bad declined. The method of increasing the virtuous and decreasing the unworthy--what we have termed a secondary means--is also delineated. Through blunt "carrot and stick" methods, the sage kings radically altered the behavior of society.[21] By rewarding desired behaviors and punishing unsuitable ones the ranks of the virtuous were greatly increased and those of the unworthy greatly depleted. What was done once can be done again; the "fact" that the sage kings created an ideal society through the exaltation of the virtuous seems sufficient proof that it can be done in Mo tzu's time--if only wise, resourceful rulers, latter-day sages, can be inspired to implement the practice. Mo tzu additionally manages to critique current practices in hiring and promotion while ostensibly describing what the sage kings did *not* do. Here and elsewhere in the text, Mo tzu condemns the practice then current of bestowing high positions and other favors on the incompetent, whose only qualifications are their wealth and nobility, their family connections, or their attractive appearance.

Mo tzu's method of increasing the virtuous reinforces the perception that the Mohist ideal man is defined by his behavior and not by any state of inner illumination or supramundane insight. Another similar passage illustrates how righteousness was produced by the sage kings:

> ....when anciently the sage kings governed they said: "The unrighteous will not be wealthy; the unrighteous will not be esteemed; the unrighteous will not be considered intimates; the unrighteous will not be allowed near." Therefore when the rich and esteemed men heard this they withdrew and consulted saying: "What we initially relied on was wealth and prestige. Now the superior promotes the righteous without avoiding the poor and lowly. If it is like this, then we have to be righteous." When the intimates heard this they also withdrew and[22] consulted saying: "What we initially relied on was intimacy. Now the superior promotes the righteous and does not avoid those far off. If it is like this, then we have to be righteous."...When those far off heard this they too withdrew and consulted saying: "We initially supposed that since we were far away we had nothing on which to rely. Now the superior promotes the righteous without avoiding the distant. If it is like this, then we have to be righteous." Reaching to the officials of the far off, rustic hinterlands as well as the officers' children in the palace, the multitudes in the state and the farmers of the surrounding area, when they heard it, they all competed in being righteous.[23]

Like his understanding of virtue, Mo tzu's definition of righteousness seems, on the surface, to be psychologically unsophisticated. Evidently the outward, objectively measurable form of the individual's behavior is all that Mo tzu seeks to regulate; if someone's actions appear acceptable then his, or her, inner motives are inconsequential. The text shows no awareness of the possibility that someone might strive to appear righteous in order to gain power and wealth that could be used for nefarious or anti-social ends; Mo tzu sees no irony in the idea of people *competing* to be righteous in order to gain rewards and avoid punishments. What matters to Mo tzu is behavior, and if the promise of rewards and the threat of punishments are sufficient to secure good behavior then Mo tzu will use them as an appropriate means.[24]

The appearance of being virtuous or righteous is not the whole basis for employment; the MT emphasizes that the abilities of the potential official must be fathomed as well. This is done through observing the individual in action: "Then the sage kings listened to their words and examined their actions; investigating their area of competence, they carefully assigned them office."[25] In the next lines we read,

> Therefore those who were competent to be assigned to rule a state were assigned to rule a state. Those competent to be senior officials were made senior officials, and those competent to be assigned to rule a district were assigned to rule a district.[26]

Mo tzu shows a strong concern throughout these chapters for the appropriate delegation of responsibilities. When an official is assigned a position requiring greater wisdom and ability than he can muster, the result is disastrous for society. The virtuous are to be promoted, but only to a level commensurate with their abilities.

Another danger lies in attempting to pursue the exaltation of the virtuous without a clear understanding of the techniques underpinning it. Mo tzu details the errors of modern rulers who incorrectly apply the principle by bestowing high rank on the virtuous without providing appropriate responsibilities and remuneration. To ensure that the "correct" techniques of the sage kings are followed, Mo tzu propounds three rules:

> If there is this method but one does not have the techniques of implementing it, then it is as if the affair is not yet successfully completed.[27] Therefore it is necessary to set up three rules. What are these three rules? I say that if their rank is not high, then the masses will not respect them; if their pay is not generous, then the masses will not trust them; if their measures and decrees are not definite, then the masses will not fear them. Therefore anciently the sage kings bestowed high rank and generous emoluments on them. Employing them in affairs, they made their commands definite. Now how could these [rank, pay, and power] be given merely for the benefit of the officials? It was that the sage kings desired the success of their affairs.[28]

These "three rules" are secondary means by which the primary means, the exaltation of the virtuous, is rendered effective. Like our other secondary means, the methods for increasing the numbers of the virtuous, the "three rules" are used by the writers of the MT as part of the effort to persuade readers that the primary means and ultimate concern of the text are realizable goals that were attained in the past under the sage kings and that can be reached again in the near future. Although many Western interpreters of Mo tzu have emphasized the anti-traditional, egalitarian aspects of his teaching, we have here a clear example of his efforts to "work within the system." Mo tzu not only accepts the current system of feudal ranks, he urges that its distinctions be accentuated. Both emoluments and real power must be given to the virtuous--a proposition that the rulers of the day presumably found congenial (rulers then as now being inclined to view themselves as living embodiments of righteousness and truth). As is usual when Mo tzu appears to endorse the status quo, his rationale for his position is true to his ultimate goal and may differ from that of his readers. Rank, wealth, and power are the currency with which the rulers' trusted officers are paid. Mo tzu knows that the masses simply will not respect, trust, and *fear* a man who fails to enjoy the full confidence of the ruler. While Mo tzu was, so far as we can tell, relentlessly ascetic in his personal life and did not regard wealth and power as desirable in themselves, he was sufficiently pragmatic to see their value for establishing the virtuous in positions of leadership. Perhaps because he was so successful in his own asceticism, he seems to have overlooked the corrupting force of wealth and power in the lives of others; here and elsewhere Mo tzu's apparent faith in the ability of humans to rise above their weaknesses and selfishness is striking.

Thus far in our examination of the MT we have seen few indications that Mo tzu desired to create a "democratic," egalitarian society. Rather it seems more likely that Mo tzu sought to establish a highly stratified meritocracy where the competent and honest would rise to the top of the social and political system and there receive rewards in keeping with their talents and efforts. What little we know of the early Mohist organization indicates that within their own ranks the Mohists demanded strict obedience to the commands of their leader, the *chü tzu*, who held the life and death of his followers in his hands. It seems probable that the Mohists' internal organization was a small-scale model of the order that they wished to bring to society at large.

As we have seen, the arguments presented in the text for exalting the virtuous and for the secondary means designed to bring this exaltation about have all been of two types: arguments based upon commonsensical observations of social behavior and arguments grounded in the practices of the sage kings; there are far more of the latter than could profitably be detailed in this study. In addition to the general references to the practices of the sage kings, the text contains numerous accounts of humble individuals, cooks, fishermen, and the like, who though living in modest circumstances were nonetheless recognized as great talents and elevated to high position by Yao, Shun, Yü, T'ang, and Wu. All along the text has also emphasized the great utility of employing and promoting the virtuous. When the virtuous are promoted, the cold are clothed, the hungry are fed, and the country is orderly. Conversely, when the wealthy, the relatives, and the handsome are promoted, the people freeze, starve, and suffer from social unrest.

However, on one occasion--almost in passing it seems--Mo tzu gives a higher sanction than social well-being for his means: "...the ancient sage kings were able to use prudently the exaltation of the virtuous and the employment of the capable to govern, thereby modeling themselves on Heaven."[29] As it turns out later in the passage, the sage kings were modeling themselves on Heaven by exalting the virtuous without regard for their social rank, so what they were imitating was the *impartiality* of Heaven. Whether they were also taking other aspects of Heaven as a model for their actions is left unstated, but we here encounter an idea that underlies much of the rest on the Essays: the ultimate justification for the Mohist means transcends utility, social benefit, and the example of the sage kings. In presenting his case to the rulers and literati of the Warring States, Mo tzu places his strongest emphasis on the arguments he thinks most likely to be effective: utility, benefit, and the precedent of the sage kings, but in his own system of values it seems probable that the approval of Heaven is the firmest support he can muster to demonstrate the suitability of his means. With this in mind we will proceed with the examination of the Essays.

Identification with the Superior[30]

> Therefore the Master Mo tzu said: "Now if the emperors, dukes, great officials, nobles, and gentlemen of the world truly wish to enrich their states, increase their population, regulate their punishments and decrees, and secure their altars of the soil and grain [metaphor for the state], then they must study this doctrine of identification with the superior. This is the basis [of government].[31]

In this passage we see a restatement of the Mohist ultimate concern and an endorsement of the primary means presented in the three extant chapters titled "Identification with the Superior." The Mohists' religious goal of securing all benefits for society and preventing all harm from befalling it is stated here in the particular form it assumes when viewed from the vantage point of the ruler. As explained earlier, increased wealth, flourishing population, regularized government, and a secure peace are concrete components of the Mohist ideal of social well-being, components especially attractive to those in positions of power, but of benefit to all members of society. The means by which these components of the goal are to be realized is now said to be the process of identification with the superior. Like the exaltation of the virtuous discussed in the preceding triad of chapters, the practice of identification with the superior is also called "the basis [of government]." The two means sharing this exclusive sounding designation are, we shall see, intimately intertwined in both theory and implementation.

In a very similar fashion all three chapters preface their exposition of the method of identification with the superior with a description of the time of political and social chaos that preceded the appointment of the first emperor by Heaven. These descriptions serve several purposes simultaneously: they illustrate the need for the unification of standards, both bureaucratic and ideological; they portray the evils of anarchy--a state abhorrent to the authors of the MT; they set the stage for the narration of the original, prototypic, Heaven-instituted exaltation of the virtuous, and, of course, provide a nice introduction to the topic of the essays. The following version is from "Identification with the Superior 2":

> The Master Mo tzu said: "From the modern vantage as we look back at the time when the human race had just come to life and did not yet have rulers, generally the saying is: 'Everyone in the world had a different *yi*.'[32] Therefore one man had one *yi*, ten men had ten *yi*, and one hundred men had one hundred *yi*. Consequently each considered his *yi* to be correct and considered others' wrong and thus people opposed each other. In the home fathers and sons, elder brothers and younger brothers became enemies, and, their hearts all being at odds, they could not come to accord. It reached the point where they discarded their surplus energy and did not use it to work together; they hid their excellent *tao* and did not use it to teach each other; they let surplus goods rot and did not divide them among themselves. The disorder in the world was like that among birds and beasts.[33] There were no distinctions between lord and subject, superior and subordinate, and elder and younger, and no proper relations between fathers and sons, elder and younger brothers;[34] that is why the world was in chaos.[35]

The text goes on to note that all this confusion arose because there was no ruler who could unify the *yi* of the world. Thereupon Heaven[36] selected the most "worthy, good, sage, wise, discriminating, and clever" man, made him emperor, and set him to unifying the *yi* of the empire. The emperor soon realized that he could not do the job alone so he picked the wisest and ablest men in the world and set them up as the Three Dukes to work together with him to unify the *yi* of the world. The Three Dukes in turn realized that the world was too big for them to manage on their own, so they divided it up among the feudal lords of the many states and set them to the task of unifying the *yi* of their states.[37] The lords too realized their inadequacy and selected the virtuous of their states and established them as retainers, generals, and officials, reaching all the way down to the level of village chiefs. All were then set to work at unifying the *yi* of their areas of responsibility.[38]

The problem set forth in this chapter is that the world is in social and political chaos because everyone follows their own *yi*, or "standards." The solution proffered is the procedure called identification with the superior, which, through a series of progressively more universal identifications, leads individuals to expand their sphere of loyalty first to the clan, then to the state, to the emperor, and finally to the will of Heaven itself. At each stage of this process the wills and standards of the people are united in ever widening circles of allegiance, producing the desired social cohesion and harmony. The procedure of identification with the superior described in the second chapter of that name runs essentially as follows:

> When the emperor, the lords of the states, and the chiefs of the people had been established, the emperor issued commands and instructed the people saying, "Whenever you hear and see good and evil acts you must report them to your superior. What your superior regards as correct you too must consider correct, and what he condemns you too must condemn. When the people[39] do good, search them out and recommend them;[40] when the superior is at fault, then admonish him. Identify with the superior and do not collude with subordinates. When the superiors and the people know of your behavior they will reward and praise it. But if you do the opposite of all this, then the superior will punish you and the people will rebuke you." Therefore in ancient times the sage kings governed with rewards and punishments[41] that were well investigated and trustworthy. The people all desired the superior's rewards and praise and feared his punishments. Thereupon the village head, in accord with the emperor, governed and unified the *yi* of his village. When this had been done, he led his people to identify with the district head saying, "all the villagers should identify with the district head and not dare to collude with subordinates. What he considers to be right and wrong all must consider right and wrong. Discard your bad words and actions and study his good words and actions. The district head is certainly the district's most virtuous man; if everyone takes him as a model, how can the district be disordered?" How was the district head able to govern his district? It was only that he could unify the *yi* of the

district. When the district was regulated, the district head led his people to identify again, this time with the lord of the state, saying, "all the people of the district should identify with the lord of the state and not dare to collude with his underlings. What the lord considers to be right and wrong all must consider to be right and wrong. Discard your bad words and actions and study his good words and actions. The lord is certainly the most virtuous man in the state; if everyone takes him as a model, how can the district be disordered?" How was the lord able to govern his state? It was only that he could unify the *yi* of his state. After the lord had regulated his state, he led his people to identify again, this time with the emperor, saying, "all the people of the state should identify with the emperor and not dare to collude with his underlings. What the emperor considers to be right and wrong all must consider to be right and wrong. Discard your bad words and actions and study his good words and actions. The emperor is certainly the most humane man in the world; if everyone takes him as a model, how can the world be disordered?" How was the emperor able to govern the world? It was only that he was able to unify the *yi* of the world. Now if they had only identified with the emperor and not with Heaven, then Heaven's calamities would not have been prevented.[42]

Both "Identification with the Superior 1" and "Identification with the Superior 2" warn of the dire consequences attendant upon ending the process of identification with the superior at the level of the emperor. A justly enraged Heaven will send down all sorts of unseasonable weather as a clear indication of its displeasure. This will in turn lead to famine and pestilence--Heaven's punishment for its wayward subjects. For Mo tzu, Heaven is the ultimate source of social order and the highest model for human behavior.

The process of identification with the superior as Mo tzu presents it seems unnecessarily laborious. Standards are first unified on the village level. Once this presumably difficult task has been accomplished, the whole process has to be repeated on the level of the district. The unified standards of the district are then reunified on the level of the state; the state's standards are then unified with the emperor's. Even this is not enough for there must be the final step of identifying the wills of the people with that of Heaven.[43] Logically it might make more sense to begin the process of identification with Heaven and work down, step by step, to the level of the village. If this were done, then instead of having to go through five separate processes of identification each person would only have to identify once--with his immediate superior, who would already have identified with his superior, reaching all the way back to Heaven. It seems probable that Mo tzu was aware of the awkwardness of his method, but I would suggest that his formulation was determined, as usual, by pragmatic considerations. Unlike the utterly impracticable schemes of some Chinese thinkers, the method of identification with the superior that Mo tzu has described could actually be implemented. By starting the process of identification on the level of the smallest practical social unit, the village, rather than legislating from the top down, Mo tzu ensures that the mechanisms for nearly total ideological control are set up from the very beginning. With each successive re-identification of the villagers' *yi*, or "standards," the village chief, and similarly the higher authorities in turn, can check and re-check the responses of their charges. Those failing to identify with the new *yi* can be identified and corrected; repeated failures can be met with increasing severity. Although the process lacks the elegance of more idealistic reforms, like Confucius's call to return to the rites of the Chou, its strength lies in its straightforward, if excessively simplified, plan of action. Given sufficient determination and the requisite degree of social organization, a society could actually be restructured along the lines detailed in the MT.[44]

In order for Mo tzu's procedure of identification with the superior to produce the desired social transformation, the "superior" must be, in fact, the ethical better of the subordinates who are to identify with him. Mo tzu makes it abundantly clear throughout the Essay and Dialogue chapters that this is not the case in his time--hence the prior necessity, both logical and practical, for the exaltation of the virtuous. In Mo tzu's pseudo-historical account of the original, prototypic exaltation of the virtuous translated above, Heaven picked the most virtuous man as emperor, the emperor picked the next three most virtuous men as assistants, and so on. Only after this had been done did the process of identification with the superior become a possibility. In the degenerate world in which the Mohists found themselves, humans would have to take the first step of exalting the virtuous--hence Mo tzu's appeal to rulers in the preceding triad of chapters--then and only then could identification with the superior be pursued. Implicit in this presentation is the Mohist attack on the entire system of hereditary officeholding. According to Mo tzu's account, the emperor, dukes, lords, officers, and village heads of antiquity were all appointed by Heaven or its official representatives. However, in the intervening centuries things have gone astray; the most virtuous are no longer in power, and the current rulers must be replaced by those of greater worth. It is not at all clear that Heaven ever intended for positions to be passed on hereditarily, but even if it did the time has come for a new exaltation of the virtuous. The ideological underpinnings of the aristocracy are effectively undercut by this merit-based system.

It is clear from the text that the superiors' standards are not to be questioned: "What the superior regards as correct you too must regard as correct, and what he condemns you too must condemn."[45] Yet on the same page we encounter the puzzling injunction, "When the superior is at fault regulate and admonish him."[46] How, if the superior is always right, can his subordinates correct his behavior? The answer seems to lie in the idea of the unification of standards. The superiors set the standards of morality, speech, and behavior for the entire populace, but once the standards are in place, all of society, from top to bottom, is held accountable to them. While the superiors are setting the standards, their judgement is beyond question--after all, they are the most virtuous and worthy men to be found--but after the standards have been decreed and unified for the final time, the superiors as well as the masses must conform to them.[47] In the regulation of society, both officials and peasants have a duty to see that the standards of Heaven are enforced on earth, and no persons are ever to place themselves above the law.

The ideal society depicted in the chapters entitled "Identification with the Superior" is one where harmony is attained through the homogenization of thought and behavior. Anyone deviating from the norms set by the superior is instantly reported and disciplined.[48] A firm system of rewards and punishments ensures that both good and bad acts bring their just deserts, and that informers receive both material rewards and social approval for their vigilance. The primary means of identification is thus supported by the secondary means of rewards and punishments, which is based in turn on a society-wide network of informers. What separates this social system from the ones propounded by Han Fei and Shang Yang is that its ultimate source is not the will of the ruler but, as stated in another passage, God (*shang ti*) and the spirits (*kuei shen*).[49]

While the degree of social control Mo tzu desires is not much different from that sought by the Legalists, the two schools uphold radically contrasting ideals of behavior. For Mo tzu, the standards of Heaven (order, benevolence, impartiality, nurture, etc.) are to be the standards of the world. A world shaped by the the Mohist vision would differ greatly from a totalitarian state where unflinching conformity to the whim of the despot is the highest norm of behavior. In fact, the

MT claims that the ruler's will can only be enforced when it is in tune with the standards of the people,[50] a point that the "Legalist" emperor Ch'in Shih Huang Ti would have done well to realize. Mo tzu seems to have assumed that identification with the superior is possible only because the superiors are, in the final analysis, modeling themselves on Heaven. The will of the people has a force of its own that is based on a sort of ethical consensus; the people cannot long be subjected to arbitrary decrees that clash with their ingrained, Heaven ordained standards of right and wrong.

> If we suppose that the superiors and subordinates have different standards, then what the superior rewards the people will condemn. I say, "As for what people in society think to be wrong, even causing it to receive the rewards of the superior will not suffice to encourage them to do it."[51]

This is then a pragmatic justification for the morality of the practice of identification with the superior; if the people do not share the superior's standards, he will be unable effectively to control their behavior through rewards and punishments.

Mo tzu also appeals directly to the self-interest of rulers to support his cause:

> In the affairs of the wise [ruler], he must figure out that whereby the nation and people are well regulated and do it, and he must calculate that whereby the nation and people are disordered and avoid it. Now what do we figure is the reason that the nation and people are well regulated? If when the superior governs he understands the conditions[52] of his subordinates, then there is order; if he does not understand their conditions, then there is chaos.[53]

Mo tzu goes on to explain that when the conditions, or feelings, of the masses are understood, the superior knows what the people like and dislike and is therefore able to recognize and reward the good and find and punish the bad. When this is done, the state is sure to be orderly. How can the ruler bring about this desirable state of affairs? "Only when one is able to govern by means of identification with the superior and the unification of standards can it be done."[54]

As we have seen, the main justification for identification with the superior is the precedent of the sage kings; according to the text, the entire elaborate process spun out by the writers of the MT was, in fact, instituted and practiced in high antiquity. Was this attribution presented with the expectation that it would be accepted as fact by the readers of the text? Perhaps not. Mo tzu adduces further "evidence" of the sage kings' practice of the identification with the superior that is so weak that it would seem to undermine the claim that the whole process was the sage kings' creation. Although there are other quotations from the *Shih ching* and *Shu ching*[55] that, even after being interpreted in a most strained manner, still do not prove that the sage kings practiced anything resembling the process Mo tzu attributes to them, the following is perhaps the clearest illustration of this point:

> Perhaps you suspect that only Mo tzu has this [teaching] and the former kings did not?[56] They also were like this. The sage kings all used the identification with the superior to govern. Therefore the world was in order. How do we know it was like this? Among the books of the former kings, the words of the "Great Oath" are like this:[57] "If an unethical person discovers wickedness and deception yet fails to speak out, he shall be punished the same [as the guilty party]." This is to say that the crime of one who sees evil yet does not report it is equal to that of the offender.[58]

It may well be that the sage kings followed the draconian practice of punishing non-informers as if they were criminals themselves, but it is surely a great leap, for Mo tzu as well as ourselves, from this juridical equivalence to the system of identifying with the superior. To punish non-informers as if they had personally committed the crimes that they concealed is not even remotely similar to Mo tzu's elaborate process of identification with the superior, though such punishment certainly would be mandated by the legal code in a Mohist state. While we cannot know with certainty what prompted Mo tzu to proffer this unconvincing evidence, the fact that he felt the need to employ it at all suggests that the case made so far in the chapters did not overwhelm readers of the early text.[59] The idea suggests itself that Mo tzu's claim that his primary means were created by the sage kings may function on several levels: (1) Mo tzu is asserting in a very literal way that the sage kings really and truly practiced all his primary means and shared his ultimate concern; (2) at the same time, Mo tzu seems to realize that not every one of his readers will share in this conviction, hence the appeals to the texts of the literati tradition, which serve a marginally supportive function; (3) the attribution of Mo tzu's primary means and ultimate concern to the sage kings serves an important rhetorical function as well, by providing an acceptable format for the presentation of Mo tzu's ideas. Just as Confucius before him had claimed to be a transmitter and not an innovator, so Mo tzu strengthened his presentation by cloaking it with the patina of age and the respectability conveyed by association with the sages of antiquity.

The modern reader has difficulty taking Mo tzu's claims for the antiquity of his teaching at face value; most likely the critical thinkers of the "One Hundred Schools" period experienced similar difficulties, yet it may well be that the teachings of the MT were rendered more palatable by virtue of the fact that the claims were made. Whatever the weaknesses of Mo tzu's arguments may be, they are relatively effective in placing the means and goals of the Mohists within the mainstream of the Chinese literati tradition as it existed in the Warring States period: even if only through constant repetition of the theme. Like the followers of Confucius, Mo tzu draws upon the "Classics" to establish the legitimacy of his positions in ways that the writers of the *Tao te ching* and *Han Fei tzu* do not.

Universal Love

The three existing chapters on universal love, while similar in import, differ sufficiently in presentation to merit separate consideration in our analysis.

Universal Love 1 is the shortest of the chapters by far and consists of a straightforward presentation of problem and solution. A sage who wishes to rule the world must know the source from which disorder arises--only then is he able to control and eliminate it. The MT states that the cause of disorder is the lack of mutual love (*hsiang ai* 相愛) which is equated with a lack of filial devotion (*hsiao* 孝):[60]

> Having once[61] investigated the source from which disorder arises, we see that it comes from the lack of mutual love. Subjects and sons failing to be devoted [*hsiao*] to lords and fathers--this is what is called disorder.[62]

Hsiao, ordinarily understood to mean "filial devotion," is here employed in a broader sense where it applies to the whole range of relationships between superiors and subordinates. Further, it makes demands on both parties in the relationship. Sons must love their fathers, but fathers in turn must show affection (*tz'u* 慈) for their sons; ministers should love their lords, but the lords should show affection for their ministers, etc. As presented in the MT, the demands of *hsiao* apply equally to both parties in a relationship; the failure of either to live up to their responsibilities leads to social disorder. The absence of *hsiao* is revealed in any situation where one seeks personal benefit at the expense of another.[63]

Mo tzu enumerates the causes of disorder in the world; in each case the disorder arises from the desire of individuals to benefit themselves, their families, their households, or their states at the expense of other persons' selves, families, households, or states. The conclusion is unavoidable: "When we examine this, whence does it arise? It all arises from the lack of mutual love."[64]

Thus far in the chapter, Mo tzu has spoken only of the need for mutual love *hsiang ai*. "Universal love" (*chien ai* 兼 愛) is first mentioned in a passage posing a hypothetical case: "Supposing that everyone in the world practices universal mutual love [*chien hsiang ai*], loving others as they love their own persons. Would there still be any unfilial ones?"[65] This sentence gives us our only definition of universal mutual love: to love others as oneself. (An alternate phrasing repeated in the chapter is to "regard" others as oneself.)[66] The term used in the MT for love, *ai*, does not admit any other translation, but from what we have seen of the text so far, it is clear that "love" is to be understood as something radically different from the romantic sentiments the term may call to mind for English speakers. Mo tzu's "love" seems to be an expanded awareness of others as really no different from oneself. "Universal mutual love," or loving others as oneself, is therefore an aspect of the process of "identification with the superior" discussed in a preceding section of this chapter. In that process, Mo tzu called upon humanity sequentially to expand its loyalties from individual self-interest to the interest of the clan, state, emperor, and Heaven. Instead of worrying about personal advantage, Mo tzu counseled his readers to identify with the interest of society at large, which aligns one with the interest of Heaven. In this first chapter on universal love, Mo tzu seems to be advocating a similar process of expanding loyalties and identifications, only here it is subsumed under the rubric of universal mutual love: "If we regard others' families as our own, who will cause disturbances? If we regard others' states as our own, who will attack?"[67]

The arguments presented in this chapter are evidently expected to stand or fall on the basis of their good sense; for the first time in the Essays we have a chapter that employs no analogies and makes no appeals to the practices of the sage kings to support its proposals. Perhaps this is a result of its extreme brevity. The more expanded second and third chapters rely on the full range of Mo tzu's rhetorical techniques.

"Universal Love 2" starts, as does "Universal Love 3," with a discussion of the motivation of the magnanimous: "The reason the benevolent man [*jen jen* 仁人] acts must be to promote the good of the world and to exclude harm from it."[68] We have already had occasion to cite this passage as a concise representative statement of the ultimate concern expressed in the Essays. From this opening the writers of the MT go on to consider those things that either benefit or harm the world. Both "Universal Love 2" and "Universal Love 3" agree that calamities do *not* arise from loving one another, but the two chapters follow rather different lines of reasoning from this point on. "Universal Love 2" details the fact that rulers, heads of households, and individuals love only themselves and not others. Loving only themselves, they do not hesitate to attack and injure others. The text sums up this idea as follows: "Generally the reason that the calamities, usurpations, resentments, and hatreds of the world have arisen is the lack of mutual love."[69] The cure proposed in "Universal Love 2" for all the ills of society is universal love and mutual benefit. In the discussion of the lamentable state of affairs brought about by the lack of mutual love, the MT asks: "How can we change it? The Master Mo tzu said: 'We can change it through the method of universal mutual love and mutual benefit.'"[70] Universal mutual love and mutual benefit are described as seeing others' states, families, and persons as if they were one's own. When this is done, all aggressive wars, usurpations, and injuries will cease, and the relationships of rulers and subjects, fathers and sons, and elder and younger brothers will be harmonized. All abuses of the weak and few by the powerful and many will likewise come to an end.[71] Universal mutual love and mutual benefit as described in "Universal Love 2" seems identical to the universal mutual love described in "Universal Love 1"; both consist of regarding others' states, families, and persons as one regards one's own. "Mutual benefit," sometimes translated "mutual aid," appears to be a component part of "universal mutual love" that does not require separate, or additional, duties of its own; it may be mentioned separately in this chapter because the authors of the text wish to emphasize to their readers the material advantages accruing from the practice of the Mohist way. In any case, though at first reading it sounds as if a new idea is being presented in this chapter, the actual means being taught in all three chapters on universal love appears to be identical.

The remainder of "Universal Love 2" comprises precedents from the lives of the sage kings and a series of cases, drawn from the historical record, that, Mo tzu argues, show that the masses can be coerced to do whatever it is that the ruler desires. Through these illustrations Mo tzu attempts to answer the critics who say that universal love may be good but it cannot be implemented throughout an entire society.[72] Mo tzu's basic reasoning runs as follows: universal love seems too difficult only because rulers do not truly understand what benefits and harms the world. In the past, the entire populations of states have performed all sorts of feats that were more difficult and less rewarding than universal love; as difficult as these feats were, men and women could perform them because they knew that their rulers desired them to do so. If rulers would only understand that universal love brings the world its greatest benefit and would accordingly urge it upon their subjects, then humanity could easily be brought to practice universal love, and all would rejoice in the ensuing benefits. The will and urging of the ruler is thus a secondary means by which universal love is to be produced. Mo tzu seems seriously to believe that rulers can exhort, reward, and punish their subjects into loving others as they love themselves.

When reading through the examples Mo tzu cites, one is struck by the fact that all recount what might be termed "physical" feats. Lord Wen of Chin liked coarse clothing, so all his officials wore sheepskin coats. Lord Ling of Ch'u liked tiny waists, so all his officials starved themselves. Lord Kou Chien of Yüeh loved bravery, so, after extensive training, more than one hundred of his soldiers marched to their death in a fire, as he urged them on.[73] While none of these feats lack a psychological component, they are nonetheless primarily physical accomplishments that can be accurately assessed by objective methods of measurement, e.g. one wears coarse clothing or one does not, one marches to one's death or one does not, etc. It seems significant that the authors of the MT see the practice of universal love as directly comparable to these acts of physical control. As with the rest of Mo tzu's religious means, universal love is manifested not in some inward emotional or spiritual state but by outwardly directed, concrete behaviors. If one acts *as if* he regards another's person as his own, then he is practicing universal love as Mo tzu defines it. The inner psychological or spiritual state of the practitioner is never considered by the authors of the MT; evidently Mo tzu, the ascetic, was concerned only with the control of outward behavior and not the inner states that many moderns believe guide that behavior.

Mo tzu asserts that universal love is easier to practice than the other difficult feats cited, because it brings clear rewards where the other difficult feats do not:

> Now one who loves others, people will also love in return; one who benefits others, people will also benefit in return; one who hates others, people will also hate in return; one who harms others, people will also harm in return. This being the case, what is the difficulty in it [universal love]?[74]

No one could read the chapters on universal love without being aware of the benefits claimed for its practice, but is Mo tzu implying that subjects follow their rulers' fancies for no other reason than that to do so is pleasing to their lord? Evidently so. No hint is given in this section of the text that its authors recognize the material inducements that motivate officials to pander to the whims of their rulers. When we read that the retainers of Lord Ling ate one meal a day in order to gratify their lord's fetish for men with narrow waists, we assume that these retainers considered it in their best interest to do so (whether from desire for rewards or fear of punishments we cannot say). It is probable that readers in the Warring States period viewed things similarly and also wondered at Mo tzu's apparent failure to notice that the desire to please one's lord is generally based on one's individual concerns rather than a selfless urge to satisfy the lord's peculiar cravings. However, Mo tzu makes an appealing point when he asserts that the benefits of universal love reach all of society; in that regard, universal love can be asserted to be more rewarding than the other examples of difficult accomplishments given in the chapter.

Finally we should consider the use made by Mo tzu of the examples of the sage kings in "Universal Love 2." Mo tzu cites three of the sage kings, Yü, King Wen, and King Wu, in turn and, after considering their conduct individually, concludes with the firm refrain, "Nowadays we *can* carry out universality!"[75] As we might now expect, Mo tzu makes no mention of the sentiment of love in his description of the behavior of Yü and Kings Wen and Wu; he simply shows them acting in an impartial, just, and benevolent manner. Yü constructed massive waterworks that benefited the people, mostly "barbarians," inhabiting the lands surrounding his own. King Wen prevented the oppression and exploitation of the underdog and therefore his people flourished. King Wu saved the Shang people from their own evil ruler and took upon himself all responsibility for any wrong existing in his realm. These actions, Mo tzu tells us, are universal love and mutual benefit as practiced by the sage kings. What Mo tzu has related seems no different from the benevolent rule praised by the followers of Confucius; only in providing a "practical" method of implementation does Mo tzu differ from his rivals. The way to bring about sagely government is for the lord and his officials to regard others' states, families, and persons as they regard their own and act on this basis. This then is "universal love and mutual benefit."

"Universal Love 3" differs from "Universal Love 2" in its analysis of the causes of the world's calamities. Where "Universal Love 2" attributes the world's woes to the lack of mutual love, "Universal Love 3" follows a different, though closely related, tack and pins the blame on "partiality" (*pieh* 別): "Thus as for this partiality, does it not in actuality give rise to all the great harm in the world? For this reason the Master Mo tzu says, 'partiality is wrong.'"[76] Since partiality, or partial love, is the cause of all the harmful behaviors in the world, any solution to the world's problems must somehow serve to eliminate partiality. When he presents his answer to the problem of partiality, Mo tzu takes a jab at those of his competitors who attack his teachings without offering their own programs:

> Those who criticize others must have something with which to replace their [teachings]. If one criticizes the [partial] man but has no [doctrine] to replace his, it is like fighting water with water and fire with fire;[77] one's speech will certainly be unacceptable. Therefore the Master Mo tzu said, "replace partiality with universality."[78]

How does one "replace partiality with universality"? By regarding the states, cities, and households of others as one regards one's own. When this is done all competition and strife will be eliminated, to the benefit of the entire world. Since universal love, regarding others as oneself, is of such great value, "Mo tzu says, 'Universality is right.'"[79]

Having outlined the great benefits to be produced through the religious means of universal love, Mo tzu dedicates most of the chapter to the rhetorical device of suggesting and then rebutting possible objections to the practice of universal love; along the way he manages to work in the praxis of the sage kings. The chapter closes with the stories of the three kings, already recited in "Universal Love 2," who desired things much harder than universal love from their subjects and were not disappointed by their underlings willingness to comply with their wishes. This second telling of the three kings' peculiarities adds nothing to the first; we will focus our attention on Mo tzu's objections and rebuttals.

Mo tzu's imaginary interlocutors open their objections by stating, "Granting that universality is good, even so how can it be useful!"[80] Mo tzu replies, "If it were not useful then even I would oppose it, but how can there be something that is good and yet useless?"[81] Not only is universal love practicable, but even its most ardent detractors will choose it when their own self-interest is at stake. To demonstrate this point, Mo tzu contrasts the behavior of the partial and the universal friend. The partial man will reason that he cannot take care of his friend and his friend's parents as he takes care of himself, so he will allow them to starve and freeze without intervening. When his friend is sick he will not nurse him; when he dies he will not bury him. The advocate of universality is in every way the opposite of the partial man. Now, Mo tzu supposes, if someone were about to go off on a dangerous mission, to whom would he entrust his family? In this situation "there are no foolish men and women in the world. Even one who opposes universality will certainly entrust his family to the universal friend."[82] So even though one may verbally object to universality, one's actions will affirm its desirability.

The next objection dealt with is that universality may be a good basis for choosing among commoners, but perhaps it does not apply to rulers. Mo tzu's response directly parallels his rebuttal of the preceding objection. First he contrasts the behavior of the king who regards his subjects as he regards himself with that of the selfish ruler. Then he observes that when times are hard even those who are opposed to universality will flock to take refuge with the universal ruler.

> Yet the words of the empire's gentlemen who are opposed to universality still do not end. They say, "Universality may be magnanimous; it may be righteous. Even so, how can it be actualized?"[83]

With this objection, the authors of the MT introduce the practices of the sage kings. Two of the four examples cited here are similar to those given in "Universal Love 2." A new example provides a startling illustration of Mo tzu's universal love in action. Mo tzu describes how Yü, against all his personal wishes, acquiesced to the will of Heaven and sent his troops to punish the ruler of the Miao, an "aboriginal" tribe. Yü exterminated the ruler of the Miao and a large number of Miao soldiers out of a sincere desire to bring order to the world. The text concludes, "the universality of Master Mo tzu takes its model from Yü."[84] Between the examples of the sage kings cited in "Universal Love 2" and "Universal Love 3," we have two instances of warfare extolled as models of "universal love." Neither of these two could convincingly be construed as purely defensive wars; both involve acts of conquest in which the conqueror claims that his justification is to be found in the bad behavior of his now vanquished foe (and the will of Heaven, of course). While we may wonder how many of Mo tzu's readers found plausible his acceptance of the rationales traditionally offered for the sage kings' acts of conquest, the fact that Mo tzu employed these wars as examples of universal love tells us much about the nature of this means. Mo tzu's "universal love" is not a sentimental feeling but a style of acting in the world, a style ideally characterized by magnanimity, righteousness, impartiality, and vigor--not by passivity, tolerance, and non-violence.

Mo tzu next anticipates Mencius's objection that universal love is contrary to filial piety. Claiming that it is not, Mo tzu points out that the filial son wants others to love, not hate, his parents. This can best be facilitated by loving the parents of others so that they will love one's parents in return. The text posits a complete reciprocity of actions, "One who loves others will certainly be loved; one who hates others will certainly be hated."[85]

The final hypothetical objection raised in the chapter addresses the difficulty of implementing universal love. The text repeats the examples already seen in the preceding chapter of feats ostensibly more difficult than universal love that were done in the past. The authors assert that in each instance the people were able to change because their ruler willed it. When with the proper application of rewards and punishments, the most common secondary means in the MT, the masses can be transformed within a generation, then certainly the people can be led to practice something relatively easy and beneficial like universal love and mutual aid: "It can be compared to the way fire goes up and water goes down--it could not be stopped in the world."[86]

The chapter concludes with the assertion that universal love is "the *tao* of the sage kings and the masses' great benefit."[87] Those who practice universal love make compassionate rulers, loyal subjects, loving fathers, filial sons, friendly elder brothers, and respectful younger brothers. The MT extolls universal love as a means of producing wealth and prosperity for the people and a clear ordering of the hierarchical relationships within society. For Mo tzu there is no conflict between universality and social stratification. Universality, viewing others as oneself, necessitates treating others fairly and decently but does not suggest to the authors of the text complete functional equality in society. In this way, Mo tzu attempts to anticipate and refute all possible objections to his religious means while showing it to be the *modus operandi* of the sage kings of antiquity.

Notes

[1] Rather than continually refer to "the authors of the text," or "the early Mohists," we will commonly use the name of our philosopher, Mo tzu, as a catch term for those persons, whomever they may be, responsible for writing the text. It should be understood that this is done as a matter of convenience and not to imply that an historical person, Mo tzu, is the author of the received text.

[2] The *Yi ching, Ch'un ch'iu fan lu, Tao te ching*, and *Huang ti ssu ching* are all early texts noted for their obscurity.

[3] It is a common literary device in writings from this period, viz. *Analects, Mencius, Tao te ching*, etc., to present prescriptions for ideal behavior as descriptions of the more or less historical actions of sages, benevolent men, or *chün tzu* 君子. These ideal actions are often presented as having taken place in the past, when humans held themselves to higher standards of morality.

[4] MTCC, p. 139. A very similar passage is found in the opening paragraph of "Universal Love 3." (Ibid., p. 152.)

[5] We will not count the "Anti-Confucianism" chapters as presenting a primary means, because even though the chapters are generally classified as part of the Essays, they appear never to have numbered more than two and are less constructive and instrumental in thrust than the other Essays.

[6] Of course, even here there is room for ambiguity, since each of these primary means is part and parcel of the religious goal of the text. For example, the exaltation of the virtuous is one of the methods by which the Mohists hope to secure an ideal society. At the same time its practice is also a characteristic of the society which the Mohists wish to create. In a similar way all the primary means can also be viewed as specific goals of the Mohist program. With a thinker and doer as deadly earnest as Mo tzu it is not surprising that a complete identity of means and ends is demanded.

[7] I have elected, though with reservations, to use the chapter title translations devised by Y. P. Mei. This will require that occasional caveats be given. The word *hsien*, here translated as "virtuous," has overtones of wisdom, knowledge, and cleverness, as well, that should be kept in mind as this section is read.

[8] See MTCC, p. 63 and p. 89.

[9] Ibid., p. 71.

[10] Bernhard Karlgren, *Grammata Serica Recensa, Bulletin of the Museum of Far Eastern Antiquities*, no. 29 (Stockholm, 1957; reprint ed., Stockholm, 1972), p. 106.

[11] *Tz'u Hai*, rev. ed. in 1 vol. (n.p., 1947; reprint ed., Hong Kong: Chung hua shu chu, 1972), p. 1276.

[12] A. C. Graham believes that the Logic chapters, written roughly one hundred years after the Essays, did at one time contain definitions of the key terms of the Essay chapters. Unfortunately, these passages have been lost. See Graham, *Logic*, pp. 235-236.

[13] Perhaps this refers to the officials' supervisory role. It is hard to imagine that even the most diligent official would spend his days in field labor.

[14] MTCC, p. 72.

[15] Yao, Shun, Yü, T'ang, Wen, and Wu, the sage kings of antiquity, can be divided into two groups. The first group, Yao, Shun, and Yü, may perhaps once have existed but clearly are more mythical than historical in origin. The last three, T'ang, Wen, and Wu, are certainly larger than life, but their historicity is generally unquestioned. Juxtaposed to the sage kings are the "wicked kings," Chieh, Chou, Yu, and Li, whose uncompromising depravity provides a convenient foil for the consistent benevolence and wisdom of the sage kings.

[16] Ibid., p. 71.

[17] Ibid., p. 77.

[18] When first reading the MT, I was struck by what seemed to be the extraordinary reliance of its authors on historical precedents, and especially the purported actions of the sage kings. Western descriptions of the MT tend to emphasize the anti-traditionalist aspects of the text rather than its marked links to the literary/historical roots that the Mohists share with the Confucians. In an admittedly crude and statistically inadequate manner, I have attempted to provide a rough estimate of the amount of text in these three chapters devoted to expounding the supposed teachings or narrating the purported actions of the sage kings. Using the English translation of Y. P. Mei, the total number of whole and partial lines of text in each chapter was counted. Then the number of lines directly related to the sage kings was tabulated. The results are as follows:

CHAPTER	TOTAL LINES	LINES DEVOTED TO SAGES
E. of the V. 1	100	56
E. of the V. 2	299	143
E. of the V. 3	160	67

Despite the weakness inherent in the method of quantification, the results are still striking. Roughly half of each chapter on exalting the virtuous is devoted to describing the actions of the sage kings--the same sages so highly revered in the tradition of the followers of Confucius. Similar results can be found for the other Essay chapters as well.

[19] Following Sun Yi jang, I am reading chin 進 as shang 尚. (MTCC, p. 71.)

[20] Ibid.

[21] It is interesting to note that the unsophisticated technology of social engineering endorsed by the MT is virtually identical to that propounded by the "Legalist" Han Fei and passionately condemned by the Confucian tradition. Mo tzu and Han Fei both thought that behavior--and possibly outlook, though that received far less attention--could be effectively molded through the firm, impartial use of generous rewards and stiff punishments. Where the two thinkers diverged was in the ends to which their engineering was directed.

[22] MTCC has misprinted che 者 for erh 而.

[23] Ibid., pp. 64-65. This extended quotation gives a good feel for the style of the Essays. It is not hard to imagine why the refined literati of Imperial China found the MT lacking in elegance.

[24] One cannot be too smug in evaluating this stance, since studies conducted by modern behaviorists suggest that by mandating specific outward behaviors over a period of time, experimenters can radically affect the internal psychological state of their experimental subjects. Although Mo tzu gives no hint of any awareness of this possibility, we cannot assume that he was completely oblivious to it.

[25] Ibid., p. 72.

[26] Ibid.

[27] Following Chang's gloss of the sentence. (Ibid., p. 73.)

[28] Ibid., pp. 73-74.

[29] Ibid., p. 83.

[30] There is some debate among Sinologists over precisely how *shang t'ung* (literally "upwardly identifying") comes to mean "identification with the superior," but no authority with whom I am familiar doubts that it means something of the sort.

[31] Ibid., pp. 121-122.

[32] *Yi* 義 is a difficult term to translate in this context. Its range of meanings includes our words "truth," "principle," "reason," "meaning," "standard," and "aim."

[33] It may be interesting to compare Mo tzu's depiction of primitive social chaos with the descriptions of earliest human society found in the *Tao te ching*. The "chaos" abhorred by Mo tzu is viewed as ideal simplicity by Lao tzu, who longed to return to the uncomplicated state of birds and beasts. Of course, in Mo tzu's version of this early time the *tao* was hidden and surplus goods hoarded. Would Lao tzu say that Mo tzu simply was not going back far enough--that his "chaos" was from a time when humans had begun discriminating and hence *no longer* resembled the birds and beasts? It is also clear that the two philosophers held to radically opposed assessments of the natural condition of human beings: Lao tzu saw the primeval human as a microcosm of the universe and beyond all considerations of good and evil; Mo tzu saw him as a contrary creature in need of firm socialization.

[34] This sentence certainly appears to indicate that Mo tzu was very concerned with maintaining the proper, traditional hierarchy of relationships in society and the home. A related concern for family relationships is expressed earlier in the quote when Mo tzu laments that, "fathers and sons, elder brothers and younger brothers became enemies and...could not come to accord." Mencius may have been *logically* correct when he attacked Mo tzu, saying that "love without distinction...amounts to a denial of one's father," but he was grossly unfair to the spirit of Mo tzu's teaching. For Mencius's criticisms see *Mencius* III. B. 9.

[35] MTCC, pp.106-107.

[36] The accounts in "Identification with the Superior 1" and "Identification with the Superior 2" do not specify the actor in this sentence. "Identification with the Superior 3" explicitly states that Heaven, *t'ien*, is responsible for what follows.

[37] Significantly perhaps, no mention of the moral character of the feudal lords is made in any of the three versions, while all the other categories of officials are composed of the most virtuous persons available.

[38] This paraphrase is based on "Identification with the Superior 2." (Ibid., pp. 107-108.) The explanation of the development of the first feudal order given in the MT provides a nice illustration of the intellectual cross-fertilization of the Warring States period. According to Leon Vandermeersch, Mo tzu's theory of feudal order arising from social chaos was later borrowed by the "legalist" Shang Yang, though the implications of the theory differed for the two thinkers. See Leon Vandermeersch, *La formation du légisme* (Paris: Ecole Francais D'Extreme-Orient, 1965), p. 215.

[39] Following Wang Nien sun, I am reading *chi* 己 as *min* 民. (MTCC, p. 109.)

[40] Following the emendation of Sun Yi jang, *p'ang* 傍 should be read as *fang* 訪. (Ibid.)

[41] Reading *yü* 譽 as *fa* 罰. (Ibid.)

[42] Ibid., pp.108-111. This is a nearly verbatim translation, though it has been edited to reduce the number of repetitions. The Chinese original is even more cumbersome and provides a clear illustration of the laborious style of argumentation employed in the Essays.

[43] Precisely how this is to be done is left to the reader's imagination, though the text does detail some of Heaven's identifying traits: impartiality, generosity, benevolence, etc.

[44] The *pao chia* system of Wang An shih was a Sung dynasty attempt at social control that, like the first step in Mo tzu's process of identification, attempted to create a self-policing of society on the village level. The modern structure of society in the People's Republic of China, with its organization into work units (*tan wei*) and block organizations, bears some uncanny parallels to the society depicted in this section of the MT. During the Cultural Revolution, the Chinese got a great deal of practice in "identification with the superior," and the survivors became adept at adjusting and readjusting their *yi*, "standards," as the party line changed.

[45] MTCC, p. 109.

[46] Ibid.

[47] The guiding assumption in this interpretation of the MT is that the text is logical, self-consistent, and intelligible until proven otherwise. This assumption necessitates the search for reasonable interpretations of passages that otherwise might be dismissed as self-contradictory or flawed.

[48] Mo tzu claims that in antiquity the process of identification with the superior was so efficacious that the sage kings could hear of good and evil deeds committed in far-off provinces and respond appropriately to them before all the residents of those provinces even knew that the original deeds had been done. This could

supposedly happen over a radius of thousands of miles. Naturally the sage kings were thought to have divine vision, but according to the MT "the former emperors each said, 'it is not mysterious but only the ability to make use of the eyes and ears of others to help me see and hear.'" (Ibid., p. 119.) In this passage the MT rationally explains away one of the superhuman powers attributed to the sage kings, possibly to demonstrate that the sage kings are not different in kind from the men of the Warring States period; their achievements are not to be admired wistfully from afar but imitated in the present. I find it fascinating that the sage kings are simultaneously idealized and de-mythologized in the MT.

[49] Ibid., p. 116.

[50] Ibid., p. 118.

[51] Ibid.

[52] *Ch'ing* 情 is hard to translate in this context. The commentaries generally gloss it as the "reality" or "feelings" of the masses.

[53] Ibid., p. 122.

[54] Ibid., p. 123.

[55] Throughout the MT there are numerous quotes attributed to the *Shih ching* and *Shu ching* that often are not found in the received texts of these works. Those quotes in the MT that can be traced to the extant texts usually do not correspond exactly to the current version.

[56] Following the emendation of Sun Yi jang. (Ibid., p. 130.)

[57] Y. P. Mei asserts that the following quotation is not found in the current text of the *Shu ching*. Mei, *Works*, p. 76.

[58] MTCC, p. 130.

[59] Of course, we may just have the case of an obsessive debater earnestly marshaling every scrap of evidence at hand and employing good and bad arguments indiscriminately.

[60] The writers of the MT here employ a term, *hsiao*, often thought to be the special property of the tradition of Confucius. As we have seen, and will continue to see, the traditions following Mo tzu and Confucius hold a great deal in common, including a reverence for the family and the relationships of its members.

[61] Reading *tang* 當 as *ch'ang* 嘗.

[62] MTCC, p. 136.

[63] Ibid., pp. 136-137.

[64] Ibid., p. 137. The reasoning applied here is circular. Mo tzu defines disorder as what is produced when people love themselves and not others. He then asks what causes disorder. His answer, "the lack of mutual love," is determined by the starting definition.

[65] Ibid., p. 138.

[66] This passage seems to refute the claim made by James Legge that, "Mo himself nowhere says that his principle was that of loving all EQUALLY." If all

others are regarded and loved as oneself, it is reasonable to expect that all others are to be regarded and loved in an identical manner and to an identical degree. See James Legge, *The Chinese Classics*, 2:118.

[67] MTCC, p. 138.

[68] Ibid., p. 139.

[69] Ibid., p. 141.

[70] Ibid. Again note the circularity of the reasoning employed.

[71] Ibid.

[72] It is a bit odd that having claimed in the previous chapter that the masses cannot long be forced to do anything that violates their standards, Mo tzu now expends so much energy to prove just the opposite.

[73] Ibid., pp. 143-145.

[74] Ibid., p. 145.

[75] Ibid., pp. 146-151.

[76] Ibid., p. 153.

[77] Following the emendation of Yü Yüeh. (Ibid.)

[78] Ibid.

[79] Ibid., p. 154.

[80] Ibid., p. 156.

[81] Ibid. Based on this passage several modern authors have asserted that, for Mo tzu, whatever succeeds is necessarily good. From this it is usually argued that Mo tzu is a "utilitarian" whose criterion for "goodness" is usability. Mo tzu does say that "good" things must necessarily be usable, but nowhere does he claim the converse. For Mo tzu everything that is usable is *not* necessarily good. For examples of the misreading of this passage see Frederick W. Mote, *Intellectual Foundations of China* (New York: Alfred A. Knopf, 1971), p. 87, and Hu Shih, *Chung kuo che hsüeh shih ta kang*, p. 155.

[82] MTCC, p. 158.

[83] Ibid., p. 160.

[84] Ibid., p. 163.

[85] Ibid., p. 166.

[86] Ibid., p. 169.

[87] Ibid., p. 170.

CHAPTER V

ANALYSIS OF THE ESSAYS 2

Condemnation of Offensive War

The three surviving chapters entitled "Condemnation of Offensive War" each take a different approach in illustrating the immorality and extravagant waste of military aggression. Though all strive to prove that wars of conquest are unrighteous, their lines of reasoning are widely divergent; we will examine them individually to reveal more clearly the reasons underlying the Mohist objections to military expansion.

The condemnation of offensive war is of course the religious means presented in the three chapters bearing that name. By urging others to condemn aggression, Mo tzu hoped to mold a society that would recognize both the unrighteousness and the economic unprofitability of wars of conquest. In such a society there might be need for defense against outsiders or punitive expeditions against troublemakers within the realm, but the most destructive and wasteful of wars would be eliminated. The ensuing state of relative peace is one of the preconditions necessary for the realization of the Mohist ideal world and at the same time is one of the attributes of the religious ideal. Perhaps it would be clearer to say that the condemnation of aggressive war is one of the Mo tzu's religious means, while the actual elimination of aggressive war is an aspect of the religious goal.

The whole of "Condemnation of Offensive War 1" presents one point: humans have no difficulty in recognizing small amounts of unrighteousness, but when faced with the greatest unrighteousness of all, aggressive war, they fail to perceive it as evil. What is most notable about this short chapter is the fact that Mo tzu restricts himself to purely logical arguments in his attempt to show that aggressive war is unrighteous. No appeals are made to the example of the sages of antiquity or the sanction of Heaven.

The chapter opens with one of the best known passages in the entire MT. In it Mo tzu describes a series of increasingly injurious, and therefore increasingly unrighteous acts. The gist of the passage is as follows: Suppose a man enters another's orchard and steals his peaches and plums. When the people hear of it they will condemn the act and the magistrates will punish the miscreant. Why? Because he injured others to benefit himself. When it comes to stealing others' dogs, chickens, and pigs the unrighteousness is greater. Why? Because the harm to others is greater and the crime is more heinous. As for entering another's stables and stealing his horses and cattle, the unrighteousness is again greater. Why? Because the harm to others is greater. If the harm done to others increases so does the unrighteousness and criminality of the act. When it comes to the killing of innocents and the theft of their belongings, the unrighteousness is the greatest yet. Why? Because the harm to others is greater, and if the harm is greater the act is more inhumane. All the gentlemen of the world know that this is so and condemn these acts, calling them unrighteous, yet when it comes to the great attacks of states they do not know to condemn them and even praise them, calling them righteous. Can this be called knowing the difference between righteousness and unrighteousness?[1]

To drive the point home, Mo tzu next employs a second, closely related illustration. The murder of one man is unrighteous and merits one death penalty; the murder of ten men is ten times worse and deserves ten death penalties; the murder of one hundred men is one hundred times worse and merits one hundred death penalties. All the gentlemen know this, yet when it comes to the great unrighteousness of states attacking each other they applaud it and consider it righteous. That they are truly oblivious to the unrighteousness of their actions is evidenced by the fact that they record their exploits in the records left for posterity.[2]

The final illustration of this point given in the text imagines the case of a man who recognizes a small amount of black as black but calls a large amount of it white, or who tastes a small amount of bitterness and calls it bitter but calls a large amount of it sweet. We would certainly claim that such a man does not know the difference between black and white or bitter and sweet. Similarly, people readily recognize and condemn small wrongs but fail to recognize and condemn the greatest of wrongs: aggressive war. For this reason Mo tzu concludes, "we know that the gentlemen of the world are confused in distinguishing righteousness from unrighteousness."[3]

This essay is quite a departure from all the preceding ones. In the others Mo tzu sets out to demonstrate, by hook or by crook, the reasonableness, effectiveness, applicability, etc., of the religious means that he is presenting. By contrast, "Condemnation of Offensive War 1" speaks directly to only one point-- that people can readily recognize small acts of unrighteousness but fail to perceive great unrighteousness and are therefore confused in their moral judgements. Mo tzu makes no effort to illustrate the evils of warfare nor does he extol the benefits to be derived from its elimination. The practices of the sage kings and the will of Heaven are likewise missing. The chapter stands or falls on the basis of its assertion that what is evil in small quantities is surely even more evil in large quantities.[4] Mo tzu again shows the high regard in which he holds the moral potential of humanity, for much of the force of his argument is dissipated if there is no universal moral sense informing the actions of all men. Having demonstrated the unrighteousness of war, Mo tzu expects his readers to understand and act. There are no indications that Mo tzu has considered the possibility that one might agree that war is greatly unrighteous and yet still encourage it for reasons of personal gain.

In "Condemnation of Offensive War 2" war is rejected on the basis of an historical argument: wars have been unproductive and destructive in the past, therefore they will continue to be so in the future. Mo tzu quotes an ancient saying to support the logic of this approach: "If one's plans do not come to fruition, then one should consider the past to know the future and consider the seen to know the hidden. When one plans like this, one can know anything!"[5] Given this introductory statement, it would be reasonable to expect the following passages to be devoted to historical anecdotes selected to demonstrate the futility and evils of offensive wars. From these concrete examples of past deeds, his readers would then be able to divine the likely results of future actions of a similar nature. What in fact comes next is a series of general observations on the wastefulness of war. From this we may infer that the phrase "consider the seen to know the hidden" must mean something like "consider what is before your eyes [or what is obvious] to know the hidden." What the text catalogues as being before the readers' eyes are the obvious drawbacks of warfare in early China: there is no season in which the predominantly peasant armies of the time can profitably be taken from their fields; the supplies gathered up for war will be expended in the conflict and squandered; animals and humans will be lost to cold and starvation, not to mention battle, and most of the army will never be seen again. Mo tzu does not comment on this litany of woe; he apparently assumes that the harm to society is self-evident. He does state, however, that all these deaths mean that the spirits will lose their worshipers-- a disaster that Mo tzu clearly felt should be taken more seriously by his contemporaries.[6]

Mo tzu then takes up a series of hypothetical objections of the sort likely to be raised by the supporters of war. While this might seem unrelated to the stated approach of the chapter, in fact it seems to be simply an extension of the process of reasoning from the visible to the unseen. When confronted with the objection "I covet the fame of being victorious in battle and the profit of new territories, therefore I do it [wage war],"[7] Mo tzu replies with a description of the "visible," the terrible carnage of conquest that leaves large tracts of land and whole cities uninhabited, and points out the "unseen," that vacant land is already abundantly available and what states need are tillers of the soil, not wasteland. As Mo tzu bluntly puts it, "this is to discard what is insufficient [workers] in order to double what is already in surplus [empty land]."[8]

While refuting objections, Mo tzu works in the concrete historical precedents that seemed to be promised when he stated that "one should consider the past to know the future." To refute the objection that Ching, Yüeh, Chin, and Ch'i have all profited from offensive wars, the writers of the MT list a number of small states that have recently perished and assert that many more have also been annihilated. This situation is seen as analogous to the case of a physician who treats ten thousand patients with a drug that proves beneficial to only four. Clearly the drug cannot be considered to be very effective. Similarly, offensive wars have not been of general benefit in the past; the reader is left to conclude that they will not be of benefit in the future.

The next objection arises directly from the preceding one and is also answered by resorting to the historical record. The hypothetical objector states that "other [states] were unable to gather and employ their masses [properly] and therefore perished. I am able to gather and employ my masses. Because of this, who will dare not submit when I attack?"[9] To show that even the cleverest and most powerful leaders are unable to remain dominant for long, Mo tzu recounts the stories of Ho Lu of Wu and Chih Po of Chin, two warriors who enjoyed initial conquests but were eventually annihilated by their enemies. The point of the telling seems to be that the relatively lackluster rulers of modern times do not stand a chance of triumphing where these great and ruthless men failed. Mo tzu concludes by quoting an ancient proverb that appears to support his claim that the future can be known through the examination of the past:

> "The gentleman does not use water for a mirror but uses man. When one uses water for a mirror, he sees the features of his face; when one uses man for a mirror, he knows what is auspicious and inauspicious." Now if you suppose that offensive war is profitable, why do you not examine it once in the mirror of the Chih Po affair?[10]

Where "Condemnation of Offensive War 1" is concerned only to demonstrate the great unrighteousness of offensive war, "Condemnation of Offensive War 2" is exclusively focussed on illustrating the waste and impracticality of aggression. This second chapter on offensive war seems indifferent to the moral and ethical consequences of aggression--its point is that war just does not make good sense. Again we see no mention of the sage kings and the way of Heaven. The fact that war casualties can no longer worship the spirits is mentioned as a logistical drawback of war, but the text is silent on the topic of divine retribution.

"Condemnation of Offensive War 3" also argues against aggressive war from the standpoint of benefit and profit but its reasons are quite different from those expressed in "Condemnation of Offensive War 2." According to "Condemnation of Offensive War 3," an act is to be praised because it is useful to Heaven, the spirits, and man. The chapter opens with a rhetorical question and its Mohist answer:

> The Master Mo tzu said: "Now as for what the world praises as good,[11] what is the theory underlying it? Is it praised because in the upper realm it benefits Heaven, in the middle it benefits the spirits, and below it benefits man, or is it praised because in the upper realm it does not benefit Heaven, in the middle it does not benefit the spirits, and below it does not benefit man? Even the stupidest man must say that it is praised because in the upper realm it benefits Heaven, in the middle it benefits the spirits, and below it benefits man. Now what the whole world agrees on is precisely the method of the sage kings.[12]

A number of observations can be made about this paragraph. Mo tzu justifies his own value system by claiming that it is shared by the world and implying that what the whole world agrees on must certainly be right. Further, he asserts that it is the method of the sage kings. In an attempt to defuse possible objections, Mo tzu claims that even the stupidest persons see the truth of his stance, for after all it is the position of nearly all men. By establishing a reasonable, tradition-based stance at the outset of his presentation, Mo tzu apparently hopes to obtain his readers' preliminary agreement. Though they may have doubts, only his most cynical readers can escape feeling that they *ought* to agree with the MT's definition of "good," especially since the readers are faced with a false dichotomy in which disagreement with Mo tzu seems to imply endorsement of the opposite position. Once they have accepted the Mohist position that what is "good" is what benefits Heaven, the spirits, and man, it becomes much more difficult to dissent from the real world applications of this standard of judgement as they are elaborated in the text.

The tactic followed in the next section of the chapter is to contrast the actions of the sage kings with those of modern rulers, evaluating both in the light of the chapter's definition of what is good. Not surprisingly, it is concluded that the actions of the sage kings blessed Heaven, the spirits, and men, while the actions of modern rulers bless no one. Most of the actions of the sage kings singled out for praise here seem vague when compared to the evils of modern rulers listed in their train. We are told that the ancient sages always "carefully considered righteousness" when planning for the world. Thus "in acting they were not in doubt" and "far and near all obtained what they desired, and in this way they accorded with the benefit of Heaven, the spirits, and the people."[13] Passages of this sort, because they have so few specific details, are open to a wide range of interpretations and are presumably understood by their readers in ways most congenial to their own values. The most concrete actions attributed to the sages were that they "led the masses of the world with agriculture [as opposed to warfare], and therefore their subjects served God, mountains, streams, and spirits. Since the benefits to humanity were many, the merit was also great."[14] As a result of the way the sage kings led the people, "Heaven rewarded them, the spirits enriched them, and the people praised them. [All this] caused them [in turn] to be esteemed as the Son of Heaven [Emperor]."[15] Mo tzu calls this way of ruling "the *tao* of the wise" and "the reason why the former kings came to possess the world."[16]

Modern rulers, the writers of the MT tell us, behave very differently. They spend their days preparing their troops to attack innocent states. When they actually enter their victim state, they engage in senseless destruction. (If warfare was actually conducted in the wantonly ruinous manner described in the MT, precious few spoils could have survived the holocaust to be taken home as loot.) Mo tzu poses three rhetorical questions: Is this warfare designed to bless Heaven? Is it designed to bless the spirits? Is it designed to bless men? He answers all three questions in the negative. The universalized sense of loyalty promoted in the preceding chapters is recalled when Mo tzu accuses the warring nobles of "gathering Heaven's men in order to attack Heaven's cities. This is murdering the people of Heaven."[17] Mo tzu's unusually strong concern for the welfare of both the spirits and the people is abundantly demonstrated:

> Now killing Heaven's people, destroying those who provide for the spirits, discarding and annihilating the former kings,[18] harming and oppressing the masses, and scattering the commoners, in the middle realm this certainly does not benefit the spirits.[19]

A bit later Mo tzu appears to indulge in a rare moment of sarcasm as he hammers home his point: "Now as for killing Heaven's people, the benefit it brings to them is indeed vast!"[20]

Mo tzu's next line of attack emphasizes that in a world mad for conquest every ruler is in a no-win situation. If he fails to prepare for war, or when fighting fails to be vigorous, he weakens his troops' morale and invites attack by others. If his men are well-prepared, they will still suffer heavy losses in battle, and the productivity of the state will be diminished. The loss in manpower and materiel is disastrous in either case. In spite of the terrible toll inflicted on the people, the rulers of the day still delight in war. This, the text tells us, "is to delight in harming and destroying the people of the world. Isn't this unreasonable?"[21]

As in "Condemnation of Offensive War 2," Mo tzu points out that the four most contentious states of the time, Ch'i, Chin, Ch'u, and Yüeh, are all long on acreage and short on manpower. It is senseless and counter-productive for them to engage in war to obtain more land while they decimate their citizenry.

The last section of the chapter is devoted to refuting three hypothetical objections to Mo tzu's doctrine of condemning offensive war. Of the three, only one also occurs in "Condemnation of Offensive War 2."

The first objection raises the difficult problem of the military actions of the sage kings as recorded by tradition:

> Do you not, Sir, suppose military aggression to be unrighteous and an unprofitable business? Anciently Yü marched against the ruler of the Miao. T'ang attacked Chieh. And King Wu attacked Chou. These men are all established as sage kings. What is the reason for this?[22]

The response of the writers of the MT is to define away the problem: what the sage kings engaged in was not offensive war but "punishment." To prove that the sage kings were not mere adventurers but were acting as Heaven's human instruments, Mo tzu cites long lists of bizarre signs and prodigies that occurred right before each of the military actions in question. The "fact" that these omens and portents appeared proves to Mo tzu's satisfaction that the police actions taken by the sage kings were demanded by Heaven. The reader is left to infer that all contemporary military action undertaken in the absence of extraordinary portents must necessarily be wrong.

The objection that offensive wars have most certainly benefited Ch'u, Yüeh, Chin, and Ch'i is dealt with here, as in "Condemnation of Offensive War 2," by citing the analogy of the physician who treats ten thousand patients but only cures four.

The final objection raises the self-righteous claim of those rulers who wish to be remembered in history as great and moral leaders who unified the empire:

> It is not as if I think that my gold, jade, children, and land are insufficient, but that I desire by means of righteousness to establish my name in the world and with my virtue draw the feudal lords to my side.[23]

This claim must have seemed especially insidious to the Mohists, for it represents nothing less than the intention to duplicate the deeds of the sage kings in contemporary times--without the sage kings' divine mandate. Rather than attack the hubris of this attempt, Mo tzu instead chooses to define the terms under which this course may be ethically pursued. What Mo tzu prescribes are, in fact, the actions expected of a ruler who truly regards others' states as he regards his own:

When a large state is unrighteous, he joins in worrying about it. When a large state attacks a small state, he joins in rescuing it. When the inner and outer walls of small states are not in good repair, he will certainly cause them to be repaired. When supplies of cloth and grain are exhausted, he will provide them. When supplies of money and silk are inadequate, he will furnish them. When he relates in this way to a big state, the lord of the big state is pleased, and when he relates in this way to a small state, the lord of the small state is pleased.[24]

By following this course of action, Mo tzu claims that a righteous leader will be able to draw the feudal lords to his side. Of course, such benevolent behavior may not be what the conquest-minded rulers of Mo tzu's day had in mind, but Mo tzu is uncompromising in his insistence upon the absolute, literal correspondence of word and deed. If rulers want to borrow the rhetoric of the sage kings, Mo tzu will hold them to sage-like behavior as well.

With this last objection to the doctrine of condemnation of offensive war refuted, Mo tzu closes the third chapter with a restatement of the Mohist ultimate concern and the assertion that the condemnation of offensive war is an important means for its achievement. War is again labeled the greatest disaster in the world and its condemnation is claimed to be the way of the sage kings.

Now if the kings, dukes, great officials, gentlemen, and lords of the world really and truly desire to seek to promote the world's benefit and eliminate the world's calamities, then as for waging numerous aggressive wars, [they should know that] this in reality is the greatest calamity in the world. Now if they desire to be benevolent and righteous and seek to become superior gentlemen, if above they desire to accord with the *tao* of the sage kings and below they desire to accord with the benefit to the state and its commoners, then as for the theory of the condemnation of offensive wars, it is something theysimply must investigate.[25]

Economy of Expenditures

Only two short chapters of the original triad entitled "Economy of Expenditures" are still in existence. The basic thrust of the two chapters is quite similar, although each presents material not contained in the other. We will treat them as a unit in our discussion, without slighting the distinctive material each introduces.

The fundamental point of the two chapters is succinctly stated in the closing sentence of "Economy of Expenditures 1": "Therefore Master Mo tzu said:

'Eliminating useless expenses, and thereby practicing the *tao* of the sage kings, is the greatest benefit for the world.'"[26] Both chapters emphasize that useless adornment and unnecessary refinement are wasteful and should be eliminated. By eliminating them, the wealth of the state is greatly increased and the populace receives great, if unspecified, benefits. The purposes and functions of clothing, houses, military hardware, boats, and carts are described in order to illustrate the practical implications of the Mohist insistence upon frugality.[27] The way houses should be made, "Economy of Expenditures 2" tells us, is "on the sides able to ward off wind and cold; above able to keep out snow, frost, rain, and dew; inside clean [enough] to be able to sacrifice; the chamber partitions adequate to separate men and women, and then stop."[28]

The prescriptions for clothes, weapons, and conveyances are equally austere; the two chapters set the standards for each, specifying in every instance that practicality and usefulness are to be valued, while all ornamentation and embellishment are to be avoided. "Economy of Expenditures 2" has a more authoritarian and ascetic tone than "Economy of Expenditures 1," claiming that the sage kings set up codes of dress, diet, and funeral expenditure to which the people were held. (Funeral expenses are not mentioned in "Economy of Expenditures 1.") For each category the sage kings determined the minimum requirements for sustenance, safety, and dignity and proscribed anything more extravagant: "Those things that add to the cost but do not add to the people's benefit the sage kings would not do."[29] In ancient times the artisans and craftsmen, the people who actually produced the consumer goods of the time, were also supposedly operating under strict orders to produce plain, sound, and functional objects. Mo tzu quotes the sage kings as saying, "[Provide] whatever is sufficient to meet the people's needs and then stop."[30] Since Mo tzu consistently attributes to the sage kings that which he himself holds most dear, we are again given a clear picture of one aspect of Mo tzu's ideal world. Drab, regimented uniformity is only part of the picture, however, for we must recall the great disparity between the opulence of the nobility and the grinding poverty of the masses in Warring States China. By limiting all members of society to an uninspiring but adequate level of consumption, Mo tzu believes it is possible greatly to enhance the conditions of the majority. Keeping in mind this disparity in wealth also helps clarify the apparently paradoxical Mohist focus on both frugality and benefit. What are the "great benefits" the Mohists hope to achieve when they eschew all ostentation and luxury, while living a life of subsistence-level toil? The great benefit of the Mohists appears to be the creation of a society where everyone enjoys an acceptable minimum of warmth, nourishment and security.

In "Economy of Expenditures 1," Mo tzu states his belief that the wealth of a state can be doubled through the simple method of curtailing all waste. (This, of course, includes offensive war.)

> When a sage governs a state, the state can be doubled.[31] When on a larger scale he governs the entire world, the world can be doubled. The way that he doubles it is not by expropriating land outside its borders, but because his state gets rid of all useless expenditures, that is enough to double it.[32]

With this doubled wealth the Mohists expect to be able to ensure a minimal subsistence for the entire population of the state; the surplus would most likely be used to assist those in other states who are in need and, perhaps more importantly, stored for future use in years of scarcity.[33]

In addition to promoting economy, "Economy of Expenditures 1" makes a major digression into population dynamics. According to the MT it is easy to increase a state's supply of clothing, housing, weapons, and vehicles; what is difficult to increase is the population. As is usual in such cases, Mo tzu presents his prescription in the guise of a description of ancient practices: "Formerly, the sage kings made a law saying, 'Males when twenty years of age must have a family; women when fifteen years old must be married.'"[34] Mo tzu laments that in modern times some men marry at twenty, while others wait until they are forty. This makes the average age of marriage thirty--a full ten years beyond that mandated by the sages. Figuring a child every three years, this means that two or three children per couple could have been born that were not. Not only do modern rulers fail to encourage maximal birthrates, they do everything in their power to boost the death rate artificially. Mo tzu uses this opening to repeat his criticisms of the exploitative rulers of his day and give a reprise of his arguments against aggressive war, emphasizing the damage that misrule and warfare inflict on the population growth rate. These evil practices are called "the *tao* of diminishing the people," and we are told that "when the sages governed, there simply wasn't such a thing."[35]

Strictly regulated frugality is obviously an important means for achieving the Mohist religious goal. To a small extent frugality is justified on the basis of commonsensical demonstrations of its practical value; however, the bulk of Mo tzu's proof is derived directly from his citation of the sage kings. (None of this material has been traced to other surviving Chou dynasty sources.) How population increase fits into the Mohist scheme is unclear; it is obviously desirable, but whether it is an end in itself or a means to some greater benefit is not stated in this section of the text. The authoritarian tone of the chapters makes it clear that the Mohists would not be adverse to promulgating frugality and fecundity by fiat were they given that power.

Simplicity in Funerals

The modern text of the MT contains only one surviving chapter of the triad entitled "Simplicity in Funerals." The religious means extolled in the chapter is that of severely curtailing the outlay of both time and materiel devoted to funerals and mourning. Mo tzu seeks to demonstrate that most of the evils of his time can be traced, either directly or more commonly indirectly, to the irrevocable loss of wealth demanded by the elaborate burial practices championed by "traditionalists" and the critical squandering of human energy and talent incurred through extended mourning. The substitution of Mohist-sanctioned funeral and mourning practices for those currently in use will lead, the text tells us, to the increase of wealth, population, and political order throughout the world--major goals of the MT.

The chapter begins with an analogy: "The way that the magnanimous plan for the world is exactly analogous to the way that filial sons plan for their parents."[36] The text follows up on this by posing and then answering a rhetorical question: "Now how does the filial son plan for his parents?"[37] In his answer, Mo tzu enumerates the "three benefits" (*san li* 三 利) that concern the filial son: "When the parents are poor, then enrich them; when the people are few, then increase them; when the masses are disorderly, then control them."[38] Similarly, the task of the magnanimous ruler is to enrich, increase, and order his population. (Or, in other words, to strive for the realization of the Mohist ultimate concern.)

These "three benefits" are the criteria by which the actions of modern rulers are to be evaluated, starting with funeral and mourning practices.

Mo tzu first broaches the topic of funerals and mourning by repeating his well-worn lament that in the years since the passing of the sage kings the world has forgotten their principles and is mired in ignorance. In their confusion, some gentlemen suppose rich funerals and lengthy mourning to be humane, righteous, and the duty of the filial son. (This group presumably includes many followers of Confucius.) Others uphold the opposite view, leading to great confusion, since both camps claim to be following the traditions of the sage kings. Mo tzu proposes to test the value of rich funerals and lengthy mourning by measuring them against the "three benefits." If elaborate funerals and extended mourning can enrich the poor, increase the few, and bring order, then they must be "humane, righteous, and the duty of the filial son." In this case they should be adopted and praised by all. If, on the contrary, rich funerals and lengthy mourning do not promote the universal realization of the "three benefits," then they are not humane, righteous and filial and must be excluded from the world.[39] Given the irrelevance of the standards of judgement to the practices being evaluated, it is not surprising that rich funerals and lengthy mourning are found deficient. The text does not stop with this early verdict, however; Mo tzu goes on to document the many ways in which the funeral customs of his time exact a tremendous economic and sociopolitical toll.

In answer to his first question--do rich funerals and lengthy mourning enrich the poor?--Mo tzu details the customary expenses of a lord's burial. The labor expended to build a massive grave mound is enormous. The manufactured goods, silks, jewels and gold, animals, etc., entombed with the corpse empty the state's storehouses. Besides the great wealth forever lost with each burial, there is also the human toll still incurred by the lingering practice of burying a lord's living retainers in their patron's tomb. The MT claims that for an emperor or a feudal lord this might entail the sacrifice of several hundred men and for a general or high official several tens of men.[40] The mourning customs described by Mo tzu are nearly as unattractive as the burial practices he critiques: the mourner should sob endlessly, live in a rude hut, eat and dress inadequately, and look like a physical wreck for three whole years. The net result of these practices is to disrupt the legitimate functions of all classes of society: rulers cannot vigorously pursue government and encourage agriculture; farmers cannot effectively plant and harvest;

artisans are unable to practice their crafts; and women cannot weave and spin. Mo tzu summarizes his dissatisfaction with the status quo saying,

> [I] calculate that rich funerals entail the burial of great wealth and lengthy mourning entails prolonged abstention from work. Goods already produced are carried off and buried while the production of new goods is prevented. To seek wealth in this way is analogous to seeking a harvest by prohibiting plowing; the theory of prosperity can derive nothing from this.[41]

Mo tzu next asks if rich funerals and lengthy mourning can increase the population. In his answer to this question Mo tzu focuses exclusively upon the detrimental effects of long mourning. (Funeral expenses evidently were not viewed as directly affecting population growth.) For the death of the lord of a state, a parent, a wife, or an eldest son, there is to be three years mourning, with lesser terms of mourning for less important relations. During this time the mourner is to be inadequately clothed and fed. Mo tzu claims that the number who die from this deprivation "cannot be counted," and "the damage this does to conjugal relations is great indeed!"[42] Again the MT closes the discussion with an analogy: "To seek population growth in this way is like causing someone to seek longevity by impaling himself on a sword; the theory of population growth can derive nothing from this!"[43]

The last of the "three benefits," improved social order, is taken up next. In his consideration of the impact of rich burials and lengthy mourning upon the regulation of society, Mo tzu focuses first on the disruption of administration caused by extended mourning and then considers the dire economic implications of the universal adoption of the custom. Mo tzu's main objection appears to lie with the practice of lengthy mourning. Elaborate funerals obviously bankrupt the state; Mo tzu wishes to establish the less apparent fact that long mourning eliminates all chance of economic recovery from the devastation of the funerals, by greatly adding to the disorganization of the state.

Mo tzu states that when "the superiors are caused to practice this [lengthy mourning], then they cannot attend to ruling; when the subordinates are caused to practice this, then they cannot work."[44] As a direct result "the jurisdiction must certainly be chaotic" and "clothing and foodstuffs must certainly be insufficient."[45] In the ensuing economy of scarcity the natural social order will collapse. Mo tzu presents a chain of actions and reactions that in their apparently inevitable unfolding reveal the early Mohists' faith in environmental determinism, or in its negative side at least.[46]

> If and as soon as there is insufficiency, the younger brother, having sought and been denied his elder brother's help, will be unbrotherly and will inevitably hate his elder brother. The son, having sought and been denied his father's help, will be unfilial and will certainly hate his father. The minister, having sought and been denied his lord's help, will be disloyal and will inevitably betray his superior. This is why wicked, depraved acting people in going out are without clothes and within the home are without food; they will therefore store up great humiliation[47] and accordingly will practice uncontrollable immorality and violence. Therefore robbers and thieves will be many and law abiders few.[48]

The authors of the MT, who elsewhere do not hesitate to demand the most severe self-sacrifice from the followers of the Mohist *tao*, here show a surprisingly tolerant recognition of the power that social and economic environments have in molding the behavior of ordinary individuals. The chapters on universal love, for instance, seem eerily divorced from the actual circumstances of the Warring States. Mo tzu makes absolute, untempered demands and expects uncompromising compliance from those who wish to follow his teachings. The clear impression is given that for Mo tzu the human will is all-sufficient; one determines a course of action and then follows it without deviation--the impact of outward circumstances is not a part of the calculations. A different side of the Mohist understanding of human nature is now presented with the recognition that in times of great hardship human behavior loses its veneer of "civilization," and humankind reverts to the primitive, chaotic conditions that prevailed before the rise of the sage kings.[49] The sage kings, and presumably other great individuals, were able to rise above the constraints of their outward circumstances, but the masses are seen as malleable, capable of good or bad, and subject to the dictates of their environment. This malleability has from the start been a part of the Mohist view of human nature, but due perhaps to the didactic nature of the text the greatest emphasis has always been on the possibilities of consciously directing the masses towards the good, not on the power of negative forces. True, the Mohists point to the powerful negative example that the "evil kings" presented to their subjects, but the passage under discussion goes further to imply that even a good ruler saddled with the burden of long mourning would encounter great, if not insurmountable, difficulties in trying to override the evil influences of the accompanying poverty and disruption.

Having analyzed rich burials and lengthy mourning using the criteria of the "three benefits" (enriching the people, increasing the population, and improving political order), the text turns to the consideration of the impact that rich funerals and lengthy mourning have on several other important Mohist means. Even here, however, the analysis is based on the "three benefits": when the three benefits are promoted then the other Mohist means are also more fully realized; when the three benefits are stifled then all phases of the Mohist program suffer.

Given the failure of rich burials and lengthy mourning to promote the three benefits, Mo tzu asks if they can perhaps prevent large states from attacking small ones. The gist of his reply can be summarized as follows. In these modern, degenerate times the big states are highly militarized and constantly on the lookout for small states to forcibly annex. The only states the aggressors leave in peace are those with good stockpiles of provisions, strong walls, and harmony between officials and subordinates. All other states are regarded as fair game. The adoption of rich burials and lengthy mourning ensures that "the state will certainly be poor, the people will certainly be few, and the government will certainly be disorderly."[50] (Or in other words, the three benefits will not be realized.) In this state of affairs goods will not be stockpiled, walls will fall into disrepair, and society will be disharmonious. Thus Mo tzu concludes that rich burials and lengthy mourning create the conditions that invite invasion. Although this is presented as a separate argument against the practices, it is really just an extension of the preceding inquiry into the impact of rich funerals and long mourning on the three benefits. Mo tzu has already shown that rich burials and lengthy mourning impoverish the people, reduce the population, and increase the disorder in a state; he is now looking at how this state of affairs influences several of his other means. The prevention of aggressive war, a previously discussed means, is clearly not favored by rich burials and lengthy mourning, at least not as the MT presents them.

Mo tzu next asks if rich burials and lengthy mourning can secure blessings from "God, ghosts, and spirits."[51] Again the answer is based on the three benefits:

If [the people] are poor, this means that the containers for millet and wine [for sacrifices] will not be clean. If [the people] are few, this means that those who serve God, ghosts, and spirits will be few. If [the government] is disorderly, this means that the sacrifices will not be done at the proper times.[52]

The three benefits, originally presented as the criteria by which the utility of rich burials and lengthy mourning are to be judged, have now taken on an expanded role and are seen as the basis upon which the success of the other Mohist means seems to lie.[53] Since the three benefits are obtained through the prevention of rich burials and lengthy mourning, this makes the Mohist primary means of simplicity in funerals and mourning a secondary means for attaining the primary means of preventing aggressive war and securing the blessings of God, ghosts, and spirits. The point of this somewhat convoluted analysis is not to create impossibly complex flow charts of cause and effect but to illustrate the subtle interdependencies of the various Mohist means and shed light on how the seemingly disorganized rhetorical assaults of the Essays are all consciously dedicated to the realization of the Mohist ultimate concern in human society. The angles of approach vary from chapter to chapter, sometimes overlapping and other times seemingly unrelated, but throughout the text there is a very consistent and single-minded purpose: to bring the greatest benefits to the world while excluding all that is harmful to it. Of course, the Mohist understandings of benefit and harm were not necessarily those of their contemporaries--as the following passage lamenting the common modern failure to serve God, ghosts, and spirits shows:

> When government is conducted like this, God, ghosts, and spirits approaching from on high will grasp them, saying "Which is more desirable, that we have these people or don't have them? There is nothing to choose between having them and not having them." Then God, ghosts and spirits will rain blame and cruel calamities down on them, punishing and discarding them.[54]

Mo tzu's fear of certain, severe punishment from God, ghosts, and spirits for the neglect of sacrifices was probably shared by few of the Warring States literati. Similarly his desire, based in part on this fear, to serve the traditionally revered spiritual beings of earlier, less cynical times must have been equally far from the daily concerns of those in positions of power.[55]

Mo tzu concludes his main opening arguments against rich burials and long mourning with a seemingly obligatory appeal to the sages of antiquity:

> Therefore the ancient sages established laws for conducting funerals saying, "The coffins shall be three inches [thick], sufficient for the decaying body. The clothes and cloths shall be three pieces, sufficient to cover the evil [smell?]. As for the burial, below [the coffin] should not reach groundwater, yet above it should not emit odors. When the mound is three feet then stop.[56] The living

should not mourn long but should quickly return to work, each doing what they best can for their mutual profit."[57]

The whole quote, and especially the last sentence, bears so clearly the Mohist imprint that one strongly suspects that these particular funeral regulations, or at least their specifics, are the creation of Mo tzu or the early Mohists. Tradition has it that among the sage kings Yü was most noted for frugality, but that he or any other of the sage kings could have passed down such specific instructions is extremely unlikely. Once again Mo tzu is probably manufacturing the sort of evidence that he himself seems to value and that apparently carried weight with his intended audience.

The final section of the chapter is devoted to the now familiar rhetorical device of posing objections to the chapter's religious means and then answering them with an overwhelming Mohist rebuttal. The first objection grants that rich burials and lengthy mourning may not enrich, increase, and regulate the population but claims that nevertheless "they are the *tao* of the sage kings."[58] Mo tzu answers this claim with the "historical" argument, giving an account of the deaths and burials of Yao, Shun, and Yü that incorporates a wealth of detail that was probably not available in the fifth century B.C.E. Not surprisingly, the burials of the sage kings conformed in every detail to the burial regulations quoted above. In contrast to the modest frugality of the sages, Mo tzu describes the extravagance of the burial of a modern ruler and states that "the degree to which this obstructs the people's work and squanders their wealth is incalculable."[59] Having demonstrated that the sage kings were terrifically frugal in burial and mourning, Mo tzu then summarizes the conclusions he draws from all his practical illustrations of the perils of rich burials and lengthy mourning: rich burials and lengthy mourning do not measure up against the criterion of the three benefits, they do not prevent aggressive war (and, in fact, encourage it), they do not bring blessings from God and spiritual beings, and they are not the way of the sage kings. Further, rich burials and lengthy mourning accord perfectly with the practices of the evil kings, Chieh, Chou, Yu, and Li, and therefore "they are not the *tao* of the sage kings."[60]

The second objection is more interesting, for it raises the question of the validity of inherited customs and the problem of cultural relativism. Mo tzu's imaginary interlocutors ask, "If rich burials and lengthy mourning in fact are not the *tao* of the sage kings, then why do the lords of the Middle Kingdom practice them without stopping and hold on to them without discriminating?"[61] In his answer Mo tzu gives us a glimpse into his understanding of the basis of the relative morality transmitted by human cultures (as opposed to the absolute morality Mo tzu claims to see in Heaven and God [*shang ti*]): "The Master Mo tzu said, 'this is what is called regarding one's customs as convenient and one's habits as righteous.'"[62] Mo tzu's point is that most people automatically accept without question the values handed down to them, never for a moment doubting their perfect design and absolute morality. To drive home the relativity of all human values, Mo tzu discusses the practices of the "barbarians" east, south, and west of China. The barbarians of the East eat their first-born son; this is said to be good for his younger brothers. When a husband dies, his wife is expelled from the tribe for she is now a "ghost's wife." A southern tribe believes that upon a parent's death a filial son should scrape the flesh from his parent's bones and discard it, burying the bones alone. A filial son of a western tribe burns his dead parents upon a bonfire. For all three tribes, these practices are regarded as fit and proper, but from a Middle Kingdom viewpoint the Mohists condemn them as wrong:[63] " How can this really be the *tao* of humanity and righteousness? This is what is called regarding one's customs as convenient and one's habits as righteous."[64] Mo tzu states that the barbarians' funeral practices are "too meagre," while the current Chinese practices are "too rich." He concludes that there must be moderation in funerals and then states his rules for burial. Not surprisingly, Mo tzu's rules for burial are identical in their stipulations to those attributed by the text to the sage kings and translated above. What is surprising, given the authors' penchant for verbatim repetition, is that Mo tzu's rules, while identical in import to those of the sage kings, are phrased quite differently.[65] Both sets mandate coffin walls three inches thick, three pieces of burial shroud, a pit deep enough to contain all odors but shallow enough to avoid hitting water, and a very modest mound over the site of interment.

Mo tzu closes the chapter with a restatement of his ultimate concern and the assertion that simple funerals are a means for its attainment:

> Therefore Master Mo tzu says, "If the gentlemen of the world truly wish to practice humanity and righteousness and seek to be superior gentlemen in the middle realm, then above they would desire to accord with the *tao* of the sage kings, and below they would desire

to aim for the benefit of the state and its people. Therefore as for governing with simple funerals, this is something that they simply must investigate.[66]

Notes

[1] This passage is a close, though abridged, paraphrase of MTCC, pp. 173-174. As mentioned earlier, paraphrases will be quite faithful to the text of the MT. They will be used primarily to smooth out the syntax and cut the redundancies and repetitions of the original.

[2] Paraphrase of ibid., pp. 174-175.

[3] Ibid., p. 175.

[4] It is interesting that many Western readers find "Condemnation of Offensive War 1" one of the most effective and persuasive of the Essay chapters. Mo tzu's elementary algebra, if X=Y then 10X=10Y and 100X=100Y, is more attractive than his strained interpretations of seemingly irrelevant passages from the Classics and his revisionist history lessons.

[5] Ibid., p. 176.

[6] Ibid., pp. 176-177.

[7] Ibid., p. 178.

[8] Ibid., p. 179.

[9] Ibid., pp. 181-182. It is significant that in his rebuttal Mo tzu does not challenge the basic assumption of the objector that one who can force others to submit, presumably without major loss of life, is behaving righteously. Rather he attempts to show that even the mightiest warriors of the past were unable to run roughshod over the world forever. *If* one could force the world to submit to his rule without wreaking great havoc, it would presumably be acceptable. Mo tzu has no objection to totalitarian rule in principle, or fact. The problem is that no one is actually capable of such unquestioned dominance; the attempt to conquer China is certain to result in great bloodshed and for that reason is wrong.

[10] Ibid., pp. 185-186.

[11] Chang Ch'un yi makes a plausible case for emending *shan* 善 "good" to *yi* 義 "righteous." (Ibid., p. 186) However, since the text makes sense either way, it is probably better to avoid unnecessary tampering.

[12] Ibid., pp. 186-187.

[13] Ibid., p. 187.

[14] Ibid., p. 188. This passage can be understood in two strikingly different ways depending upon one's punctuation of the text and gloss of the word *nung* 農. *Nung* ordinarily means "agriculture" but according to Yeh Yü lin it is also defined in the *Kuang ya* as "exhort." By breaking the sentence after "world" and glossing *nung* as "exhort," we obtain the following: (The sages) "led the masses of the world, exhorting their subjects to serve God, mountains, streams, and rivers." (MTHS, p. 119.)

[15] Ibid.

[16] Ibid.

[17] Ibid., p. 189. Again we see the importance of Heaven in the value system of the early Mohists, where it is viewed as the highest power to which all humans owe ultimate allegiance. The relationship of Heaven and humankind is, of course, reciprocal; in return for humanity's obedience to its will, Heaven acts as a father to the world.

[18] "Discarding and annihilating the former kings" could mean several things. Since those attacked are the descendants of the former kings, the kings are being harmed when their progeny is destroyed. Also the former kings depend on the sacrifices of their offspring, which are interrupted, perhaps permanently, by war. A third meaning might be that war runs counter to the teachings of the sages, so by engaging in wanton murder the aggressors are discarding and destroying the *tao* of the former kings. Mo tzu's reproval is unmistakable even if his exact meaning is unclear.

[19] Ibid., p. 190.

[20] Ibid. Most editors have emended *po* 博 "vast" to *po* 薄 "meagre." This does not necessarily improve the text. Since most commentators assume *po* "vast" to be unintelligible in this context, it appears that sarcasm is not, in their view, part of Mo Ti's rhetorical arsenal.

[21] Ibid., p. 192.

[22] Ibid., p. 193.

[23] Ibid., p. 202.

[24] Ibid., pp. 202-203. The translation of this last sentence follows Chang's extensive emendation.

[25] Ibid., p. 204.

[26] Ibid., p. 212.

[27] These four categories--clothes, houses, military hardware, and vehicles--do not appear to have been chosen at random. Rather they are the basic groups of manufactured goods considered essential by the Mohists, for we are subsequently told (in "Economy of Expenditures 1") that the sages relinquished all their expensive hobbies in order to increase the state's supply of clothing, housing, military equipment, and vehicles. (Ibid., p. 209.) This is a clear indication of the fundamental importance assigned to these categories by the writers of the text.

[28] Ibid., p. 216.

[29] Ibid., p. 214.

[30] Ibid., p. 213.

[31] That Mo tzu means that the *wealth* of the state can be doubled is made abundantly clear by the following lines.

[32] Ibid., p. 207.

[33] The need to store food for times of shortage is a recurring minor theme in the MT. For an example see ibid., pp. 39-40.

[34] Ibid., pp. 209-210. In his commentary Chang cites several other early Chinese texts that contain similar injunctions attributed to the sage kings. In some,

the age by which males must be married is thirty; for females it is twenty, but twenty and fifteen seem to be the most frequently cited ages. In a similarly authoritarian manner the current leaders of China are legislating higher marriage ages in a desperate attempt to lower China's birth rate.

[35] Ibid., p. 211.

[36] Ibid., p. 219.

[37] Ibid.

[38] Ibid. Mo tzu seems to have jumbled up his analogy here, confusing the concerns of the filial son with those of the ruler. Y. P. Mei tries to sort the analogy out by translating "If the parents have few people (descendants) he would increase them; if the members (of the family) are in confusion he would put them in order." Mei, *Mo tzu*, p. 123. Whether the analogy works or not, the meaning is clear enough.

[39] MTCC, pp. 220-221. Mo tzu is being less than fair to the opposing camp by establishing an inappropriate standard, the "three benefits," against which funeral and mourning practices are to be judged. It is obvious that funeral and mourning customs were never expected to enrich, increase, and pacify the realm--at least not directly. (The role of these practices in securing the assistance of the ancestors is not considered in this chapter.) To judge the practices by these standards while ignoring the social purposes that they had evolved to fulfil is to bypass the substance of the issue. Unfortunately, we have no way of knowing how these lines of attack played to a Warring States audience. Were arguments of this sort effective with his readers?

[40] Ibid., p. 222. The numbers of retainers buried with their lords mentioned in this passage seems rather high, especially since the custom is thought to have been "dying out" at this time--at least in the center of the Chinese cultural sphere. H. G. Creel suspects that because of their opposition to the practice, the followers of Confucius suppressed all references to it in the literature that they edited. This makes it very hard to to judge its prevalence. Perhaps Mo tzu's numbers are a more accurate indication of what was actually happening at the time. See H. G. Creel, *Confucius and the Chinese Way* (New York: Harper and Row, 1949), p. 119.

[41] MTCC, p. 224.

[42] Ibid., p. 225.

[43] Ibid.

[44] Ibid., p. 226.

[45] Ibid.

[46] The text clearly seems to say that bad times create bad people but stops short of saying that in good times people are *necessarily* good. Certainly the likelihood that people will be good is greater in times of prosperity, but even then effort and correct teachings are required for the ideal society to be created.

[47] Following the gloss of Wang Yin chih quoted in Yeh Yü lin, MTHS, p. 145.

[48] MTCC, p. 226.

[49] See the preceding discussion of chaos in the section on "Identification with the Superior."

[50] Ibid., p. 227.

[51] Ibid. The Chinese terms used are *shang ti, kuei, shen* 上帝, 鬼, 神.

[52] Ibid., p. 228.

[53] Although it is not mentioned in the text, Mo tzu could plausibly have argued that the implementation of universal love is also strongly based upon the three benefits. For the other Mohist means, viz. identification with the superior, anti-fatalism, etc., the connection is tenuous.

[54] Ibid.

[55] Mo tzu's credulity, of which we shall see more later, stands in strong contrast to the hard-nosed skepticism evinced by most of the writers of his time whose works have survived till the present. In his pious acceptance of traditional beliefs, many modern writers see evidence for the theory that Mo tzu was of lower class origins--their assumption being that the poorer, less educated strata of society are inherently more conservative than the elite.

[56] Following Sun Yi jang's gloss. (Ibid., p. 228.)

[57] Ibid., pp. 228-229.

[58] Ibid., p. 229.

[59] Ibid., p. 232.

[60] Ibid., p. 233.

[61] Ibid.

[62] Ibid. Sun reads *yi* 義 "righteous" as *yi* 宜 "proper." Both cognates and homophones in ancient Chinese, the two characters are often defined in terms of one another, e.g. 義 者 宜 也. See Legge, *The Chinese Classics*, 1:405. Sun's emendation is not only unnecessary but trivializes the meaning of the passage. For the Mohists, what is righteous must also be appropriate to the circumstances at hand, but righteousness is more than mere appropriate behavior. Of course in the Logic chapters the later Mohists define *yi* "righteousness" as *li* 利 "benefit." (MTCC, p. 493.) Following this definition we get, "This is what is called regarding one's customs as convenient and one's habits as beneficial." If *yi* is taken to mean *li*, then the term is without moral significance in this passage.

[63] It is interesting that Mo tzu is appealing to the gut-level revulsion that his readers would experience when reading of practices so different from their own. The "barbarians'" practices seem wrong to Mo tzu's readers because the "barbarians'" relative morality offends the relative morality of the Chinese, not because any absolute standard of right and wrong has actually been invoked.

[64] Ibid., p. 235.

[65] It seems possible that the two passages were written differently to strengthen the claim that the first set of rules actually originated with the sage kings and are not just the words of Mo tzu placed in the sage kings' mouths--which is what one

might suspect reading two identically worded passages. This is yet another small indication that the writers of the text took their appeals to precedents very seriously and were not just mechanically repeating implausible attributions.

[66] Ibid., p. 236.

CHAPTER VI

ANALYSIS OF THE ESSAYS 3

Will of Heaven

In the past two chapters, an attempt was made to give a feel for both the content of the MT and the manner in which the content is presented. In order to allow the text to speak for itself, extensive use was made of quotations and rather linear summaries of the chapters being analyzed. From this point on, we will move through the text more expeditiously, approaching the content of the chapters being studied more or less thematically. Consequently, less use will be made of long quotations, and we will be concerned more with the conclusions of the text rather than the processes by which the conclusions are reached. However, points that do not fit into this thematic approach will still be introduced where appropriate.[1] Where all three versions of a chapter have survived ("Will of Heaven" and "Anti-Fatalism"), they will be discussed simultaneously. (For the other three Essays to be discussed in this chapter, only one version of each is extant.)

All three surviving chapters entitled "Will of Heaven" forcefully proclaim that Heaven exists, is aware of and concerned with the actions of *all* humankind, and actively intervenes to reward and punish humans for their behavior: "Now humans all live in the world and serve Heaven. If people offend Heaven, then there is truly nowhere they can go to flee from it."[2] While it may appear that moral standards are legislated by the emperor and other rulers, in a deeper sense this is false. Heaven is the true source for the highest standards of human behavior, and the will of Heaven is the ultimate source of moral guidance. The authors of the MT reason that standards never come from the lowly and humble but are given to the lower orders by the higher. Therefore scholars (*shih*) rectify the common people, ministers rectify the scholars, feudal lords rectify the ministers, and so forth. The process ends when Heaven rectifies the emperor.[3]

The religious means presented in the chapters is following the will of Heaven and adhering to the standards Heaven sets.[4] In "Will of Heaven 3" we are given an explicit, if abbreviated, definition of following the will of Heaven: "What is it like to follow the will of Heaven? I say it is universally to love the people of the world."[5] In each of the chapters, Mo tzu says that for him the will of Heaven is a measuring tool analogous to the wheelwright's compass and the carpenter's square; with it Mo tzu can separate righteousness from unrighteousness.

A great deal of space is devoted to describing the will of Heaven and demonstrating that what Mo tzu has labeled the will of Heaven is, in fact, what he claims it to be. Mo tzu asks: "Then what does Heaven desire and what does it hate? Heaven desires righteousness and hates unrighteousness."[6] We know that this is so because righteousness makes the world live, prosper, and be orderly, while unrighteousness makes it die, become impoverished, and grow disorderly. "Now Heaven desires [the world] to live and hates for it to die, desires it to be wealthy and hates for it to be impoverished, desires it to be orderly and hates for it to be disorderly."[7] The standard of righteousness given to men by Heaven is "universal, mutual love and mutual benefit."[8] As depicted by Mo tzu, the standard of Heaven is mostly concerned with the way humans treat one another; however, when describing the model righteous behavior of the sage kings, Mo tzu adds another dimension to the practice of righteousness. We are told that in their affairs the sages "above revered Heaven, in the middle served ghosts and spirits, and below loved men."[9] It would seem that "universal, mutual love and mutual benefit" extends beyond the human plane and is fully implemented only when Heaven, ghosts, and spirits are included among its beneficiaries. Following the will of Heaven then requires humans to consider the well-being of Heaven, ghosts, and spirits as well as displaying universal love for humankind.

The relationship of humans and Heaven is a major theme of the chapters. As with most concepts presented in the MT, it is not without its ambiguities. On the most fundamental level, the relationship between humans and Heaven is based on the principle of *quid pro quo*: "When I do what Heaven desires, then Heaven also does what I desire."[10] In a later passage we read that "there are those who do not do what Heaven desires but do what Heaven hates. Therefore Heaven also does not do what they desire but does what they hate."[11] The MT is quite specific on the rewards and punishments meted out by Heaven. Those who follow the will of Heaven receive "blessings and wealth"; those who do not are visited by "calamities and evil influences."[12] Mo tzu feels that people are insufficiently appreciative of all that Heaven does for them and likens the gentlemen of the age to unfilial sons.[13] Humanity is remiss in fulfilling its share of the bargain that Heaven has entered into on its behalf. The balance can be righted only if humans also love universally and provide reverent sacrifice to Heaven. The Heaven of the Mohists is omniscient and utterly impartial in its dealings with humanity; there is no hint of unpredictability or caprice in its actions. However, although Heaven is a stern judge of human behavior, it is also asserted that Heaven loves humanity: "Now Heaven universally loves the entire world."[14] While there is no necessary conflict between the role of divine judge and loving deity, this depiction adds a measure of complexity to Mo tzu's otherwise straightforward theology.

The nature of Heaven and its love for humans is revealed in the proofs of Heaven's love presented in the MT. In all three chapters entitled "Will of Heaven" we are told that Heaven's love for humanity is shown by the divine retribution visited upon the murderer of an innocent person. In this instance, Heaven's actions as judge and executioner are viewed as proof of Heaven's love, for if Heaven did not love humankind it would not care that an innocent had been wronged.

A less forbidding aspect of divine love is revealed in the passage in "Will of Heaven 2" that claims that Heaven's love for humanity is shown in the way that Heaven has structured the world for the benefit of all humans. The order of nature, the regular progression of the seasons, the harmonious interactions of the human, animal, and environmental spheres are all clear indicators of Heaven's solicitude and concern.[15] Heaven is depicted as the conscious organizing power responsible for all that is right in the world. While Heaven is not quite considered the creator of the universe, it is clearly the general manager with complete responsibility for all aspects of the world's operation.[16]

The logic of a train of reasoning found in the first and third chapters on the will of Heaven is rather opaque. In both passages Mo tzu writes that we know that Heaven loves the masses because "it universally enlightens them." How do we know that it does this? "Because it universally possesses them." How do we know this? "Because it universally eats from them [accepts their offerings]." The passage goes on to note that all the civilized peoples of the world prepare sacrifices for God, ghosts, and spirits;[17] from this Mo tzu infers that Heaven must possess and love the people of the world.[18] The reasoning seems to be that because Heaven accepts their sacrifices, it must necessarily love those who make offerings to it; since this includes all the civilized world, Heaven must love everybody.[19]

The last proof of Heaven's love for humankind is found in the sure rewards given to the deserving and the unfailing punishments visited upon the guilty. The certainty of the heavenly *quid pro quo* is illustrated by the contrasting fates of the sage kings and their evil counterparts, the wicked kings of the Three Dynasties. We read that the sage kings "universally loved the world, and therefore, benefiting it, they transformed the will of the people and led them in revering God, mountains, streams, ghosts, and spirits."[20] As a result, Heaven piled up rewards on them "installing them as emperors."[21] The wicked kings behaved in a formulaically opposite manner and were punished by Heaven; their infamy reaches to the present.[22] That Heaven sees fit to punish bad rulers and reward good ones shows Mo tzu that Heaven is concerned for the fate of the commoners who are the subjects of these kings.

In addition to illustrating the benefits that individuals receive from following the will of Heaven, Mo tzu also provides a glimpse of his ideal world, a world achieved when all follow Heaven's will and governments are based on the Mohists' version of righteousness.[23] Neither of the two descriptions of the Mohist ideal world are particularly vivid or visionary by modern standards, but, given the chaos and uncertainty of the Warring States period, any account of a secure world where peace and basic sustenance are guaranteed must be viewed as utopian. In the state founded upon following the will of Heaven, the superiors and subordinates will both work diligently at their respective tasks; as a result, the state will be orderly and wealthy. The surplus wealth will be used to prepare sacrifices to "Heaven and ghosts" and to buy the friendship of neighboring states.[24] With internal and external peace secured, the masses will be well fed and rested; the rulers and bureaucrats will be kind and loyal, and the relationships of fathers and sons, elder and younger brothers, will be characterized by affection and filialness respectively.[25] The passage sums up the benefits of the universal adoption of the practice of following the will of Heaven as follows: "Then punishments and governmental decrees will be orderly, the masses will be harmonious, the states will be prosperous, goods will be sufficient, the people will all have warm clothes and filling food, and [all] will be peaceful and free of worries."[26]

More than the other two chapters, "Will of Heaven 3" places a strong emphasis on the Mohist means of condemnation of offensive war. This impression is strengthened by the fact that the concluding portion of "Will of Heaven 3" recapitulates the entire contents of "Condemnation of Offensive War 1," a short chapter composed of two extended analogies, while adding its own injunctions and exhortations.[27] The point made in "Condemnation of Offensive War 1" is that humans recognize small amounts of unrighteousness for the evil that it is, but when faced with great unrighteousness they paradoxically fail to recognize it as evil but praise it as good. This is illustrated by the story of the thief who breaks into a garden and makes off with some vegetables. This is recognized as evil by all. In both chapters the text recounts a series of progressively more injurious crimes, and in each case affirms that society recognizes the increasing severity of the offense. The final crime recounted, offensive war, is inexplicably praised and seen as virtuous by the conquest-mad rulers of the day. The second illustration concerns the man who sees a little black and calls it black, but when faced with a large quantity of black calls it white. In "Condemnation of Offensive War 1" these stories are used to demonstrate the fact that the people of Mo tzu's time cannot distinguish righteousness from unrighteousness.[28] These same analogies are used in "Will of Heaven 3" to a slightly different effect. Mo tzu's point is no longer simply that humans are confused in their moral judgements. His conclusion is that absolute standards have been given to humanity by Heaven, though people fail to recognize them. Mo tzu closes the chapter with these words: "The will of Heaven is the standard of righteousness."[29]

In summary, the primary problem addressed in the chapters entitled "Will of Heaven" is that the people of the world, both high and low, fail to follow the will of Heaven. The chaos that ensues from this failure is the cause of much of the injustice and misery that plagues the world. The solution is, of course, to lead the people of the world back to the sage kings' practice of following the will of Heaven, which is understood to embrace the practice of another Mohist means, universal love. The logical outcomes of practicing universal love, such as the opposition to war and all other forms of aggression, are also included as part of practice of following Heaven's will. Additionally, it is stated that all righteous action must benefit Heaven and the ghosts and spirits as well as humankind. Therefore humans must respect Heaven and the spiritual beings and sacrifice to them. Heaven is depicted as sentient and actively concerned with human affairs. A divine and infallible judge, Heaven keeps track of both merit and guilt and sees that all are punished or rewarded appropriately. By following the will of Heaven, and all the other Mohist means subsumed under it, an ideal world can be created. Characterized by order and stability, the Mohist ideal is a world where everyone is provided with a sufficiency of the basic necessities, with the surplus returned to Heaven and the spiritual beings or used to buy the goodwill of neighboring states.

On Ghosts

The religious means presented in the one surviving chapter entitled "On Ghosts" is to teach humanity to worship ghosts and spirits reverently and believe in their power to reward good and punish evil. When this is done the world will again be orderly: "Now if the people of the world all believed in the ability of ghosts and spirits to reward virtue and punish wickedness, then how could the world be in chaos?"[30] The widespread propagation of the worship of, and belief in, ghosts and spirits will lead directly to the realization of the Mohist ultimate concern:

> Therefore Master Mo tzu said: "Now if the kings, dukes, great officials, scholars, and gentlemen truly seek to promote the world's benefits and remove that which harms the world, then as for the existence of ghosts and spirits they must reverently proclaim [it]. This is the *tao* of the sage kings."[31]

In addition to teaching about ghosts and spirits and their divine rewards and retribution, the practice of this religious means requires sincere worship from the practitioner.

The problem addressed in this chapter is the breakdown of social mores and traditional standards of behavior that Mo tzu believes began with the passing of the sage kings: "Since the death of the sage kings of the ancient Three Dynasties, the world has lost its righteousness and the feudal lords have forcefully attacked [one another]."[32] This has led to the destruction of the relationships of superior and subordinate, father and son, and elder and younger brothers. The officials do not attend to their duties and the masses fail to work; the world has fallen into violent chaos as a result. Although the timing of this decline coincides with the death of the sage kings, Mo tzu believes that the root cause is to be found in the breakdown of the traditional beliefs in ghosts and spirits:

What is the reason for all this? It is all due to doubts over the distinction between the existence and non-existence of ghosts and spirits and ignorance of their ability to reward virtue and punish wickedness.[33]

The solution proffered by Mo tzu is the revival of traditional sacrificial practices and the renewal of the peoples' faith in ghosts and spirits. If the people believe that good is invariably rewarded and evil is unerringly punished, then, Mo tzu reasons, self-interest will cause them to transform their behavior and the world will regain its former harmony.

What are these ghosts and spirits in which Mo tzu so earnestly desires the people of the world to believe? Like Heaven, the ghosts and spirits are depicted as omniscient, omnipresent witnesses to all that humans do: "Even if there is a deep river valley, a wide forest, or a secluded ravine--places where there are no people--one's actions must not be improper, for ghosts and spirits will see them."[34] However, ghosts and spirits do not appear to be exactly equivalent to Heaven, for in several other places in the MT we find a recurring formula stating that all truly good things must "in the upper realm be beneficial to Heaven, in the middle realm benefit ghosts and spirits, and below benefit humanity."[35] At the very least, we must assume that even if their functions overlap, Heaven and the ghosts and spirits occupy different levels of a hierarchy that descends from Heaven through the level of ghosts and spirits to humankind. It must be noted, however, that Mo tzu's use of what we would consider to be technical terms is very imprecise.[36]

In one abrupt passage in "On Ghosts," Mo tzu briefly attempts a typology of ghosts and spirits: "The ghosts of all times are not other [than this]: there are heavenly ghosts, and also the ghosts and spirits of mountains and water, and also there are men who have died and become ghosts."[37] Unfortunately, no further clarification is provided, so there is little basis for distinguishing between these various ghosts and spirits, and perhaps little need as well.[38] So far as the Mohist program is concerned, there is apparently no functional difference separating these categories of ghosts and spirits; all serve to put humans on their guard and ensure good behavior.

As we have seen, in their actions ghosts and spirits duplicate Heaven; however, it appears that ghosts and spirits are responsible only for enforcing standards; setting them is Heaven's task. (There is also no indication in the MT that ghosts and spirits universally love human beings.) Since the ghosts and spirits are aware of everything that humans do, they are ideally positioned to reward and punish people on the basis of their actions. How this differs from the rewards and punishments of Heaven is uncertain; perhaps there is no difference at all. Heaven provides the standards, but ghosts and spirits share with Heaven the task of observing, judging, and responding to human actions. Many of the ghosts and spirits are tied to specific localities (mountains, rivers, etc.), and the ghosts of men seem restricted in their influence to their immediate families and lifetime acquaintances.[39] It is tempting to think of ghosts and spirits as the footsoldiers out in the field doing Heaven's bidding within their personal jurisdictions, but Mo tzu has already indicated in the previous chapter that Heaven is perfectly capable of doing its own police work. It does seem that Heaven is usually more concerned with universal questions and that ghosts and spirits generally mete out individual punishments, but the evidence is ambiguous. In this instance we are restricted in our understanding of Mohist theology by the spotty and inconclusive nature of the evidence.

As already indicated, Mo tzu repeatedly stresses the morally uplifting influence produced by the belief in ghosts and spirits--this is one of the reasons that Mo tzu is sometimes labeled a "utilitarian"--but in addition Mo tzu is also a strong advocate of sacrifice for the service that it provides to the ghosts of one's ancestors: "If ghosts and spirits truly exist, then this [sacrifice] is to meet one's father, mother, elder brothers and their wives and feed them. Then how could this not be the beneficial affair of the world?"[40] Just as humanity has failed in its duties towards Heaven, so it has been remiss in its sacrificial responsibilities to ghosts and spirits; Mo tzu is determined to set the world back on the proper course of service and reverence.

In most of the chapter, Mo tzu is adamant that ghosts and spirits do in fact exist; a great deal of effort is expended to convince a skeptical readership of this Mohist verity. In this endeavor several different kinds of reasoning are employed. The first strategy is to examine the "proof of the ears and eyes of the masses."[41] Although this sounds admirably empirical, in practice it amounts to little more than collecting improbable tales from various books that were circulating in Mo tzu's time.[42] What, to Mo tzu, gives these stories credibility is the claim that the events narrated were witnessed by large crowds; this is the "proof of the ears and eyes of the masses." Mo tzu concedes that his more sophisticated readers might not be overwhelmed by the evidence of these stories and rhetorically asks, "Can the sage kings of the former Three Dynasties, Yao, Shun, Yü, T'ang, Wen, and Wu, adequately serve as a model?" To ensure that the evidence about to be presented will be accepted, Mo tzu suggests that "those men average and above *all* say that [men] like the sage kings of the former Three Dynasties are sufficient as a model.[43]

The evidence educed from the deeds of the sage kings is largely circumstantial: the sage kings worshiped, sacrificed, and showed deference to ancestral altars, therefore they must have believed in the existence of ghosts and spirits. After presenting this evidence, Mo tzu turns to the writings attributed to the sages, claiming that the sage kings left written evidence of their devotion to ghosts and spirits for the benefit of their descendants. Why did they write so repetitively about the worship of ghosts and spirits? Because, Mo tzu claims, "the sage kings were concerned about it."[44] To seal his case, Mo tzu presents selections from writings he attributes to sage kings from each of the Three Dynasties. Since sage kings from all of the Three Dynasties left testimony to the existence of ghosts and spirits, Mo tzu infers that they all were sincere believers in spiritual beings.

The last of Mo tzu's proofs is found in the accounts of the swift and terrible punishments visited upon two of the evil kings of antiquity. In both cases the evil kings offended Heaven and were punished by sage kings operating under a commission from Heaven. No amount of earthly power could save them from their Heaven-ordained fates. Somewhat discordantly, Mo tzu concludes: "This is why I say that when it comes to the punishment of *ghosts* and *spirits*, it isn't influenced by wealth and nobility, numbers and strength, bravery and power, martial strength, and tough armor and sharp weapons."[45] It appears that Mo tzu views these cases of punishment by Heaven-appointed sage kings as being tantamount to punishment by ghosts and spirits. Taken at face value, this passage indicates that Mo tzu sees no difference between punishment by Heaven (or its human agents) and punishment by ghosts and spirits, just as in earlier passages the other roles of the two presumably distinct classes of divinities are blurred. Chang Ch'un yi claims that the "benevolent hearts" of the vanquishing sage kings are the "ghosts and spirits" referred to in this passage, but this seems like an elaborate rationalization.[46]

In most of "On Ghosts," Mo tzu confidently and authoritatively asserts that ghosts and spirits definitely exist, yet here and there traces of uncertainty are found. Near the close of the chapter, Mo tzu says that if ghosts and spirits do not exist then sacrifices would appear to be a waste of food and wine. However, this is not really the case, he claims, for sacrifices have great social utility: "Even if ghosts and spirits really do not exist, then this [sacrifice] still can draw the multitudes together for group enjoyment and the making of friends among neighbors."[47] Later in the same passage, Mo tzu reiterates that sacrifices do not waste food but serve to seek blessings from ghosts and spirits and to provide for group enjoyment and the making of friends. Mo tzu concludes: "If ghosts and spirits truly exist then this [sacrifice] is to meet one's father, mother, elder brothers and their wives and feed them."[48] For someone who is so certain of the existence of ghosts and spirits, Mo tzu employs a great deal of hypothetical language and seems excessively concerned to demonstrate the social utility of practices that should need no mundane justification. Of course, it has already been noted that Mo tzu takes great pains to ingratiate himself with his audience; this admission that spiritual beings might not exist may be just a stratagem to enhance his credibility among the more skeptical of his readers.[49]

In common with the other chapters we have examined, "On Ghosts" takes a religious means--in this case teaching reverence for, and belief in, ghosts and spirits--and attempts to demonstrate its potential effectiveness in curing the ills of the time and ultimately in realizing the Mohist religious goal. The means is justified by appeals to common experience, tradition, literary documents, and the records of the kings of antiquity. Mo tzu depicts the functioning of the means in a way that embraces the implementation of the other religious means as well (following the will of Heaven, opposing aggressive war, etc.). As usual, the practice of one Mohist means implies the practice of them all. The chapter concludes with the familiar refrain: "[This] is the *tao* of the sage kings."[50]

Condemnation of Music

The one surviving chapter entitled "Condemnation of Music" is fundamentally an attack on extravagant, non-productive expenditures presented in the form of a critique of a complex of activities that Mo tzu has collectively termed "music." Apparently the activities composing "music" formed an outstanding example of the general waste and profligacy of the ruling class and therefore were singled out for this special attack. As a critique of waste, "Condemnation of Music" in many respects parallels "Economy of Expenditures" and "Simplicity in Funerals."

The religious means taught is the complete elimination of music. This is to be done not because music is unpleasant, but because it is seen as a major impediment to the attainment of the Mohist ultimate concern:

> Thus when examined above it does not accord with the affairs of the sage kings, and when measured below it does not conform to the benefit of the masses. For this reason Master Mo tzu says, "Making music is wrong."[51]

The chapter starts with a statement of the Mohist ultimate concern, here phrased as a description of the business of the humane person (*jen che* 仁 者): "In the affairs of humane persons, [they] must devote themselves to seeking the flourishing of the world's benefit while eliminating all harm from the world."[52] With this as a starting assumption, Mo tzu mounts various attacks on music, all of which are based on music's negative impact on the commonweal. It soon becomes apparent that Mo tzu is operating with an unfamiliar definition of music. What is this music to which Mo tzu is so vehemently opposed?

We know that the music to which Mo tzu objects is orchestral, for he complains that large numbers of men and women must be taken from their natural occupations of farming and cloth making to play the instruments involved (various string and wind instruments, gigantic bells and drums). This music is performed in lengthy concerts before large audiences. Mo tzu claims that it cannot be enjoyed alone--hence the large audiences--and that by holding its listeners captive for long periods of time it seriously disrupts the functioning of government and the pursuit of agriculture. If this were not bad enough from the Mohist point of view, music also requires a very elaborate setting; Mo tzu speaks of the "carvings and ornaments" and "high towers, pavilions, and spacious houses" that are apparently an integral part of the music that the Mohists wish to eliminate.[53] Evidently no music is complete without a banquet as well, for Mo tzu also disapproves of the expense of the requisite meat dishes.[54] From Mo tzu's criticisms it can be inferred that the music to which he objects is an enormous, formal production that combines an extended orchestral concert with a sumptuous banquet, often involving heavy drinking and, in some cases, dance performances.[56] In addition, special grounds and buildings must be prepared for the staging of these musical events. Clearly, when Mo tzu attacks music he is not condemning the singing of peasants working in their fields, though it is always possible that he might also be opposed to modest pleasures of that sort. The Mohist criticism is founded on the moral, political, and above all economic drawbacks of music as practiced by the aristocracy; it is misleading at best to make statements like the following: "Mo tzu had absolutely no sympathy for foolishness like music."[56] Based on this chapter, it is impossible to say what, if anything, Mo tzu thinks about the simple musical amusements of the commoners, which are after all closer to what modern readers of the text commonly think of as music. We do know that in "On Ghosts," Mo tzu extolls the social benefits of sacrifices and notes that even if spirits do not exist, sacrifices provide an occasion for group enjoyment and fellowship. Should villagers decide to dance and sing at a harvest festival, Mo tzu might well approve. For the rest of our discussion when we speak of music, we will mean the complex of activities that Mo tzu lumps together under this rubric; it must be remembered that for the Mohists, music is something very different from anything brought to mind by our current lexical uses of the term.

In form, the chapter consists of a series of arguments against the extravagant excesses of music. Most of these arguments have been briefly alluded to above; we will present them in slightly fuller form here but without going into exhaustive detail.

Mo tzu first rejects music on the grounds that it is not in harmony with the acts of the sage kings and is not beneficial to the people.[57] In this rejection Mo tzu appears most outraged by the expense of musical performances and the ensuing hardships endured by the masses. The remaining criticisms are all specific examples of excessive expense and attendant hardship used by the chapter's authors to flesh out the original complaint.

The heavy taxes exacted from the peasantry in order to fund the construction of musical instruments are contrasted with the taxes the sage kings levied to support the development of transit systems. In the latter instance, the taxes could be readily borne, for the benefits were shared by all; the taxes raised to construct instruments only benefit those lucky enough to hear the concerts, so naturally they are resented.[58]

Mo tzu next asks how music influences the chaos of the day and the "three worries" (*san huan* 三 患) of the people, viz. that the hungry will not be fed, that the cold will not be clothed, and that the toilers will not rest. Predictably, Mo tzu concludes that the high cost of music only aggravates the problems of the commoners and does not lead towards the realization of the Mohist ultimate concern of promoting the world's benefit while excluding all harm from it.[59]

By taking healthy young workers away from their fields and looms to play in the orchestras or sit in the audiences, music actually reduces the productivity of society and leads to shortages of food and clothing. In addition, the gentlemen will neglect their role in government, leading to further chaos.[60]

The authors of the MT then didactically recount the tale of Duke K'ang of Ch'i, a man who loved dance so much that he maintained a large troupe of dancers at great expense. Since this particular duke reigned several decades after Mo tzu's probable date of death, we can assume that his example was not personally cited by Mo tzu; however, it is probably safe to assume that dance was one of the specific components of the Mohists' music--and by this account not the least wasteful of them. Again, the authors' argument is that music takes people from their work and requires unjustifiable expense.[61]

In a sort of summary, Mo tzu contrasts humans with the birds and beasts. The birds and beasts can survive without engaging in labor, since food and clothing are naturally provided for them; however, humans are not in this enviable position and must toil for a living. With this introduction, Mo tzu then reviews all the harm to agriculture, industry, and government caused by the practice of music. In every case cited, the main complaint is that music takes people away from their allotted tasks. Either Mo tzu is guilty of extraordinary exaggeration or music was remarkably time-consuming, for these criticisms seem to assume the loss of a large block of time on a daily or near daily basis.[62]

Mo tzu finishes his attack on music by quoting two passages from ancient books. The first passage is a criticism of dance performances and does not mention music at all: "As for constant dancing in the palace, this is called the practice of sorcerers."[63] Behavior of this sort is to be punished by both humans and God, according to Mo tzu's source. The second passage tells of Ch'i, the son of

Emperor Yü of the Hsia dynasty. Ch'i lost himself in immorality, music, excessive eating and drinking, and thus he offended Heaven.[64] From this Mo tzu reasons that music is neither pleasing to Heaven nor beneficial to the people. The conclusion of the chapter is that music must be eliminated if the Mohist ultimate concern is to be achieved:

> This is why Master Mo tzu says, "Now if the scholars and gentlemen of the world really desire to cause the flourishing of the world's benefit and remove all that harms it, then they ought to investigate the character of music, and having done this they cannot but prohibit and stop it."[65]

Anti-Fatalism

Whether intentional or not, it seems significant that the first chapter on anti-fatalism, the last of the Essay means,[66] starts with nearly the exact same words as the first of the Essay chapters, "Exaltation of the Virtuous 1":

> The Master Mo tzu said, "Nowadays, when emperors, dukes, and great officials govern their states, they all desire their states to be wealthy, their people to be plentiful, and their jurisdictions to be orderly, yet they do not gain wealth but obtain poverty; they do not increase their population but decrease it; they do not gain order but obtain chaos. This is fundamentally to lose what they desire and obtain what they hate. What is the reason for this?"[67]

Although we cannot be certain of the intentions of the authors of the MT, the effect of this literary parallel is to give a sense of closure to the Essays and subtly stress the unity of concern underlying the seemingly disparate emphases of the chapters. The basic question is the same throughout the Essays no matter how it is phrased: How can the greatest benefits be brought to the world while all calamities are removed from it? Each triad of Essay chapters suggests a different means for the rectification of the specific problems raised in the chapters and, by extension, the transformation of society at large; the chapters currently under consideration are no exception.

The problem focussed on in the three surviving chapters titled "Anti-Fatalism" is that the belief in fate allows people to deny responsibility for the results of their actions and inevitably leads to an attitude of laziness, irresponsibility, and indifference.[68] As we have already seen, the Mohists are firm believers in the value of personal industry, willpower, and endeavor. From their perspective, the belief in fate insidiously undercuts their entire program, for people who can blame all their failures on fate will never be motivated to undertake the strenuous actions necessary to transform society. For the Mohists, it is essential that men and women believe in their ability to ameliorate their conditions through individual and collective effort. Speaking of the enviable lot of the subjects of the sage kings, Mo tzu states: "Now how could it possibly be their [the people's] fate? It was definitely due to their [the sage kings'] effort."[69] It is repeatedly emphasized throughout the chapters that effort, not fate, is the reason for the success or failure of all human enterprises.

The means taught in the chapters is the refutation of the doctrine of fate, which is seen as a root cause of the world's misery:

> Now if the scholars and gentlemen of the world desire to discern the causes of right and wrong and benefit and harm, then as for the existence of a heavenly fate, they cannot but violently oppose it. As for upholding the existence of fate, this is the world's great harm. For this reason Master Mo tzu opposes it.[70]

What is the doctrine of fate objected to here? Judging from the many examples given in the MT of the wayward behavior of those who believe in fate, it appears that the Mohists' definition of the doctrine of fate is virtually identical to our common lexical usage. When discussing the behavior of the evil kings of the Three Dynasties, Mo tzu describes how they lusted and indulged themselves uncontrollably, immersed themselves in wine and music, neglected government, oppressed the people, etc., but when they were finally brought to punishment they were not willing to say: "'I am feeble and unworthy, and my administration of government was bad.' Rather they invariably said: 'It is definitely my fate to be annihilated.'"[71] Belief in fate denotes acceptance of the idea that all one's successes and failures are predetermined; the result that will ensue from any initiative is settled beforehand. If this is really believed, then there is no reason to make more than the most modest of efforts in any undertaking, for no amount of striving, or slacking off, will change the inevitable outcome. However, the Mohist conception of fate does not seem to include the belief that all one's actions are predetermined: it appears that humans are generally free to chose what they will do, on a day-to-day basis; only the final outcomes, the successes and failures, appear to be preordained.[72]

All three chapters declare the need for standards to evaluate the legitimacy of any doctrine (though in this case it is only the doctrine of fate that is destined to come under scrutiny). The "three tests" (*san piao* 三 表 in "Anti-Fatalism 1" and *san fa* 三 法 in "Anti-Fatalism 2" and "Anti-Fatalism 3") are roughly comparable in each of the versions, though differences exist.[73] The three versions all state that every doctrine must have its basis (*pen* 本), its evaluation (*yüan* 原), and its application (*yung* 用).[74] Like other methods of evaluation presented in the Essay section of the MT, the "three tests" sound more rigorous than they actually are. We read that any legitimate doctrine should be based (*pen*) on "the affairs of the sage kings of antiquity,"[75] or alternately on "the will of heaven and ghosts and the affairs of the sage kings."[76] The evaluation (*yüan*) of any doctrine is found in "the books of the former kings."[77] (The other two chapters agree that the evaluation of any doctrine is found in "investigating the testimony of the ears and eyes of the masses."[78]) The application (*yung*) of any doctrine is the only test that is even vaguely empirical, consisting of "promulgating it in order to govern, and observing its benefits for the state and the people."[79] The remainder of each of the chapters is devoted to refuting the doctrine of fate, presumably on the basis of the tests just enumerated, though in actual practice the "three tests" are applied so unsystematically that their boundaries blur, and it is often uncertain which of the tests is being applied to the example at hand.

The first test is that of the "basis" of the doctrine. All three chapters look to the deeds of the sage kings to test the basis of the doctrine of fate:

> Thus nowadays some among the scholars and gentlemen of the world believe that fate exists. Why not investigate it in the affairs of the sage kings? Anciently, that which Chieh [a wicked king] had brought to chaos was restored to order by T'ang; that which Chou [another of the wicked kings] had disordered was rectified by King Wu. The times were not transformed, and the people were not changed, yet under Chieh and Chou the world was in chaos, while under T'ang and Wu the world was ordered. How can it be said that there is fate?[80]

In this passage, the point is that the lives of the people can be transformed by a change of rulers, therefore there can be no such thing as an immutable fate, for without any other alterations the lot of the people has changed from desperate to enviable. The transforming power of the sage kings proves that there is no fate.

Another argument presented in the chapters may also be employing the test of the "basis" of the doctrine, though in a seemingly unrelated manner. Throughout the chapters, Mo tzu tries to demonstrate that on the grounds of their respective patterns of behavior it is clear that the wicked kings believed in the doctrine of fate, while the sage kings did not. In "Anti-Fatalism 3" Mo tzu states that "Anciently, the wicked kings instituted it [the doctrine of fate], and the poor people followed it."[81] From this and other passages we can infer that Mo tzu may have been trying to claim that the "basis" of the doctrine of fate lies in the practices of the wicked kings. However, these passages appear primarily to have been intended to serve as illustrations of the third test, the "application" of a doctrine.[82]

The second of the "three tests," the "evaluation" of a doctrine, is to be determined by two different things: in the first and third chapters the evaluation is to be based on the "testimony of the ears and eyes of the masses"; in the second chapter fate is to be evaluated by "the books of the former kings." Despite the clarity of the tasks set for themselves by the authors of the MT, the three chapters of "Anti-Fatalism" mix all kinds of proofs in their "evaluation" of the doctrine of fate.[83] In one of the most perplexing arguments in the entire Essay section of the MT, Mo tzu asks if anyone has ever seen the "form" of fate. Using the same process that led him to conclude that ghosts and spirits exist, viz. the investigation of the testimony of the ears and eyes of the masses, Mo tzu asks if "From antiquity up till the present, since the origins of the people, has there perhaps once been someone who has seen the form of fate or heard its sound?" Mo tzu answers his question, "Not once."[84] The problem seems to lie in the question being asked. If Mo tzu had asked if anyone had ever seen what they believed to be the influence of fate in human lives, the answer he would have received--especially, one suspects, from those same persons who believe in ghosts--would certainly have been yes. Since fate has never been envisioned, then or now, as having a form or sound, the question appears to be inappropriate; however, it is possible that the import of this argument was perceived quite differently by Mo tzu's contemporaries.

Having disposed of the sensory data of the masses, Mo tzu turns to the feudal lords and the sage kings. They too have never seen or heard fate; neither their recorded words nor their deeds give any hint of a belief in fate (as a "thing").[85] A large number of examples are drawn from the writings of the sage kings to demonstrate that the sage kings did not believe in fate, and that therefore the test of "verification" shows that fate does not exist.

The final test is that of "application." Mo tzu takes two tacks in employing this test. One, which we have already seen, is to claim that the doctrine of fate was instituted and institutionalized by the wicked kings of antiquity, with disastrous results. The other, more hypothetical, is to speculate how the believers in fate would respond in a variety of situations and then contrast this response with the behavior of those who deny fate and value human effort. The main point made is that believers in fate deny that virtue is rewarded and evil punished. Therefore they are never willing to make the effort to do what is right but only do what is easiest and least dangerous.[86] In a later passage, Mo tzu details the chain of reactions that would follow from the institutionalization of the belief in fate: "superiors would not attend to governing, and subordinates would not work"; as a result the government would be in shambles and essential goods would be unavailable. This would make it impossible to sacrifice properly to God, ghosts, and spirits and take care of both the virtuous and the needy of the world.[87] Mo tzu concludes this analysis saying:

> Therefore above fate does not benefit Heaven, in the middle it does not benefit ghosts, and below it does not benefit mankind; the strong upholding of this is the source from which especially baneful teachings arise and the *tao* of wicked men.[88]

In summary, the doctrine of fate is rejected by the Mohists for a variety of reasons but above all for what it leads to: the shirking of individual responsibility for the betterment of the world. Mo tzu does not object to the "superstitious" connotations of the belief in fate--after all, Mo tzu seems to have believed every ghost story he ever heard--but goes to great lengths to demonstrate that the belief in fate was not a part of the glorious legacy of the sage kings. Mo tzu introduces three criteria, or "tests," for use in determining the legitimacy of any doctrine and attempts to utilize them to discredit the belief in fate. His final conclusion is that the belief in fate prevents the realization of the Mohists' ultimate concern and must be refuted: "Now if the scholars and gentlemen of the world truly seek to cause the flourishing of the world's benefit while removing all harm from it, then as for this teaching that fate exists, they cannot but strongly oppose it."[89]

150

<u>Anti-Confucianism</u>

The last chapter that we will consider in this analysis of the Essays, "Anti-Confucianism," is quite probably not an "Essay" at all. However, since the editors of the text have appended "Anti-Confucianism" to the Essay section of the MT, it is incumbent upon us to consider it here.[90] As already indicated on several previous occasions, "Anti-Confucianism" differs from the other Essays in numerous ways. Unlike the ten triads of Essay chapters, "Anti-Confucianism" appears never to have existed in more than two versions; moreover, it does not present a problem or a religious means, nor does it make any mention of the Mohist ultimate concern. Students of the MT have often observed that the style and structure of "Anti-Confucianism" is at odds with that of the other Essays; though these subjective impressions are not quantified, they are nonetheless solidly grounded in years of textual study and should be respected.[91] Stephen Durrant's grammatical analysis of the Essay chapters is inconclusive on this point: "Anti-Confucianism" lacks several grammatical features common throughout the Essays; however, several other chapters lack these features as well.[92] In any case, the garbled "facts" and dates, including numerous anachronisms, recorded in the historical illustrations given in the chapter provide strong evidence suggesting that "Anti-Confucianism" was not written by Mo tzu or his immediate disciples and was therefore a late addition to the text.[93] For all these reasons, "Anti-Confucianism" will not be accorded the attention given to those chapters that focus on the presentation of a Mohist religious means; however, a synopsis of its contents may be in order.

"Anti-Confucianism" comprises a series of attacks, often intemperate, on the practices and beliefs of those whom the text labels "Confucians." (It is quite unlikely that many self-proclaimed followers of Confucius would recognize themselves in the caricatures lampooned by the chapter's authors.) In addition to these forays against Confucian ideology and praxis, the chapter also includes a fair number of vitriolic *ad hominem* attacks on Confucius and several of his disciples. One example of the latter should suffice to give a feel for the lack of concern for historical accuracy displayed by the authors of "Anti-Confucianism," while also showing the polemical nature of the chapter:

His [Confucius's] followers and disciples all modeled themselves
on a certain K'ung [Confucius]. Tzu Kung and Chi Lu assisted
K'ung Li [a rebel] and reduced Wei to chaos. Yang Huo[94] was
seditious in Lu. Fu Hsi took Chung Mou [a district that he was
governing] and rebelled.[95]

The passage goes on, but this is enough for our purposes. The acts of sedition and
rebellion charged in the passage just quoted are either not documented in other
sources or badly distorted in this passage.

Other tactics used to attack the followers of Confucius include exaggerating
Confucian practices, extending them to their logical extremes in order to make them
appear ridiculous, and, more fairly, pointing out the logical contradictions in
Confucian beliefs and practices. One of the cleverest passages in the chapter
addresses the inconsistency inherent in the "Confucian" belief that "the superior
man must be antique in speech and dress and only then is he magnanimous." The
authors of the chapter point out that "this so-called antique speech and dress were
once surely new, therefore when the ancients spoke that way and wore those
clothes they were not superior men." The passage concludes by asking: "Must one
therefore wear the dress and speak the speech of the non-superior man in order to
be magnanimous?"[96]

Throughout the chapter, the characteristic concerns of the Mohists are
raised, and the Confucians are condemned for actions that are opposed to the
Mohist means. The followers of Confucius are criticized for believing in fate, for
promoting music, for being non-productive parasites living off the labor of others,
for practicing partial, graded love, and for advocating extended mourning and
elaborate rituals. Although "Anti-Confucianism" does not fit the pattern followed
by the other Essay chapters, there is little doubt that it is a product of the Mohist
school and accurately reflects their criticisms of the Confucian schools of the
Warring States period. However, there is very little in the chapter that adds to our
understanding of the religion espoused by the authors of the Essays--the last topic
that we will consider in this chapter.

The Religion of the Essays

Having surveyed every one of the surviving Essay chapters, we can now
summarize what has been learned about the religion of the Essays.[97] The

ultimate concern of the Essays--to promote all that benefits the world while excising all that harms it--has been encountered in virtually every chapter examined. In order for this ultimate concern to be realized, a number of conditions must be met: wars of aggression must cease, good government must be secured, extravagance in all its forms must be curtailed, the population must be increased, the economy strengthened, etc. These desiderata are the concrete manifestations of the Mohist ultimate concern and at the same time can be viewed as means for its attainment. The Essays provide a comprehensive system, comprising ten different means, that is designed to bring about the restructuring of society and the achievement of the Mohist ultimate concern. Though the religious means taught in the Essays seem at first to be unfocussed and haphazard, further study reveals that they were consciously understood by the authors of the MT to form a comprehensive program for resolving the most pressing problems of Warring States China.

The exaltation of the virtuous is the first religious means presented in the Essays. It has been placed at the head of the Essays for both logical and practical reasons: the exaltation of the virtuous is the basis for creating the society-wide ideological conformity necessary for the realization of the Mohist ideal world. Once truly superior men are elevated to positions of authority, society will be on the way to restoring the ideal conditions enjoyed during the Hsia dynasty of antiquity.

The second of the Essay means, identification with the superior, can only take place after morally outstanding men have been placed in positions of authority. The procedures for identification with the superior seem excessively cumbersome, but by proceeding in a series of small steps with constant checking and rechecking for compliance, the system of social control that the authors of the MT have posited could conceivably work in the real world. This attention to applicability is one of the many factors that separates the Mohist means from those of the Confucians. In the chapters on identification with the superior, we first encounter the Mohist means of extending the boundaries of one's sense of loyalty and identification until it embraces all of humanity; at this point one has identified with the *yi* of Heaven and shares in Heaven's universality and impartiality. This ability to regard the lives, families, and possessions of others as one regards one's own--for this is the end result of the process of identification with the superior--is critical to the realization of most of the Mohist means. It forms the basis of Mo tzu's "universal love and mutual benefit" and provides the perspective on life that informs and empowers the other means, for without a divinely inspired vision of the oneness of the human race--a sense that all humans are in the same boat and are all deserving of the basic necessities of life--the Mohist means lose their moral force and urgency.

The remaining religious means presented in the Essays are all aimed at producing a better world in the short run. In the long haul, the collective implementation of these religious means will lead to the realization of the Mohist ultimate concern. Many of the means, if fully implemented, include the implementation of several of the others. For instance, the full realization of universal love would necessarily mean the end of offensive war and might also lead people to practice greater economy of expenditures, greater simplicity in funerals, etc., out of the realization that waste and extravagance are detrimental to society as a whole. However, it is clear that the authors of the MT intended for the means to be adopted *en masse* as a package of mutually supporting methods for societal transformation. Since the means are so intimately interrelated, it does not matter which of the means is implemented first in any particular situation; the necessity for the others will soon become apparent. For this reason, Mo tzu advises his disciples to start with the most pressing need faced by the state in which they are working, rather than inflexibly insisting on the exaltation of the virtuous as the logical beginning for their work.[98] The early Mohists demand the complete identity of word and deed, so it is not surprising to find that the ten Mohist means presented in the Essays become, when implemented, primary distinctive characteristics of the Mohist ideal world.

Mo tzu claims that his means and religious goal can be justified by the benefits that they bring to society, but benefit is not the highest justification for the Mohists' program. The source for the ultimate concern of the Mohists and for the means leading to its realization is the will of Heaven. Mo tzu seems sincerely to believe that the program he espouses is based on the will of a sentient, if somewhat amorphous, deity, variously named Heaven or God. Heaven, God, ghosts, and spirits all share in the task of watching humanity, punishing the bad and rewarding the good. In return, humans should respect and sacrifice to these spiritual beings. In his understanding of Heaven and the spiritual beings, Mo tzu seems to be adopting the practices and piety of an earlier age, or perhaps revealing beliefs current among the lower classes during the Warring States period.

The ideal world envisioned by Mo tzu is a highly stratified meritocracy. Those in positions of authority are to be given great wealth, status, and power, for without these three things the rulers will not be respected, trusted, and feared by the masses. Great ideological uniformity is to be demanded, with every member of society identifying his standards with those of his immediate superior. The emperor, the highest human authority, is required to identify with the standards of Heaven, so in effect all his subjects are also ultimately identifying with the will of Heaven. In the ideal world, all the religious means of the Essays will have been put into place, resulting in a peaceful, populous world where everyone enjoys adequate, but not extravagant, food, clothing, and shelter. Traditional social hierarchies will all be upheld, for filial reverence (*hsiao*) and other duties based on status and degrees of relationship appear to have been highly valued by the Mohists.

The ideal man of the Essays is defined by his behavior. He is competent, diligent, and ascetic but in no way "mystical." The one "super-normal" ability demanded of him by Mo tzu is the capacity to view the property and needs of others as if they were his own and act on that basis. The Mohists give great credit to the power of the human will and believe that anyone should be able to follow the "right" course once it has been pointed out to him or her. Human nature, however, is malleable; without the proper influences, ordinary people can be led astray. Mo tzu believes that he has found the ultimate moral compass and source of true values in the will of Heaven; with this as a guide, humans are capable of great disciplined action.

In summary, the religion espoused in the Essays is largely "mundane" in its concerns. Its ultimate goal is to rebuild the "paradisiacal" world that existed in the past when the sage kings ruled. However, the Mohist religion does not derive its highest values from the desires and values of human beings, rather the will of Heaven is viewed as the source both of the Mohist ultimate concern and of the means for its realization. Belief in Heaven and the spiritual beings is an essential part of the Mohist creed; performing sacrifices with reverence and respect is an important means for securing the Mohist ultimate concern and is a characteristic of the ideal world the Mohists sought to achieve. The Mohists believe that Heaven and the spirits function in the here and now of this world; they do not relegate spiritual beings to a remote and aloof plane of existence. Heaven is the source of the

Mohist ultimate concern and the religious means leading to its achievement; all the topics of the Essays are means for attaining the realization of a religious goal. It is therefore misleading to analyze the Essay means in terms of modern categories like economics, political science, etc. From the religious point of view, all the Essay topics are religious in nature, for the primary function of all is to realize the Mohists' ultimate concern.

156

<u>Notes</u>

[1] While it might seem more consistent to continue the examination of the Essays in exactly the same manner in which we began, I hope that it is no longer necessary to proceed in such a laborious fashion. This study set out to uncover the ultimate concern of the Essay and Dialogue sections of the MT; in order to establish the primacy of the actual contents of the MT over our *opinions* about the text, it was necessary to go through the text in a very linear way, thereby uncovering the guiding concerns of the text's authors. It is hoped that this has been done in an acceptably impartial manner. Since we have now established the main themes expressed in the first half of the text, we believe it possible to conduct the rest of our analysis by looking for those same themes in the rest of the text. When new themes arise, we will, of course, introduce them as well.

[2] MTCC, p. 259.

[3] Ibid., p. 260. Notice the clear stratification of society assumed in this reasoning and presented as part of the Heaven-instituted world order. The process of rectification is essentially a recapitulation of the formula presented earlier as "identification with the superior"; in both cases Heaven is the highest authority and the source of ultimate standards.

[4] When researching this work, I was tempted to call following the will of Heaven the ultimate concern of the MT, for all the religious means presented by Mo tzu find their highest justification in the fact that they are demanded by Heaven. However, it soon became clear that this interpretation is denied by the organization of the text. Following the will of Heaven is presented as just another of the Mohist means; it does not expressly occur in all the other Essay chapters, and where it is found it is treated no differently from the other means. *Logically*, following the will of Heaven should perhaps be regarded as the ultimate concern of Mo tzu and his early followers, but this does not appear to be their view of the matter.

[5] Ibid., p. 261. In this passage, one Essay means is defined by another, pointing to the interdependence of all Mo tzu's religious means. In other places in the chapters, following the will of Heaven is equated with both practicing universal love and opposing offensive warfare. (Opposing offensive warfare is itself subsumed by universal love, since one who loves others as himself would never engage in military aggression.)

[6] Ibid., p. 241.

[7] Ibid., pp. 241-242. The desires and dislikes of Heaven narrated in this passage add up to yet another restatement of the ultimate concern of the Mohists. It seems that Heaven and Mo tzu share the same concerns and wish to bring about the same state of affairs on earth.

[8] Ibid., p. 243.

[9] Ibid., p. 244.

[10] Ibid., p. 241.

[11] Ibid., p. 251.

[12] Ibid., p. 241.

[13] Ibid., p. 252.

[14] Ibid.

[15] Ibid., pp. 252-253. Were he alive today, Mo tzu would likely be an ardent environmental activist, probably of the Earth First! sort. Our materialistic, greed-driven economy has greatly overstepped the bounds Mo tzu believes Heaven has set for human activity, with grievous effects on the balance of the natural world.

[16] At several points in this extended passage it almost sounds as if Heaven is responsible, at least in part, for some of the process of creation. We read that "even down to the level of the tip of a hair, there is nothing that Heaven does not do," and "Heaven divided the mountains, streams, ravines, and valleys." The actual creation of the world is not described in the MT, but dividing up the mountains and streams seems perilously close to the later stages of the process of creation.

[17] It appears that Heaven is directly equivalent to "God, ghosts, and spirits." The exact identity of God (*shang ti*) is even less clear in the MT than that of Heaven. At times, it seems that Mo tzu uses the terms interchangeably, almost generically, to refer to a general order of spiritual beings responsible for overseeing human existence. However, in our discussions and translations *t'ien* is always translated as Heaven, and *shang ti* is always translated as God.

[18] Ibid., p. 245. A second version of this passage is found on p. 261.

[19] If Mo tzu is simply claiming that Heaven loves those who sacrifice to it, it seems unnecessary and a bit odd to present the tortured reasoning recounted above. If Heaven accepts sacrifices from all (and how could it refuse them?), does this imply that Heaven *possesses* all those who sacrifice?

[20] Ibid., p. 262. Note the apparent malleability of the masses.

[21] Ibid., p. 263.

[22] Ibid.

[23] Righteousness has already been equated with the practice of universal love, so the description that follows is that of a world where both individuals and governments practice universal love and mutual benefit.

[24] The pragmatist in Mo tzu is revealed in this passage. After all his emphasis on doing what is moral and right with no regard for attendant hardship, Mo tzu now without a trace of self-consciousness suggests using surplus wealth to buy "rings, jade pendants, pearls, and jades" with which to sooth the resentments of the neighboring feudal lords. The casual way this practice just happens to be mentioned here, and nowhere else, suggests the possibility that Mo tzu might have endorsed a full range of manipulative techniques to calm potential adversaries that the authors of the MT did not think worth mentioning in the text. Mo tzu expects uncompromising uprightness from his followers, but the hereditary rulers of the day are to be bought off--at least until they can be replaced!

[25] Again we see that, so far as the Mohists are concerned, universal love does not cause the breakdown of the traditional family relationships but is actually a way of ensuring that the relationships are realized in fact, not just in word.

[26] Ibid., pp. 249-250. A second version of the ideal world is described in ibid., p. 264. This second version approaches the ideal from the perspective of opposing

offensive warfare rather than practicing universal love; it is therefore more negative in tone, telling what will not happen rather than describing what will.

[27] Of course, since the chronology of the composition of the individual chapters of the Essays has not yet been determined, we have no way of ascertaining which of these two similar passages was written first. In light of the complementary functioning of the Mohist means, it is not surprising that material used to illustrate the necessity of one means is used to make a similar point for another means.

[28] The problem here is the conflict between the standards of individual morality and the standards adhered to by the governments of states in their international intrigues. Mo tzu expects both individuals and governments to follow exactly the same uncompromising standards. Many of Mo tzu's contemporaries obviously thought otherwise, as do most modern heads of state!

[29] Ibid., p. 271. The reprise of the contents of "Condemnation of Offensive War 1" runs from p. 267 to p. 271.

[30] Ibid., p. 275.

[31] Ibid., p. 301.

[32] Ibid., p. 274. Following Pi Yüan I am reading *cheng* 正 as *cheng* 征.

[33] MTCC, pp. 274-275.

[34] Ibid., p. 285. Heaven seems to share overlapping functions with the ghosts and spirits. As we shall see, if Mo tzu had a clearly thought-out understanding of the divinities ruling his world, he failed to articulate it in any documents that have survived till the present.

[35] Ibid., p. 186.

[36] In the first section of this chapter we saw a passage where Heaven (*t'ien*) and God (*shang ti*) are equated and used as different names for the same amorphous deity. (This is very common in Chou dynasty writings and not unique to Mo tzu.) Throughout the Essays, Mo tzu appears more concerned with broad principles and generalized plans of action than with precisely worded doctrines and specific, detailed programs. His theology seems true to his overall approach.

[37] Ibid., p. 299. This passage fits poorly in its present context and may perhaps be an interpolation.

[38] The category of "heavenly ghosts" (*t'ien kuei* 天鬼) is especially puzzling. "Heavenly spirits" (*t'ien shen* 天神) are often mentioned in Chou dynasty literature, but "heavenly ghosts" appears to be a new term. It is also unclear whether there is any difference between the ghosts of mountains and water and the spirits of mountains and water. One suspects that Mo tzu is using "ghosts and spirits" as a generic term for "spiritual beings" taken *en masse*.

[39] We refer here to the "ghosts of men" because no specifically female ghosts or spirits are mentioned in the MT.

[40] Ibid., p. 301.

[41] Ibid., p. 276.

[42] Mo tzu attributes these stories to the "Spring and Autumn" annals of five different states: Chou, Ch'in, Yen, Sung, and Ch'i. These texts no longer exist; however, the stereotyped style in which these tales are recounted may reflect their written origins in works of the "Spring and Autumn" genre.

[43] Ibid., p. 286.

[44] Ibid., p. 289. If Mo tzu is to be believed, the sage kings all shared a deep concern for the welfare of ghosts and spirits. Mo tzu's reasoning is very similar to that of this study on the same point: if an author mentions something repeatedly, it must be because it is important to him. The fact that Mo tzu claims that the sage kings repeatedly spoke of that which was most important to them reinforces our assumption that in their writing the authors of the MT consciously followed this principle and placed greatest emphasis on what was most important to Mo tzu.

[45] Ibid., pp. 298-299.

[46] Ibid., p. 299.

[47] Ibid., p. 300.

[48] Ibid., p. 301.

[49] Unfortunately, we cannot determine what Mo tzu's "real" attitude towards spiritual beings might be. At times he seems motivated by sincere piety, but other passages show a distinctly pragmatic outlook. Mo tzu also seems willing to employ any argument he can contrive, whether good or bad, to make his points, so it is conceivable that these "pragmatic" passages are only inserted to win the intellectual assent of his "utilitarian" readers. Does Mo tzu actually wish to convince people of the existence of ghosts and spirits or merely to convince them of the inevitability of swift and certain supernatural rewards and punishments? Although the latter seems possible at times, in other passages he seems sincerely concerned to promote the practice of the traditional sacrifices. Did he have any alternative? Could he have convinced his fellow Chinese of the inevitability of rewards and retribution without the agency of ghosts and spirits? Though intriguing, these questions do not have historical answers.

[50] Ibid.

[51] Ibid., p. 303.

[52] Ibid., p. 302.

[53] Ibid., p. 303.

[54] Ibid.

[55] Two of Mo tzu's attacks on music are directed exclusively at the expense and immorality of large scale dance presentations.

[56] Mote, *Foundations*, p. 87.

[57] "Condemnation of Music 1" never deals with the problem of the sage kings and their use of music: it was universally believed in the Warring States period that music was one of the primary amusements of the sage kings and was one of their greatest cultural innovations, yet Mo tzu claims that making music is contrary to the *tao* of the sage kings. This glaring contradiction is the sole subject matter of the seventh of the Epitomes, "Threefold Argument." In this chapter, Mo tzu is

confronted by a scholar named Ch'eng Fan who takes issue with the claim that "the sage kings did not make music." (Ibid., p. 58.)

The reply attributed to Mo tzu appears uncharacteristically weak. Mo tzu concedes that not only did the sage kings listen to music, but they also composed it on occasion; Mo tzu even gives the names of compositions attributed to the sage kings. Smelling victory, Ch'eng Fan retorts: "You say that the sage kings were without music, but after all this is certainly music. How can you say that the sage kings were without music?" Part of Mo tzu's reply appears to have been lost; what remains is an unusual analogy:

> The Master Mo tzu said: "The sage kings' command was to reduce excesses. The benefit of eating lies in knowing that one is hungry and then eating. This is its wisdom. But this is certainly without [real] wisdom. Now [in an analogous manner] the sage kings had but little music; this is also to be without [music]. (Ibid., pp. 61-62.)

As it is currently written this analogy is not effective, yet Mo tzu's point can be discerned: just as a little wisdom is no wisdom at all, so a little music counts as no music. The sage kings practiced music in such moderation that they could be regarded as not having music. Evidently, Mo tzu felt it was hopeless to argue that the sage kings prohibited music. Instead he chose to claim that their music was so modest an expenditure that it fell into an entirely different category of extravagance than that of the music of his contemporaries.

In the "Kung Meng" chapter of the Dialogues, Mo tzu is shown debating the value of rites and music with Kung Meng tzu, a Confucian. In their debate Kung Meng claims that when a country is wealthy and orderly, then music should be pursued. Mo tzu's rebuttal is that wealth and order disappear almost instantly once music is taken up. (Ibid., pp. 587-588.) In part, this is why music does not benefit the people.

[58] Ibid., pp. 303-305.

[59] Ibid., pp. 305-306.

[60] Ibid., pp. 306-307.

[61] Ibid., pp. 307-308.

[62] Ibid., pp. 309-311. As the following passages suggest, Chou dynasty aristocrats indulged their fancies with great energy and unbridled enthusiasm. Perhaps music actually could be as disruptive as the Mohists claim it to be.

[63] Ibid., p. 311.

[64] Ibid., p. 312.

[65] Ibid., p. 313.

[66] This is assuming that the chapters entitled "Anti-Confucianism" do not count as "proper" Essays. The two chapters entitled "Anti-Confucianism" are a bit of an enigma. Neither presenting a problem and its Mohist solution nor upholding a religious means, they seem to have been placed at the end of the Essay section by default: they do not fit better anywhere else. We will consider them briefly in the following section of this chapter but without placing great weight on their message, since it is so different from those of the other Essays.

[67] Ibid., p. 316.

[68] The authors of the MT have approached this problem of irresponsibility on several previous occasions, most recently in "On Ghosts." There it was argued that humans cannot escape the consequences of their actions because Heaven and the spiritual beings are constantly watching, judging, and responding to the actions of all people. Here Mo tzu is trying an approach that does not require belief in supernatural sanctions. If fate is denied, then it cannot be used to rationalize failure, and everyone will be forced to assume responsibility for their own success or failure. The Mohists assume that this will lead to an aggressively industrious society where poverty and want are unknown.

[69] Ibid., p. 332.

[70] Ibid., p. 330.

[71] Ibid., p. 328.

[72] It is not at all certain that the authors of the MT thought through the implications of the belief in fate with any rigor. The fate against which they are struggling appears to be the relatively unsophisticated belief of the masses--and an equally world-weary aristocracy--not a well-developed philosophical position.

[73] The "three tests" described in "Anti-Fatalism 1" and "Anti-Fatalism 3" appear most similar, though they are presented under different rubrics. The second and third chapters both call their "three tests" the *san fa*, but differ in other ways. This, when coupled with the fact that the first chapter promises proofs that are only found in the second chapter, suggests that these three chapters may be at least partially scrambled. See note 83 below.

[74] Ibid., p. 317, p. 325., p. 331. In all cases *yüan* 原 "origin" is read as *yüan* 源 "to evaluate."

[75] Ibid., p. 317.

[76] Ibid., p. 325.

[77] Ibid.

[78] Ibid., p. 317 and, with different wording, p. 331.

[79] Ibid.

[80] Ibid., p. 318.

[81] Ibid., p. 334.

[82] As already indicated, it can be quite frustrating to attempt to determine which of the "three tests" Mo tzu is employing in any one passage. This is due in part to what appears to be a predilection for rhetorical overkill that leads the authors of the text indiscriminately to use every weapon at their disposal (much as if a modern army were to throw sticks and stones in between launching waves of guided missiles).

[83] A. C. Graham argues persuasively that "Anti-Fatalism 1" and "Anti-Fatalism 2" as they are now preserved are garbled, with a section of "Anti-Fatalism 1" placed in "Anti-Fatalism 2" and vice-versa. Assuming that Graham is correct, the three chapters still show the mixed reasoning and confusing structure noted above,

though to a lesser degree. For Graham's reasoning, see Graham, *Divisions*, pp. 12-16.

[84] Ibid., pp. 325-326.

[85] Ibid., p. 326.

[86] Ibid., pp. 321-322.

[87] Ibid., pp. 323-324.

[88] Ibid., p. 324.

[89] Ibid., p. 338.

[90] For the purposes of this analysis, it would have been far more convenient if "Anti-Confucianism" had been placed among the Epitomes. Unfortunately it was not, so we are obligated to treat it as part of the Essays. However, for reasons soon to be discussed, "Anti-Confucianism" will not be treated with the detail accorded the other Essay chapters.

[91] For an example, see Mei, *Mo tzu*, p. 200.

[92] A table showing the distribution of distinctive grammatical particles in each of the Essay chapters is found in Durrant, "Examination," p. 248.

[93] Mei, *Mo tzu*, p. 200.

[94] MTCC, p. 358 prints *hu* 虎 for *huo* 貨.

[95] Ibid.

[96] Ibid., p. 345.

[97] This summary will not attempt to recapitulate every insight drawn from the text in the course of this analysis but will be confined to the *religion* of the Essays, narrowly construed.

[98] In an ideal situation, the Mohists would, I suspect, start with the exaltation of the virtuous, since it provides the basis for the implementation of the other means. However, in the less than perfect conditions of the Warring States, they can start wherever the need is greatest and work in the other means as suitable occasions arise. Although Mo tzu is very absolute in his pronouncements, he is also a pragmatist who will accept whatever legitimate opportunities he is offered to put all, or part, of his program into effect.

CHAPTER VII

ANALYSIS OF THE DIALOGUES

Introduction to the Dialogues

The five chapters that compose the Dialogue section of the MT differ greatly in form from the Essay chapters and will have to be approached in a manner that takes account of these differences. With the exception of the chapter entitled "Kung Shu," which is a sustained narrative dealing with a single presumably historical incident, the Dialogues are all composed of numerous distinct passages that recount conversations or recall incidents from the teaching career of Mo tzu. Overall, these passages do not appear to have been organized by subject matter or edited to present clear expositions of Mohist themes, though several passages on related topics are sometimes placed contiguously in the text. Three of the Dialogues are named for persons who are featured prominently within the chapters that bear their names, but even here the editors seem to have been rather loose in their attributions. (For instance, the "Keng Chu" chapter could perhaps better have been named after Wu Ma tzu, a man who appears in more passages than Keng Chu himself.) All in all, the organization of the Dialogues seems rather haphazard, especially when contrasted with the Essay chapters.[1] Since the Dialogues appear to be records of actual incidents and conversations participated in by Mo tzu and not formal lessons, they contain no systematic presentations of the Mohist ultimate concern or the Mohist religious means; however, Mo tzu was a man with an intense focus to his life, so naturally many references to his goal and means are scattered throughout the chapters. In the Essays, we see the relatively systematic presentation of the doctrines and strategies of a teacher and theoretician. In the Dialogues we see glimpses of that same man in action; the fascination of the Dialogues lies in the insights they provide into the real-world application of the dry ideology of the Essays. Accordingly we will not simply use the Dialogues to confirm the understanding of Mo tzu's religion that has been derived from our study of the Essays. Rather we will look to the chapters for a heightened sense of what the Mohist means really meant to Mo tzu and his disciples. Therefore it will not be necessary to note every passage in the Dialogues that supports our interpretation of the Essays; to do so would be exhausting and repetitious in the extreme, for virtually every passage in the Dialogue chapters confirms, illuminates, or extends our understanding of the Mohist religion.[2] Yet due to their anecdotal character, the Dialogues are not readily analyzed on the basis of religious goals and means either. How then should the Dialogues be approached?

One possible method of dealing with the Dialogues is to examine each incident or passage individually, attempting to classify them by content and didactic intent. There are many obvious problems with this approach, the most fundamental of which is that many passages defy ready classification. Numerous conversations are of an *ad hoc* nature, dealing with specific circumstances and individuals in ways that are probably not intended for universal application.[3] Other passages touch upon so many of Mo tzu's religious means and characteristic illustrations that the would-be systematizer is overwhelmed by the richness of the material.[4] Although this method is inadequate for the analysis of the Dialogues, its tentative utilization is revealing.

A preliminary survey of the Dialogue chapters shows that every one of the religious means of the Essays is found in the Dialogues, the condemnation of offensive war occurring with greatest frequency.[5] Passages defending or explaining the Mohist belief in ghosts and spirits are next in number, with seven occurrences by my count. The remaining Mohist means are found with less frequency, though all occur more than once. In addition, there are three clear statements of the Mohist ultimate concern in the Dialogues. Besides these statements of the means and ultimate concern of the Mohists, one can find numerous passages dealing with other typical Mohist concerns: the nature of righteous conduct, the moral blindness and general perversity of the gentlemen of the Warring States, the need to follow the teachings of the sage kings while avoiding the bad example of the wicked kings, etc. As already indicated, this method of classifying and quantifying the contents of the Dialogues is inadequate on many counts; however, it does provide us with a quick overview of the general subject matter of the chapters in question and is therefore reviewed here.

The approach to be followed in the rest of this chapter is to examine each of the Dialogue chapters in turn, citing those passages that add materially to our understanding of the religion of the Essays as it has been presented in the preceding chapters. This method is similar to that followed in the analysis of the Essays, with the exception that it will be more selective in the material cited. It is to be understood that all passages that appear to contradict or complicate our understanding of the religion of the MT will be included, while we will ignore material that either simply confirms or is irrelevant to the points that have been made.

Keng Chu

As already mentioned, one of the most interesting aspects of the Dialogue chapters is the insight they provide into the way the Essay doctrines are translated into action. Similarly, the Dialogues also give us a glimpse into the everyday activities of Mo tzu (as edited by his disciples, of course). Reading these chapters, it quickly becomes apparent that Mo tzu spent a good deal of time arguing with, and refuting the doctrines of, a large number of rival theoreticians, most of whom are traditionally believed to have been followers of Confucius.[6] Occasionally, Mo tzu's rivals ask him questions, and some of his answers shed new light on his belief system. One of these questions is posed by Wu Ma tzu, who asks: "Which have brighter wisdom, ghosts and spirits or the sages?" Mo tzu replies that "The way the bright wisdom of the ghosts and spirits compares with that of the sages resembles the way that those with sharp hearing and sight compare with the deaf and blind."[7] Mo tzu justifies this statement by pointing out that even the greatest sages were unable to predict the future over the span of many centuries, while an oracle conducted by the Hsia emperor predicted the eventual rise of the Yin (Shang) and Chou dynasties. For Mo tzu, this proves that the wisdom of ghosts and spirits greatly exceeds that of the best men. From this passage, it is clear that Mo tzu places great faith in imperial oracles as a method for communing with the ghosts and spirits. (We shall see later that Mo tzu rejects a different form of prognostication as irrational superstition.)

Two conversations recorded in the chapter show that Mo tzu is aware of the difficult, almost quixotic nature of the task that he has set for himself and his followers. Wu Ma tzu initiates one conversation by charging that: "[Although] you behave righteously, men do not follow you and ghosts do not bless you, yet you continue doing it. You must be mad." Mo tzu replies:

> Now suppose you have two servants right here. One works when he sees you and does not work when he does not see you. The other works both when he sees you and when he does not. Which of these two men would you value?

When Wu Ma tzu answers that he would value the man who works whether he is observed or not, Mo tzu retorts: "Then you too value the madman."[8] In the other passage, Mo tzu responds to the criticism that "You universally love the world but cannot yet be said to have benefitted it" by comparing himself to the man who is rushing to put out a fire, while Wu Ma tzu is compared to the bystander who adds more fire to the blaze. What matters is not what one accomplishes but what one attempts. Mo tzu concludes his argument by saying: "I consider my own intentions to be right but condemn your intentions."[9] These passages suggest that Mo tzu was fully aware of how radical his religious means appeared to be, from the perspective of the literati of the Warring States, and how thankless the task of proselytizing could be.

The Mohist emphasis on action over speculation is seen in the injunction found in this and the following chapter to speak often of doctrines that lead to action and to speak infrequently of doctrines that do not.[10] Mo tzu evidently practiced what he preached, for in two separate passages he attempts to persuade and embarrass Lord Wen of Lu Yang (a district in the state of Ch'u) into adopting the Mohist means of opposing aggressive wars. As we might expect, Mo tzu is blunt and uncompromising in his efforts; if he was worried that he might offend Lord Wen, it certainly does not show in either passage. One can almost picture the lord of Lu Yang staring at his toes as Mo tzu forces him to admit that Ch'u must be suffering from "kleptomania" (ch'ieh chi 竊疾), since it keeps annexing other states while its own fields lie fallow and untended.[11] Throughout this and the following Dialogue chapters Mo tzu displays the depth of his commitment to his vision of the ideal world and to the means that he feels will bring it about. The Mohist religion depicted in the Dialogues is urgently activist to an extent that one might not suspect on the basis of the Essays alone.

Esteem for Righteousness

The chapter "Esteem for Righteousness" starts with the declaration that "of all the ten thousand things nothing is more valuable than righteousness."[12] This is demonstrated by the fact that no one is willing to trade their life for the ownership of the world, while many people are willing to sacrifice their lives for a doctrine. (This seems to be especially true of the followers of Mo tzu.) Elsewhere Mo tzu claims that the employment of righteousness in government leads to population increase, orderly government, and security, so it appears that righteousness leads directly to the realization of the Mohist ultimate concern and is valued for that reason.[13] As in the previous chapter, Mo tzu seems to realize that his teachings are not wholly in keeping with the tenor of the times, but despite all criticism Mo tzu is determined to follow the path of righteousness. In one passage Mo tzu is confronted by an old friend who says: "Nowadays there are none in the world who practice righteousness. You alone are inflicting pain on yourself by practicing righteousness. You ought not cause suffering for yourself." Mo tzu answers:

> Now suppose that there is a man right here who has ten sons. One son plows while the other nine are cloistered at home. As a result the one who plows cannot but strive harder. Why? Because those who eat are many, while those who plow are few. Now since there are none in the world who practice righteousness, you ought to encourage me. Why do you stop me?[14]

Later in the chapter, Mo tzu exhorts several of his disciples with these words: "Though you are not able to practice righteousness, you ought not discard this *tao*. This is analogous to the case where the carpenter is unable to cut yet does not reject his chalk line."[15] Together with the quotations from the previous chapter translated above, these passages present a more human view of Mo tzu. In the Essays, Mo tzu seems utterly insensitive to human weaknesses and failings; he acts as if he truly expects the world to adopt his teachings simply because doing so would make the world a better place. He is consistently unwilling to acknowledge that for many people a huge gulf lies between knowing what is righteous and doing what is righteous. Here he admits that his *tao* is beyond the reach, and even the desire, of most persons and seems almost quixotic in his determination to continue struggling against daunting odds. That this sense of being a righteous man fighting alone for the good of the world might lead towards megalomania is suggested by the last passage in the chapter:

> The Master Mo tzu said: "My doctrines are sufficient for [all] uses. Discarding my doctrines to think on your own is like discarding the harvest to pick up individual grains. Taking other doctrines to oppose my doctrines is like throwing eggs at a rock. After all the eggs in the world are exhausted, the rock will still be the same; it cannot be destroyed.[16]

These are strong words, but unfortunately we have no way of knowing if they were actually spoken by Mo tzu or merely added to the text by overzealous followers.

The ascetic stance of the Mohists is amplified in a passage discussing the "six perversities:"

> Master Mo tzu said: "You must discard the six perversities. When silent, then reflect. When speaking, then teach. When acting, then serve [some useful purpose]. When you employ these three things you will certainly become a sage. You must discard joy, anger, pleasure, grief, love, and hate, using [instead] benevolence and righteousness. When your hands, feet, mouth, nose, ears, and eyes all work for righteousness, you will certainly become a sage.[17]

In this passage Mo tzu exhorts his followers to rid themselves of all emotions, calling them "perversities." Interestingly, we find "love" (*ai* 愛) listed among the emotions to be purged. In the discussion of the Essay means of "universal love," it was noted that the Mohist understanding of "love" appears to have little or nothing to do with the lexical English and Chinese meanings of the word; rather it denotes an expansion of one's normal sense of identity: viewing others as one views oneself. This passage suggests that Mo tzu was aware that he had given the word a special, technical sense in his system--one quite distinct from its ordinary meaning of warm, personal feelings of attachment and affection. Here he is claiming that "love" in its common lexical meaning is one of the human emotions, or "perversities," that must be eliminated if one would become a sage. This conception of the sage as one who has denied and excised the human emotions of joy, anger, pleasure, grief, love, and hate is unique in this period of Chinese intellectual history.[18]

Mo tzu's understanding of Heaven, ghosts, and spirits is clarified by his reaction to the prognostications of a fortuneteller (*jih che* 日者). In this passage Mo tzu is travelling north to Ch'i when he encounters a fortuneteller. The fortuneteller says, "On this day God kills the black dragon in the North; your color is black, so you cannot go north."[19] Ignoring this advice, Mo tzu continues on his way, until he reaches a raging river and is forced to turn back. On their second meeting the fortuneteller exults, "I told you that you could not go north." Mo tzu retorts that:

> The people in the South cannot go north, and the people in the North cannot go south. In color there are dark ones and light ones. Why are they all unable to proceed? Moreover, on the days *chia* and *yi* God kills the green dragon in the East. On the days *ping* and *ting* God kills the scarlet dragon in the South. On the days *keng* and *hsin* God kills the white dragon in the East. On the days *jen* and *kuei* God kills the black dragon in the North. If we adopt your doctrine, this means prohibiting all travel in the world.... Your theory cannot be used.[20]

From this passage it is clear that Mo tzu shows some selectivity in his acceptance of "traditional" folk beliefs. Ghost stories are taken at face value, as are imperial oracles, yet this form of divination, with which Mo tzu is evidently familiar, is rejected outright. Why? Although we cannot know for certain what reasons inform Mo tzu's judgement, it seems likely that Mo tzu's belief or disbelief is determined at least partly on the basis of the function of the practice or concept being considered. If this is true, then Mo tzu believes in the existence of Heaven, God, and ghosts and spirits, not because he is a superstitious member of the lower classes, but, in part, because of the essential role that they serve in his religious system. These spiritual beings are ethical forces in the Mohist universe that function to keep human behavior within acceptable limits; without the threat of retribution from the various spiritual beings, humans would be far more likely to indulge in non-productive license and immorality. For Mo tzu's means to work, it is essential that humans believe that their actions are constantly being monitored and that all deeds, both good and bad, receive just compensation. A revival of faith in the power of Heaven, God, and ghosts and spirits is the agency through which Mo tzu hopes to propagate this belief. Similarly, the oracles that Mo tzu quotes generally convey ethical morals. However, beliefs and practices that do not further the Mohist means are uniformly rejected. The belief in fate and the divination practices refuted in the passage translated above are examples of "superstitions" that Mo tzu sees as impediments and would like to eliminate.[21] Yet this is not the whole story, for Mo tzu also seems sincerely concerned to ensure that humans act in ways that benefit the spiritual beings. This is to be done for the sake of the spiritual beings and not just for producing salutary influences on humankind.

In a minor variation not previously encountered in the MT, Mo tzu rephrases his ultimate concern as a code of action:

> The Master Mo tzu said, "Whatever doctrines and actions benefit Heaven, ghosts, and the masses should be employed. Whatever doctrines and actions harm Heaven, ghosts, and the masses should be discarded. Whatever doctrines and actions accord with the sage kings of the Three Dynasties, Yao, Shun, Yü, T'ang, Wen, and Wu, should be employed. Whatever doctrines and actions accord with the wicked kings of the Three Dynasties, Chieh, Chou, Yu, and Li, should be discarded."[22]

From this passage it is clear that the Mohist ultimate concern of "promoting all that benefits the world while removing all that harms it" is designed to serve the good of Heaven and ghosts as well as humanity. Although this has been implied in a number of passages in the Essays, this is perhaps the most explicit statement yet encountered. Furthermore, it appears that *all* the actions of the sage kings are to be imitated, for they all promote the good of Heaven, ghosts, and the masses. Mo tzu has consistently used the precedent provided by the actions of the sage kings to justify his means, but he has not previously claimed that everything that they did was necessarily good.

In the rest of "Esteem for Righteousness," a number of attacks on "the gentlemen of today" are found. As in the Essays, Mo tzu criticizes these hapless fellows for their vanity, irrationality, and laziness. Additionally, several of the analogies found in the Essays are presented here as they might have occurred in actual conversations. Though it is fascinating to observe the way Mo tzu's illustrations and analogies vary as they are presented in different contexts, this material does not provide new insights into the religion of the early Mohists.

Kung Meng

As previously noted, the chapter titled "Kung Meng" contains a large number of attacks on the beliefs and practices associated with the Confucian schools. (Many of these same criticisms have already been seen in the "Anti-Confucianism" chapter.) Since these attacks do not add to our understanding of the

Mohist religion, they will not be summarized here.[23] However, in the course of criticizing the Confucians, the Mohists reveal something of their own values.

In contrast to the "Confucian" doctrine that the loyal minister speaks only when called upon, Mo tzu asserts that the gentleman must provide counsel whenever he sees the lord embarking upon an unrighteous course of action.[24] The Mohist ideal man must be absolutely uncompromising in his dedication to righteousness and the commonweal; if this means that he must break the rules of courtly etiquette and risk his life by providing unwanted advice, then that is a price he is willing to pay. This commitment to principle seems absolute, though it is tempered somewhat in a passage found in the next chapter, "Lu's Question," in which Mo tzu advocates making decisions on the basis of common sense and long-term benefit rather than rigidly principled idealism.[25]

Mo tzu gives a definition of wisdom in the course of a conversation in which he claims that Confucius was notably lacking in that quality: "The Master Mo tzu said, 'Now the wise person must honor Heaven, serve the ghosts, love humankind, and be economical in expenditures. When combined, this constitutes wisdom.'"[26] Like many of Mo tzu's definitions, this has a rather spontaneous quality and does not necessarily give the final word on the matter, but it does suggest that these are some of the most important characteristics of the ideal Mohist. In a later passage discussing the four Confucian principles that are "sufficient to destroy the world," these same qualities are shown to be absent in the followers of Confucius, with the difference that the Confucians are accused here of believing in fate, while no mention is made of their lack of love.[27] Based on the attention that they receive in this chapter, it seems that belief in and worship of the ghosts and spirits and economy of expenditures hold especially important positions among the Mohist means. (This may be because so many of the other means can be viewed as emanating from these two.)

In a further clarification of Mo tzu's attitude towards the "supernatural," we learn that unlike the Confucian Kung Meng tzu, Mo tzu believes that there really are auspicious (*hsiang* 祥) and inauspicious actions. As it turns out, this belief is just the logical extension of the Mohist doctrine of moral cause and effect. Mo tzu reasons that since Heaven, ghosts, and spirits reward good actions and punish bad ones, all actions that bring rewards are propitious; those actions the spiritual beings punish are then unpropitious. To deny that there are propitious and unpropitious actions is tantamount to denying the existence of ghosts and spirits and leads to the belief that fate is responsible for all that happens to humanity. Mo tzu illustrates his point with the examples of the kings of antiquity. Believing that some actions are propitious and others are not, the sage kings and their ministers behaved responsibly and the world prospered. The evil kings denied that actions could be auspicious or inauspicious; they consequently allowed the government to disintegrate and the state to fall into ruin.[28]

Several other stories in the chapter recount conversations that further add to our understanding of the actions of ghosts and spirits and their role in the Mohist universe. We read that an unnamed disciple of Mo tzu claims that after serving Mo tzu for a long time, the promised blessings have failed to materialize. He challenges Mo tzu, saying "Could it be that your doctrine has flaws and that ghosts and spirits are not sentient? For what reason have I not received blessings?" The point that Mo tzu makes in his answer is that one receives blessings only in response to truly meritorious actions. That this particular disciple has received no blessings provides no cause for wonder, for he is shown to be seriously deficient in virtue.[29] From the second story we learn that ghosts and spirits are only one of many factors that can influence a person's life. This is an important clarification, for from the Essays alone it would be easy to assume that all good or bad fortune is controlled by supernatural forces. The passage begins with Mo tzu lying ill. A man approaches him and rather gracelessly asks,

> You suppose ghosts and spirits to be sentient and able to confer calamities and blessings. They reward the good and punish the bad. Now you are a sage. Why are you sick? Could it be that your doctrine has flaws and the ghosts and spirits are not sentient?[30]

Mo tzu's reply shows a recognition of the natural forces affecting humans' health and longevity and hints at a more elaborate view of causality than the Essays reveal:

> Even if I am sick, how then are [ghosts and spirits] not sentient? There are many different ways that people contract illness. Some get sick from [extremes of] cold and heat; some get sick from toil and hardship. This is like having one hundred gates and closing one of them.[31] How would burglars not be able to enter?[32]

The last passage from "Kung Meng" that we will consider has already been cited in the second chapter of this study; the interest in this passage for us now lies in the suggestion it provides that the absolute standards of the Mohists are, in practice, considerably more flexible than one might expect from reading the Essays.

The story in question recounts Mo tzu's deception in tricking a promising student into studying in his school. Mo tzu promises the student an official post as a reward for his studies but fails to deliver on his pledge. When called to task by his student, Mo tzu tells the story of an alcoholic eldest son who was tricked into burying his deceased father by his brothers, who offered him wine as payment for his performance of the rites. When the father was safely interred, the brothers refused to hand over the wine, telling the brother that they had saved his reputation by getting him to do what was right. Similarly Mo tzu claims that he has tricked the student into doing what is right: "Now you have done righteousness, and I have also done righteousness. How could I alone be righteous? If you did not study, then people would have laughed at you. Therefore I urged you to study."[33]

What is perplexing about this passage is Mo tzu's glib justification of a case of admitted deception. Throughout the Essays, Mo tzu insists upon the absolute identity of means and ends. There seems to be no room for deceit in the Mohist program; Mo tzu says exactly what he means and holds himself uncompromisingly to the standards that he claims to have received from Heaven. Yet here we see Mo tzu behaving like the "gentlemen of today" that he elsewhere accuses of hypocrisy. Mo tzu's justification for his actions is the claim that the end justifies the means--a claim he would probably reject were it offered by one of his rivals.[34]

Lu's Question

The largest part of "Lu's Question" is devoted to arguments against offensive war. In this chapter more than any other we see Mo tzu in action, rushing about China dissuading bellicose rulers and ministers from attacking their neighboring states. In several of the passages it appears that an offensive attack is imminent; in the others Mo tzu may be engaging in preemptive persuasion, derailing aggressive impulses before any commitment to a plan of action has actually been made.

In his efforts to dissuade rulers and their ministers from attacking other states, Mo tzu employs four basic arguments. The most direct argument is that aggressive war is wrong. This is stated as a fact without much elaboration, e.g. "To attack Lu will be Ch'i's great transgression."[35] A second argument stresses that the evil consequences of warfare inevitably rebound upon the aggressor. This line of attack may have been especially effective, for it is repeated in many different forms. At its simplest it runs as follows: "When a large state attacks a small state it injures them both, and disaster will necessarily return to the [large] state."[36]

The third line of reasoning attempts to invalidate the claim that in their military adventures modern rulers are simply assisting Heaven by punishing miscreants. Mo tzu insists that Heaven can take care of its own business and needs no help from modern bullies.[37] As we have noted, throughout the Essays Mo tzu discusses the numerous occasions on which the sage kings attacked and vanquished neighboring kingdoms. In every case, Mo tzu claims that the sage kings were assisting Heaven by administering divine chastisement to the guilty parties. What is different now? Mo tzu seems to be saying that, in some cases at least, it is no longer appropriate for mortals to assist Heaven in its work.[38] At the very least, it seems likely that Mo tzu had very little tolerance for modern rulers who sought to fabricate noble-sounding rationalizations for their reprehensible actions. The final class of arguments opposing aggressive war draws its force from the Mohist axiom that the governments of states are held to the same Heaven-instituted moral standards that govern individual behavior. Mo tzu believes that what is immoral for the individual is immoral for the state and makes his point with a number of analogies, all of which are also found in the Essays.[39] The radical nature of this Mohist belief is reflected in the surprise shown by prince Wen, who says "When I look at it from your point of view, then what the whole world says is permissible is not necessarily so."[40]

In one passage Mo tzu gives his formula for avoiding attack from hostile states in response to an inquiry from the lord of Lu. Mo tzu says:

> I desire that the lord reveres Heaven and serves the ghosts above and that he loves and benefits the masses below, preparing valuable furs and money, and with humble speech quickly presenting these gifts to the neighboring lords on all sides. [If he does all this] and leads the people in serving Ch'i [the threatening state in this particular instance], then the calamity can be averted. Besides this, there is definitely no recourse.[41]

Successful statecraft, as understood by Mo tzu, has both a supernatural and a natural aspect; the wise ruler must see that both are taken seriously. Bribing the neighbors is not enough; one must also buy off the spiritual beings if one wishes to find peace and security in a time of turmoil.

For Mo tzu, obtaining the good will of the spiritual beings is a serious business that must be conducted with scrupulous fairness. Mo tzu criticizes the presumption of an official in charge of sacrifices in Lu who sacrificed one small pig and asked for one hundred blessings. This sort of giving is enough to make anyone, human or spirit, afraid of presents, Mo tzu reasons. The ideal, exemplified by the sage kings, is to sacrifice with no strings attached; it is implied that if one is going to make requests, they must be in proportion to the sacrifice tendered.[42] This further illustrates the reciprocity governing relations between the human and spirit realms that is introduced in the Essays.

Mo tzu's personal understanding of his mission is clarified in an extended, and rather one-sided, conversation that he has with a rustic named Wu Lu. Wu Lu, apparently a man of few ideas, repeatedly exclaims, "Righteousness, that is all. Righteousness, that is all. What is the point in talking about it?" In response to this obnoxious refrain, Mo tzu lists a number of occupations that might benefit the world and concludes that the path he has chosen for himself is the most useful of all. What Mo tzu sees himself as doing is "explaining the *tao* of the sage kings and seeking their principles, understanding their doctrines and investigating their words; above persuading the kings, dukes, and officials, and below persuading the ordinary fellows and wandering scholars."[43] Mo tzu obviously views himself as a teacher and thinker, first and foremost. If the Mohists were actively intervening in unjust wars at the time of this conversation, Mo tzu gives no hint of it.[44] Teaching the *tao* that he has discovered in the tradition of the sage kings is the best thing that Mo tzu can offer the world and is what he regards to be of ultimate importance, for by convincing the world to follow the *tao* of the sage kings, Mo tzu hopes to restructure human society in the image of an idealized past. In this way, humanity will be led to follow the will of Heaven, and all that benefits the world will be promoted, while all that harms it will be prevented.

Two of the remaining passages in "Lu's Question" have already been cited in the second chapter of this paper. In one, Mo tzu contrasts his useful skills with the clever, but impractical, artifice of Kung shu P'an, concluding that "what benefits humans is called skillful; what does not benefit humans is called clumsy."[45] The other passage has already been translated in its entirety (see above p. 41) but is sufficiently important to be mentioned again. In response to the question, "Since you have now seen the gentlemen of the four quarters, what will you speak of first?,"[46] Mo tzu gives his speech detailing the proper course of action to be followed after entering a state. Mo tzu's followers are to examine the conditions of the state, find the most pressing need, and then respond to that need by teaching the appropriate Mohist means. This passage provides the clearest illustration in the MT of the process by which the Mohist means are to be introduced to the leaders of a state. By focussing on the immediate needs of the states, the first means can be introduced; the other, related means are presumably to be employed after some initial success has been reached with the first and most critical means.

The last passage in "Lu's Question" to be considered here is puzzling. P'eng Ch'ing Sheng tzu (a disciple of Mo tzu?) states: "The past can be known, but the future cannot." Mo tzu evidently finds this proposition objectionable and responds with a seemingly inappropriate analogy that can be summarized as follows: Suppose your parents have had an accident one hundred *li* from here and you have one day to rescue them. Would you choose a strong horse and good cart or an old nag and a cart with four-cornered wheels for your rescue attempt? When P'eng Ch'ing Sheng tzu says that he would choose the good cart and horse, Mo tzu concludes, "How is the future not known?"[47] The puzzle here lies in Mo tzu's intent. Does he really wish to demonstrate that the future can be known, is he simply trying to outargue his disciple, or is he trying to establish some other point? It is obvious that by choosing the good cart and horse, P'eng is more likely to effect a successful rescue, but prudent foresight is certainly not the same thing as detailed knowledge the future. We have already seen that Mo tzu believes in the accuracy of the predictions of imperial oracles, but this is not at issue here. Mo tzu is claiming that the future can be known through logical inference from present circumstances. Why? The answer appears to lie in Mo tzu's opposition to the doctrine of fate. By claiming that intelligent choices in the present set the conditions leading to knowable future outcomes, Mo tzu is undercutting the intellectual foundations of the doctrine of fate. He does not appear to believe that all future events can be known but may simply be saying that foresight and planning are sure to bring rewards, while failure to pursue the most promising course of action will lead to disaster--an essential point if the men of the Warring States period are to be inspired to make disciplined efforts to transform their world.[48]

Kung Shu

The chapter entitled "Kung Shu" is devoted in its entirety to the story of Mo tzu's successful efforts to prevent Ch'u from attacking Sung. In the narration of the tale, Mo tzu appears to be the moral and intellectual superior of both Kung shu P'an, the inventor of the "cloud ladders" to be used in the attack, and the king of Ch'u, the presumed originator of the plot. Though it has been claimed that this story is a late addition to the text, its content is certainly in keeping with the rest of the MT. To convince first Kung shu P'an and later the king of Ch'u of the unrighteousness of their plans, Mo tzu employs many of his most characteristic lines of reasoning.

As the tale begins, Kung shu P'an has just completed the construction of "cloud ladders," with which the armies of Ch'u plan to attack Sung. Mo tzu has recently arrived at the capital of Ch'u, having walked for ten days and nights with the intention of thwarting the projected attack on Sung. In a conversation with Kung shu P'an, Mo tzu uses with great effectiveness his argument that states are governed by the same moral rules as individuals. Mo tzu begins by asking Kung shu P'an to kill a man who has insulted Mo tzu. This request displeases Kung shu P'an. Adding insult to injury, Mo tzu offers Kung shu P'an one thousand *chin* (ten *chin* in some versions) to perform the execution. Kung shu P'an replies, "I am righteous and definitely do not kill men."[49] Once Kung shu P'an has said this, Mo tzu has won the contest, for there is no way that Kung shu P'an can now claim that it is righteous to cause the death of thousands of innocents in the attack on Sung. Mo tzu relentlessly points out the contrast between Kung's indignantly moral words and warmongering actions. In addition he throws in several other arguments from "Condemnation of Offensive War," but they are unnecessary; Kung shu P'an is already defeated. However, Kung shu P'an claims that the matter is out of his hands; only the king can stop the attack.

Mo tzu next uses his "kleptomania" analogy on the king. The gist of this analogy is that if a rich man puts aside all his wonderful carriages, clothes, and food in order to steal the broken-down carriage, ratty clothes, and unsavory food of his poor neighbor, people will think that he has a serious problem. The same is true, or should be, for states. Mo tzu further points out that for a rich state to steal the miserable possessions of a poor one makes no sense and is unrighteous as well.

The king concedes these points but is still determined to attack Sung, for after all "Kung shu P'an has made cloud ladders for me; I must attack Sung."[50] Mo tzu is able to convince the king to desist only after he has demonstrated successful counterstrategies to all of Kung shu P'an's plans of attack and told the king of his three hundred trained disciples waiting on the walls of Sung to repel the "Ch'u bandits."

So far as the religion of the MT is concerned, there is little new information in this chapter, with the exception of the remarkable revelation that Mo tzu's disciples formed a corps of experts in defensive technology ready to rush to the rescue of besieged states. (The existence of Mohist defense corps has long been known from other sources, but this is the only clear mention of the fact in the Essays and Dialogues.[51]) Besides this, we see Mo tzu pursuing his goals with great energy and ingenuity, employing his best anti-war arguments with an undeniable elan and flair.

The Religion of the Dialogues

Since the Dialogues make no attempt to present the doctrines of Mo tzu in a systematic manner, their religious content cannot easily be compared to that of the Essays. However, we have seen that the same religious means and ultimate concern are prominently featured in both. It is significant that at no point are the doctrines of the Essays contradicted, either in word or in spirit, in any of the Dialogue passages. The moral absolutes so characteristic of the Essays become a little fuzzy when put to actual practice, and Mo tzu shows himself to be less rigid and quite a bit craftier than he appears in the Essays, but the two sections of the text are remarkably consistent in outlook and content. It seems safe to say that the Dialogues are a faithful, or at least plausible, record of the actual words and actions of Mo tzu as he taught the religious doctrines and attempted to secure the implementation of the religious means that are systematized in the Essays.

Notes

[1] Perhaps it is safer to say that the criteria used by the editors of the MT in organizing the Dialogue chapters are not immediately apparent. Is there some reason that there are more passages discussing righteousness in "Lu's Question" than in "Esteem for Righteousness"? Did the editors deliberately concentrate most of the passages attacking Confucian doctrines in the "Kung Meng" chapter? Many similar questions regarding the organization of the chapters can be raised, but resolving them is beyond the scope of this study.

[2] One of the most outstanding features of the Dialogue passages is their plausibility; they really seem to be accounts drawn from the life of the same fellow who preached the themes presented in the Essays. Though few writers admit to it, I suspect that this is the main reason scholars are so sure of the authenticity of the Dialogues. The Mo tzu of the Dialogues talks and behaves exactly as one would expect based on a close reading of the Essays; we see the same concerns expressed and the same unflinching dedication to righteousness at any cost. Favorite parables and illustrations from the Essays are repeated in the Dialogues, often with variations and embellishments apparently designed to enhance their persuasive impact. One receives the strong impression that one is seeing a teacher at work, revising and rethinking his material as he speaks but always remaining true to his vision of an ideal world.

[3] Mo tzu's assessments of the character of several of his disciples and rivals fall into this category; however, there is some value in these passages, for Mo tzu reveals a good deal about himself by the kinds of judgements he makes.

[4] A single anti-Confucian passage may also mention the Mohist means of condemnation of music, simplicity in funerals, economy of expenditures, and more. Since the references to Mohist means and characteristic concerns are often quite oblique, quantification becomes subjective and therefore questionable.

[5] Unless anti-Confucianism is considered a means. I have counted fourteen different passages with clear anti-Confucian messages. This is several more than the number of passages condemning wars of aggression. Even more passages could be considered anti-Confucian if attacks on persons thought to be "Confucians" are included. (I have only counted criticisms of individuals as examples of anti-Confucianism when the grounds for attack are expressly linked to "Confucian" beliefs or practices. Making this determination is one of the many subjective factors that render this attempt at analysis unreliable.)

[6] The commentaries to the MT identify nearly all of Mo tzu's antagonists as "Confucians," while some of his questioners appear to have been adherents of his own school. These debates were presumably engaged in before an audience of disciples and may have played a large role in the curriculum of Mo tzu's academy. Even after allowing for the favorable editing likely to have been given to these passages by his disciples, Mo tzu emerges as a formidable debater.

[7] MTCC, pp. 553-554.

[8] Ibid., p. 557.

[9] Ibid., p. 556.

[10] Ibid., p. 561 and pp. 570-571.

[11] Ibid., pp. 565-566.

[12] Ibid., p. 567.

[13] Ibid., p. 559.

[14] Ibid., pp. 567-568.

[15] Ibid., pp. 571-572.

[16] Ibid., p. 578. At the very least, this passage reinforces the impression that Mo tzu was a true believer in his own cause.

[17] Ibid., p. 571.

[18] Before the doctrines of Buddhism were transmitted to China, there were philosophical texts that advocated minimizing emotions (*Lao tzu*) and even transcending them (*Chuang tzu*), but, so far as I know, no one besides the Mohists proposed *eliminating* the emotions by brute force of will.

[19] This passage is often cited by writers who wish to argue that Mo tzu was dark-skinned. From this they then infer that he had been branded as punishment for some crime or that his skin was blackened by sun and labor.

[20] Ibid., pp. 577-578.

[21] This "functionalist" analysis of Mohist beliefs is not inspired by the school of anthropologists who reduce the meaning of all religious data to their function for the society being studied. Rather it is derived directly from the observation of the thought processes of the early Mohists, as revealed in the MT: the claim is that Mo tzu sometimes appears to be a "functionalist" in his approach to matters of belief and practice.

[22] Ibid., p. 570.

[23] The importance of these criticisms of "Confucian" doctrines and practices, like the chapters on defensive warfare, lies not so much in their content as in the fact that they were written. The existence of these criticisms supports the belief that the Mohists were active debaters and proselytizers who worked unstintingly to promote the practices that they believed would bring the world its greatest benefits, while opposing all those doctrines that harmed the world. The doctrines and practices of the "Confucians" fall into the latter category, of course.

[24] Ibid., pp. 579-580.

[25] In this passage, Mo tzu refutes the claim of one of his disciples that prince Tzu Lu of Ch'u behaved in a praiseworthy manner when he refused the throne offered to him by a rebel general and chose instead to die with honor. Despite the fact that the rebels had killed both his parents, Tzu Lu should have accepted the throne and then, after consolidating his rule, executed the rebel general. This way, Mo tzu appears to think, the prince could have saved the state, his honor, and his life. (Ibid., pp. 610-611.) Every so often, one encounters a passage like this in the MT that suggests that Mo tzu is not the inflexible moralist he appears to be in the rest of the text. The most literal-minded of Mo tzu's followers appear to have made a virtue of martyrdom for the sake of principle, as we have seen in the case of the disciples of Meng Sheng who insisted on returning to a beleaguered city to die with

their leader; however, Mo tzu himself sometimes reveals a shrewd and calculating side to his personality.

[26] Ibid., p. 583.

[27] Ibid., pp. 588-589. In this passage, the non-economical expenditures of the Confucians include funeral and mourning practices, music, and dance.

[28] Ibid., pp. 584-585.

[29] Ibid., pp. 591-592. It may be significant that although the questioner in this passage claims that he has served Mo tzu for a long time, he is not referred to by name and is treated more or less as an outsider by the compilers of the text. Mo tzu may also be making the point that merely claiming to be a Mohist confers no benefits; the ghosts and spirits look to deeds, not affiliations.

[30] Ibid., pp. 592-593. Note that both questioners close their inquiries with the exact same words, viz. "Could it be that your doctrine has flaws and the ghosts and spirits are not sentient?" Even in the Dialogues, which supposedly represent actual conversations, the editors of the MT tend to rely upon stereotyped formulae.

[31] Evidently Mo tzu believes that being in the good graces of the ghosts and spirits is like closing one of the hundred gates through which sickness enters.

[32] Ibid., pp. 591-592.

[33] Ibid., pp. 590-591.

[34] Throughout this study, we have observed the general imprecision of definition and analogy that characterizes the older textual layers of the MT. As A. C. Graham has observed: "One of the interesting things in pre-Han, as in early Greek philosophy, is that we can watch over several centuries a people learning how to think." (Graham, *Logic*, p. 5, n. 7.) Assuming that this passage accurately reports an actual incident from Mo tzu's teaching career, we may be seeing a case where Mo tzu simply does not realize the implications of his words and actions.

[35] Ibid., p. 589.

[36] Ibid.

[37] Ibid., p. 600.

[38] Mo tzu clearly idealizes the sage kings of antiquity, attributing all virtue to them and interpreting their actions in the most sympathetic manner imaginable. Seeing the current crop of rulers and schemers at close range, it is perhaps impossible for Mo tzu to envision them competing in virtue with his long-dead heros. We have seen that Mo tzu views the high antiquity of the Hsia dynasty as a kind of "golden age," but it is not clear that he believes the present to be necessarily and inevitably degenerate and corrupt. One of the ways of understanding Mo tzu's program is as an attempt to recreate the ideal state that existed in the past, so it is puzzling that he appears to deny the possibility that a modern ruler is capable of assisting Heaven. Of course, the case in question concerns prince Wen of Lu Yang; perhaps Mo tzu is simply saying that prince Wen is not a suitable candidate for the job of Heaven-appointed enforcer.

[39] For example, Mo tzu points out that if it is immoral for an individual to steal and kill, then it must certainly be even more immoral for states to institutionalize the

practice on the massive scale of wars of conquest; this is comparable to calling a little white white and a lot of white black. (Ibid., pp. 600-601.)

[40] Ibid., p. 601. How many citizens of the U.S.A. would be equally bemused to hear this argument seriously presented? For a law-abiding people, we certainly seem unconcerned by the "collateral damage" our "smart" (but immoral) bombs recently inflicted on Iraq. One wonders what Mo tzu thought of the Confucian doctrine of "rectification of names." The MT's failure to discuss this presumably congenial Confucian doctrine seems an unusual omission in an otherwise thorough text.

[41] Ibid., p. 597.

[42] Ibid., pp. 609-610. When it comes to securing the blessings of the spiritual beings, the behavior of the supplicant is more important by far than sacrifices. Just as in "Kung Meng," "Lu's Question" also contains a long passage in which a follower of Mo tzu claims that the ghosts and spirits have not been treating him terribly well. Again Mo tzu adamantly proclaims that righteous action is what brings the greatest blessings, not sacrifices. (Ibid., pp. 608-609.)

[43] Ibid., p. 605.

[44] As we have noted in the second chapter of this study, this passage contains the line: "Ti has thought of shouldering armor and picking up a sword to relieve the calamities of the feudal lords." Mo tzu points out the futility of this action, claiming that one man makes no impact on the battlefield. If Mo tzu has an army of trained disciples, this is where he should mention it.

[45] Ibid., p. 614.

[46] Ibid., p. 607. The questioner is apparently asking Mo tzu what he now believes to be the most urgent problems of the day.

[47] Ibid., p. 610. The wording of this last sentence is obscure, but this appears to be its meaning.

[48] Passages like this demonstrate the difficulty of interpreting the Dialogues. It would be easy to dismiss Mo tzu's rebuttal as a willful misinterpretation of Peng's thesis or as a non sequitur, but it is also possible, as we have suggested, that Mo tzu has an ulterior motive for his response. The goal of this analysis is to neither overinterpret nor underinterpret the text, but it is obvious, especially in cases like this, that there are great opportunities for error.

[49] Ibid., p. 615. I confess to some difficulty in translating this sentence.

[50] Ibid., p. 617. It seems that there are certain rationalizations common to the thinking of military men in all times and places.

[51] It is really quite odd that there are no other mentions in the MT of the early Mohists taking on the role of defenders of the innocent. This coupled with the sustained narrative style of the "Kung shu" chapter, unique in the MT, suggests that this chapter might be the product of a later time. I know of no conclusive evidence to this effect however. As suggested in the second chapter of this paper, it may be that the Mohists took on the task of defending innocent states late in the life of their founder, or even after his death.

CHAPTER VIII

CONCLUSION

In the first chapter of this book, it was stated that the goal of this study is to analyze the ultimate concern of the Essay and Dialogue sections of the MT, the oldest strata of the text. This has now been done. Along with determining the ultimate concern of the early followers of Mo tzu, we have also investigated the means by which the Mohists hoped to achieve their goals and the justifications presented in the MT for both the Mohist means and goals. Since the entire thrust of this analysis is exploratory, we did not set out to prove the correctness of any predetermined hypotheses; however, in the course of this examination of the text, a number of observations have been made--some very general, others quite restricted in scope. By necessity, the bulk of our investigation has been based on the Essays; the anecdotal and sometimes cryptic nature of the Dialogue chapters makes them less suited for analysis than the systematic and didactic Essays. Our understanding of Mohist theory has therefore been derived in large part from the Essays, while the Dialogues have given us insights into the application of that theory in an imperfect world. While it would be impractical, and probably unnecessary, to reiterate every point made in the course of this analysis, it may be worthwhile to recall the most important insights provided by our method.

By defining religion as ultimate concern, we have been able to view the MT in all its parts as a religious document, though we have chosen to focus on only two sections of the text. In this way we have avoided compartmentalizing the doctrines taught in the MT into reified Western categories that, while arguably adequate for defining modern academic disciplines, are totally foreign to the China of the fifth and fourth centuries B.C.E. This in turn has allowed us to perceive the fundamental unity of purpose expressed throughout every chapter of the Essays and

Dialogues. We hope to have shown that the Mohist religion is both systematic and reasonably coherent, embracing every aspect of life and therefore placing enormous demands upon its followers.

The ultimate concern of the early Mohists is to create an ideal world, or as they put it "to promote all that benefits the world while removing all that harms it." The benefits that the Mohists seek include sensible economic growth, population increase, the end of offensive warfare, the establishment of well-ordered government, and the prohibition of all wasteful expenditures. The Essays present ten interrelated, and in some cases overlapping, means by which this ideal state can be achieved. These religious means have, of course, been examined in great detail in the body of this analysis. The ultimate source from which the means and ultimate concern of the Mohists are derived is the will of Heaven, though penultimately they can be justified by the benefit they bring to society. Together, the Mohists' means form an integrated program of action for the transformation of society (or, as Mo tzu would have it, for restoring the world to the conditions enjoyed in antiquity during the reigns of the sage kings).

The essential insight of the Mohist religion is the unity of the human race. This is not received in mystical vision but is the product of the conscious strategy of regarding the lives and possessions of others as one regards one's own. Therefore, it is within the reach of all humans willing to make the requisite effort. It is this insight that enables the Mohists to put aside all self-interest for the sake of righteousness, and this insight that, in the final analysis, makes or breaks the implementation of the Mohist means. Judging from the historical record, it would appear that Mo tzu and his followers met with little long-term success in popularizing this way of viewing the world.

Although the later Mohists created a remarkably sophisticated corpus of logical propositions, the early Mohists appear to have just muddled along, proving most of their points by means of analogies, appeals to ordinary, everyday reasoning, and especially through reliance upon the pseudohistorical precedents provided by the deeds attributed to the sage kings. The worst of the Mohist arguments are almost non sequiturs, at least in the view of modern readers, but at their best the early Mohists were powerful and compelling proponents of their profoundly moral, Heaven-instituted model for individual human behavior and world social order.

The point with which this study should close, and the most important insight derived from this investigation as a whole, is a simple idea that has, I fear, been bludgeoned to death in the body of this monograph, namely that the uniqueness of the MT lies in its presentation of a coherent, employable (in theory at least) system of means for the transformation of society and the creation of an ideal world. The MT is held together by the thread of one overriding ultimate concern-- to create an ideal world--and all the multifarious and seemingly disjointed doctrines that it contains are consciously designed to serve this one end. It is by asking the religious question of the text and taking the time to see what the text itself says that we are enabled to see the transparent system and structure of the MT. From a religious point of view anyway, the MT stands alone as the first Chinese attempt to project a complete view of an ideal society and provide a comprehensive system of means for its realization.

BIBLIOGRAPHY

Editions and Translations of the Mo tzu

Chang Ch'un yi. *Mo tzu chi chieh.* Shanghai: World Book Company, 1936; reprint ed., Taipei: Wen shih che ch'u pan she, 1982.

David-Neel, Alexandra. *Socialism chinois: le philosophe Meh-ti et l'idée de solidarité.* London: Luzac and Co., 1907.

Graham, A. C. *Later Mohist Logic, Ethics and Science.* London: University of London, 1978.

Harvard-Yenching Institute. *A Concordance to Mo tzu.* Harvard-Yenching Institute Sinological Index Series, supplement no. 21. Peking, 1948.

Legge, James. "The Opinions of Mo Ti," The Chinese Classics. Vol. 2: *The Works of Mencius,* pp. 100-122. Oxford: Clarendon Press, 1895; reprint ed., New York: Dover Publications, Inc., 1970.

Mei Yi pao. *The Ethical and Political Works of Motse.* London: Arthur Probsthain, 1929.

Pi Yüan. *Mo tzu chu.* N.p., 1783; reprint ed., Taipei: Kuang wen shu chu, 1965.

Sun Yi jang. *Chiao pu ting pen Mo tzu hsien ku.* Addendum by Li Li. N.p., 1922; reprint ed., Taipei: Yi wen yin shu kuan, 1969.

Watson, Burton. *Mo Tzu: The Basic Writings.* New York: Columbia University Press, 1963.

Yeh Yü lin. *Mo tzu pai hua chu chieh.* Taipei: Hua lien ch'u pan she, 1969.

_____. *Mo tzu hsin shih.* Tainan: Ta hsia ch'u pan she, 1982.

Other Works Cited

Baird, Robert D. *Category Formation and the History of Religions.* The Hague: Mouton, 1971.

Ch'en Ku ying, ed. *Chuang tzu chin chu chin yi.* Taipei: Shang wu yin shu kuan, 1975.

Ch'en Kung. *Mo hsüeh yen chiu.* Taichung: Tung Hai University, 1964.

Ch'en Yüan te. *Chung kuo ku tai che hsüeh shih.* Taipei: Chung hua shu chu, 1962.

Cheng Te k'un. *Chou China.* Archaeology in China, vol. 3. Cambridge: W. Hefler and Sons, 1963.

Chiang Ch'üan. *Tu tzu chih yen.* Quoted in Ch'en Yüan te, *Chung kuo ku tai che hsüeh shih*, pp. 191-192. Taipei: Chung hua shu chu, 1962.

Ch'ien Mu. *Mo tzu.* Shanghai: Commercial Press, 1931.

Chou Fu mei. *Mo tzu chia chieh tzu chi shih.* History and Chinese Literature Series, no. 6. Taipei: Taiwan University, 1965.

Creel, H. G. *Confucius and the Chinese Way.* New York: Harper and Row, 1949.

Durrant, Stephen W. "An Examination of Textual and Grammatical Problems in *Mo Tzu.*" Ph.D. dissertation, University of Washington, 1975.

Fang Shou ch'u. *Mo hsüeh yüan liu.* Taipei: Chung hua shu chu, 1957.

Forke, Alfred. *Me Ti: des Socialethikers und seiner Schuler philosophische Werke.* p. 23. Quoted in Stephen W. Durrant. "An Examination of Textual and Grammatical Problems in *Mo Tzu*," pp. 19-20. Ph.D. dissertation, University of Washington, 1975.

Fung Yu lan. *A History of Chinese Philosophy*, trans. Dirk Bodde. Princeton: Princeton University Press, 1962.

_____. *Chung kuo che hsüeh shih hsin pien.* Peking: Jen min ch'u pan she, 1964.

Graham, A. C. *Divisions in Early Mohism Reflected in the Core Chapters of Mo-tzu.* Singapore: National University of Singapore, Institute of East Asian Philosophies, 1985.

_____. *Disputers of the Tao: Philosophical Argument in Ancient China.* La Salle, IL: Open Court, 1989.

_____. "How Much of *Chuang tzu* Did Chuang tzu Write?" *Journal of the American Academy of Religion.* Vol. 47, no. 3S. *Studies in Classical Chinese Thought* (September 1979): 459-501.

Griffith, Samuel B. *Sun Tzu: the Art of War.* Oxford: Oxford University Press, 1963.

Han Fei tzu. Chu tzu chi ch'eng. Vol. 5. N.p.: Chung hua shu chu, n.d.

Hsin Kuan chieh, Meng Teng chin, and Ting Chien, eds. *Chung kuo ku tai chu ming che hsüeh chia p'ing chuan.* Vol. 1. N.p.: Chi lu shu she, 1980.

Hsü Cho yün. *Ancient China in Transition.* Stanford: Stanford University Press, 1965.

Hu Shih. *Chung kuo ku tai che hsüeh shih.* N.p., n.d.; reprint ed., Taipei: Commercial Press, 1970.

_____. *The Development of the Logical Method in Ancient China.* Shanghai: n.p., 1922; reprint ed., New York: Paragon, 1963.

Huai nan tzu. Chu tzu chi ch'eng. Vol. 7. N.p.: Chung hua shu chu, n.d.

Jen Chi yü. *Mo tzu.* Shanghai: Jen min ch'u pan she, 1961.

Karlgren, Bernhard. *Grammata Serica Recensa. Bulletin of the Museum of Far Eastern Antiquities,* no. 29. Stockholm, 1957; reprint ed., Stockholm, 1972.

Kojima Kenkichiro. *Chu tzu pai chia k'ao,* pp. 186-187. Quoted in Stephen W. Durrant. "An Examination of Textual and Grammatical Problems in *Mo Tzu,*" p. 45. Ph.D. dissertation, University of Washington, 1975.

Lau, D. C., trans. *Mencius.* Middlesex: Penguin Books, 1970.

Legge, James. *The Chinese Classics.* Vol. 1. *Confucius: Confucian Analects, The Great Learning, and The Doctrine of the Mean.* Oxford: Clarendon Press, 1893; reprint ed., New York: Dover Publications, Inc., 1971.

Liang Ch'i ch'ao. *Mo tzu hsüeh an.* N.p., 1921; reprint ed., Taipei: Chung hua shu chu, 1966.

_____. *Tzu Mo tzu hsüeh shuo.* N.p., 1936; reprint ed., Taipei: Chung hua shu chu, 1956.

_____. *Intellectual Trends in the Ch'ing Period.* Translated by Immanuel C. Y. Hsu. Cambridge, MA: Harvard University Press, 1959.

Lo Ken tze. *Chu tzu k'ao so.* Peking: Jen min ch'u pan she, 1958.

Lü shih ch'un ch'iu. Chu tzu chi ch'eng. Vol. 6. N.p.: Chung hua shu chu, n.d.

Maspero, Henri. "Notes sur la logique de Mo-tseu et son école." *T'oung Pao,* 25 (1928):1-64.

_____. *La chine antique. Annales du Musée Guimet,* no. 71. Paris: Presses Universitaires de France, 1965.

Mei, Yi pao. *Motse: the Neglected Rival of Confucius.* London: Arthur Probsthain, 1934.

Mote, Frederick W. *Intellectual Foundations of China.* New York: Alfred A. Knopf, 1971.

Needham, Joseph, gen. ed. *Science and Civilisation in China.* 7 vols. Cambridge: Cambridge University Press, 1954-. Vol. 2.

_____, gen. ed. *Science and Civilisation in China.* 7 vols. Cambridge: Cambridge University Press, 1954- . Vol. 6, pt. 2 (1984): *Agriculture,* by Francesca Bray.

Pan Ku. *Erh shih wu shih.* Vol. 1. Reprint ed. Taipei: Kai ming shu tien, 1969.

Peking University. *Hsün tzu hsin chu.* Peking: Chung hua shu chu, 1979.

Rubin, Vitali A. *Individual and State in Ancient China.* Translated by Stephen I. Levine. New York: Columbia University Press, 1976.

Robinson, Richard. *Definition.* Oxford: Oxford University Press, 1950.

Schwartz Benjamin I. *The World of Thought in Ancient China.* Cambridge, MA: Harvard University Press, 1985

Ssu Ma Ch'ien. *Shih chi.* Reprint ed. N.p.: T'ung wen ying tien k'an, 1903.

Teiser, S. F. "Engulfing the Bounds of Order: the Myth of the Great Flood in *Mencius.*" *Journal of Chinese Religions.* Nos. 13 and 14 (Fall 1985 and 1986):15-43.

Ts'en Chung mien, *Mo tzu ch'eng shou ke p'ien chien chu.* Peking: Ku chi ch'u pan she, 1958.

Tseu, Augustinus A. *The Moral Philosophy of Mo-Tze.* Taipei: China Printing, Ltd., 1965.

Tz'u Hai. Rev. ed. in 1 vol. N.p., 1947; reprint ed., Hong Kong: Chung hua shu chu, 1972.

Vandermeersch, Leon. *La formation du légisme.* Paris: Ecole Francaise D'Extreme-Orient, 1965.

Watson, Burton. *Early Chinese Literature.* New York: Columbia University Press, 1962.

Yates, Robin R. E. "The Mohists on Warfare: Technology, Technique, and Justification." *Journal of the American Academy of Religion.* Vol. 47, no. 3S. *Studies in Classical Chinese Thought* (September 1979): 549-603.

APPENDIX

CHARACTER LIST OF NAMES AND BOOK TITLES

Chan kuo ts'e 戰國策
Chang Ch'un yi 張純一
Ch'en Chen sun 陳振孫
Ch'en Chu 陳柱
Ch'en Ku ying 陳鼓應
Ch'en Kung 陳拱
Ch'en Yüan te 陳元德
Ch'eng Fan 程繁
Ch'i 齊
Chi Lu 季路
Chiang Ch'üan 江 玉泉
Chiao pu ting pen Mo tzu hsien ku 校補定本墨子閒詁
Chieh 桀
Ch'ien Han shu 前漢書
Ch'ien Mu 錢穆
Chih chai shu mu 直齋書目
Chih Ch'eng 芝城
Chih Po 智伯
Ch'in 秦
Ch'in Ku li 禽滑釐
Ch'in Shih Huang Ti 秦始皇帝 (The First Emperor of the Ch'in dynasty)
Ching 荆
Chou 周
Chou (Dynasty) 周

Chou Chi chih 周繼旨
Chou Fu mei 周富美
Ch'u 楚
Chu tzu chi ch'eng 諸子集成
Chu tzu k'ao so 諸子考索
Chu tzu pai chia k'ao 諸子百家考
Chuang tzu 莊子
Chuang tzu chin chu chin yi 莊子今註今譯
Ch'un ch'iu fan lu 春秋繁露
Chung kuo che hsüeh shih hsin pien 中國哲學史新編
Chung kuo ku tai che hsüeh shih 中國古代哲學史
Chung kuo ku tai chu ming che hsüeh chia p'ing chuan 中國古代著名哲學
    家評傳
Erh shih wu shih 二十五史
Fa 法
Fang Shou ch'u 方授楚
Feng Yu lan 馮友蘭
Fu Tun 腹 黃享
Han Fei tzu 韓非子
Han shu 漢書
Ho Lü 闔閭
Hsin Kuan chieh 辛冠洁
Hsiang Tzu Niu 項子牛
Hsün tzu hsin chu 荀子新注
Hu Shih 胡適
Huai nan tzu 淮南子
Huang ti ssu ching 黃帝四經
Hui (King of Ch'u) 楚惠王
Jen Chi yü 任繼愈
Ju 儒

K'ang (Duke of Ch'i) 齊康公
Kao Shih tzu 高石子
Kao Sun tzu 高孫子
Kao Yu 高誘
Keng Chu 耕柱
Kojima Kenkichiro 兒島献吉郎
Kou Chien (Lord of Yüeh) 越王句踐
Ku Yen wu 顧炎武
Kuan Ch'in ao 管黔今敖
K'ung Li 孔悝
Kung Meng 公孟
Kung shu P'an 公輸盤
Lao tzu 老子
Li 厲
Li Li 李笠
Liang Ch'i ch'ao 梁啟超
Ling (Lord of Ch'u) 楚靈王
Lo Ken tze 羅根澤
Lü shih ch'un ch'iu 呂氏春秋
Lu 魯
Mao K'un 毛坤
Meng Sheng 孟勝
Mo hsüeh yüan liu 墨學源流
Mo Ti 墨翟
Mo tzu 墨子
Mo tzu ch'eng shou ke p'ien chien chu 墨子城守各篇簡注
Mo tzu chia chieh tzu chi shih 墨子假借字集釋
Mo tzu chu 墨子注
Mo tzu hsin shih 墨子新釋
Mo tzu hsüeh an 墨子學案

Mo tzu pai hua chu chieh 墨子白話句解

Mu Ho 穆賀

Nung 農

Pan Ku 班固

P'eng Ch'ing Sheng tzu 彭輕生子

Pi Yüan 畢沅

Shang Yang 商革央

Sheng Ch'o 勝棹

Shih chi 史記

Shih Chiao 史角

Shih ching 詩経

Shu ching 書経

Shun 舜

Ssu ma Ch'ien 司馬遷

Sui (Dynasty) 隋

Sun Yi jang 孫詒讓

Sung (Dynasty) 宋

T'ai p'ing yü lan 太平御覽

T'ang 湯

T'ang (Dynasty) 唐

T'ang Yao ch'en 唐堯臣

Tao 道

Tao te ching 道德経

Tao tsang 道藏

T'ien Hsiang 田襄

Tsa 雜

Ts'en Chung mien 岑仲勉

Tsung Heng 縱衡

Tz'u Hai 辭海

Tzu Mo tzu hsüeh shuo 子墨子學說

Wang An shih 王安石
Wang Nien sun 王念孫
Wang Yin chih 王引之
Wei 魏
Wen (Lord of Chin) 晉文公
Wen (Lord of Lu Yang) 魯陽文君
Wen (Sage King) 文王
Wu (Sage King) 武王
Wu Lü 吳盧
Yang Ch'eng Chün (Lord of Yang Ch'eng) 陽城君
Yang Chu 楊朱
Yang Huo 陽貨
Yao 堯
Yeh Yü lin 葉玉麟
Yen t'ieh lun 鹽鐵論
Yi ching 易經
"Yi Wen Chih" 藝文志
Yin Yang 陰陽
Yü 禹
Yu 幽
Yü Yüeh 俞越
Yüeh 越

INDEX